Low-Water Landscaping

by Teri Dunn Chace
Award-Winning Horticulture Author

for
dummies®
A Wiley Brand

Low-Water Landscaping For Dummies®

Published by: **John Wiley & Sons, Inc.,** 111 River Street, Hoboken, NJ 07030-5774, www.wiley.com

Copyright © 2023 by John Wiley & Sons, Inc., Hoboken, New Jersey

Media and software compilation copyright © 2023 by John Wiley & Sons, Inc. All rights reserved.

Published simultaneously in Canada

For general information on our other products and services, please contact our Customer Care Department within the U.S. at 877-762-2974, outside the U.S. at 317-572-3993, or fax 317-572-4002. For technical support, please visit https://hub.wiley.com/community/support/dummies.

Wiley publishes in a variety of print and electronic formats and by print-on-demand. Some material included with standard print versions of this book may not be included in e-books or in print-on-demand. If this book refers to media such as a CD or DVD that is not included in the version you purchased, you may download this material at http://booksupport.wiley.com. For more information about Wiley products, visit www.wiley.com.

Library of Congress Control Number: 2022949552

ISBN: 978-1-119-98580-8 (pbk); ISBN 978-1-119-98581-5 (ebk); ISBN 978-1-119-98583-9 (ebk)

SKY10039614_120822

Contents at a Glance

Table of Contents

Introduction

There comes a day when you reckon with the state of your yard. Your lawn is turning brown and the other plantings look distressed. Meanwhile, your water bill creeps higher, and the news about low reservoirs and depleted aquifers grows more alarming. You look up at the blue, cloudless sky, you look down at the dry sights around you, and you wonder what to do.

This book is here to help you adapt to the reality of low water in your landscape. I assure you, you can act in many ways.

You can make all sorts of tangible changes, like taking steps to help your garden ground retain water better and to reduce runoff.

You can tackle a project as large as installing an in-ground irrigation system and as seemingly minor as planting some attractive native wildflowers in the part-day sheltering shade of a boulder or wall.

You can try clever innovations pioneered by gardeners who grow crops in arid regions, from using strategically placed clay pots or pipes to get water right into root zones to creating watering zones to positioning thirstier plants on the down-hill side of a slope.

You can — once and for all, no more dithering — take out that scraggly lawn and not look back.

It's time to explore and install a whole new range of (yes, beautiful!) plants that are adapted to minimal water.

I promise you the results won't look barren and scrubby; the landscape will come alive as you shift your approach and change the ways you plant and maintain everything. Now it's time to stop fretting, delve in, and do it. Soon you'll be delighted with your yard's new, improved look — and proud and relieved that it was accomplished while consuming substantially less water.

About This Book

Low-Water Landscaping For Dummies provides you a mixture of ideas, step-by-step instructions, and answers to practical questions like:

>> How do I stop water from running off and away from my yard?

>> Which dry-adapted plants are the most durable, most colorful, most long-blooming?

>> What's the best method for installing and watering a new plant?

>> Is there a better way to deliver water to my plants?

>> Is there a way to landscape with large and small rocks that doesn't look like a gravel pit?

>> What's involved in removing a lawn? What are suitable replacement plants?

>> What material makes a good mulch and how thick should I apply it?

>> When's the best time of day to water and why?

>> What's the best way to install a dry streambed so it looks natural?

>> How should I collect rainwater?

>> What is gray water, and is it safe to use in the yard?

>> What's the best way to raise edible plants with limited water? What are the recommended plants?

>> Are there tricks for watering moisture-greedy potted plants?

>> Can I add a water feature without consuming a lot of water?

>> What is xeriscaping, and how can I apply its principles to my own yard?

This handy guide addresses all of these matters and more — no question is too elementary, no concern too trivial! This book also gives you a handle on the best practices and explains what has worked best for others in similar situations.

As you proceed through this learning curve, you'll find a common and reassuring theme: Being careful and frugal with outdoor water use leads to a successful home landscape. I'm here to help you get the groove on!

Cultivated varieties (*cultivars*) have been chosen or developed for superior or alternative qualities; some call these selections *nativars*. In the lists in this book, I indicate these in 'single quotes' because that's the industry standard, in web listings, catalogs, and nursery tags.

Foolish Assumptions

When writing this book, I've made a few assumptions about you, dear reader:

>> Plants you've installed in the past have struggled and failed, and you're tired of wasting money and effort. You wonder what you've been doing wrong and/or what would be better choices.

>> Boring "desert dot" (you know, a spread of gravel with an occasional succulent plunked in at random) landscaping doesn't inspire you. Sure, it's probably low-maintenance, but it also isn't very attractive.

>> Although you've seen colorful dry-climate gardens, you don't have a clue where to begin, in terms of plant selection and plant placement.

>> You're fed up with your lawn and its many demands, but you're not sure what you can or should do next.

>> You want to fashion a landscape where you can actually sit outside and enjoy the sights and sounds. Perhaps a bit of cooling shade . . .

>> Landscaping in an ecologically sensitive way appeals to you, but you don't know how or where to begin.

>> You've experienced success with DIY indoor projects and feel ready, willing, and able to tackle a water-wise approach in your yard, but you need guidance and information.

Icons Used in This Book

Throughout this book, you can find icons — small pictures next to the text that point out extra-important information. Here's what they all mean:

TIP

For gems of accumulated wisdom — quite often the kind learned by painful experience! — follow this icon.

WARNING

Consider this icon like a stop sign: When you see it, stop and pay extra attention, because I only use it to help you avoid serious mistakes or bodily harm.

REMEMBER

You're trying to work correctly and efficiently *and* to be sensitive to the environment. Problem is, you may not always know what's right and what isn't. This icon steers you in the proper direction.

TECHNICAL STUFF

This icon highlights the jargon and concepts that are interesting but not essential to understanding low-water landscaping.

Beyond This Book

This book is chock-full of tips and other pieces of helpful advice you can use as you tackle water-wise projects and make water-wise choices. If you want additional tidbits of wisdom, check out the book's Cheat Sheet at www.dummies.com. Just search for "Low-Water Landscaping For Dummies Cheat Sheet."

Where to Go from Here

If you're excited about making good and practical changes in your landscape and the creative juices are starting to flow, flip through the index or Table of Contents to find a subject that interests you.

Or you can turn to whatever section looks to have the answers and information you're wanting most, whether it's Part 2's descriptive plant lists, Chapter 16's tour of mulches, or Chapter 15's instructions on how to install an attractive dry streambed. Later you can backtrack to the lowdown on rain barrels (Chapter 2) or divert to my tips for potted plants (Chapter 17). In trawling through Part 3, you may surprise yourself by being drawn to the updated information about artificial turf in Chapter 13.

When you're ready, put on your hat and sunscreen, roll up your sleeves, and let me empower and guide you into water-wise landscaping. It's easier than you think and more gratifying than you can imagine.

1

Getting Started with Low-Water Landscaping

Chapter **1**

Lacking Water? No Problem

This book is all about landscaping with less water. No matter whether you're trying to sustain an established yard in a desertlike climate or you're wishing to make changes while adjusting to a limited or unpredictable water supply, the message is the same: You can do it!

Having a beautiful landscape isn't just nice, it's also important. The plants in and around the area are more than décor, they're alive — even in times when water is scarce. We humans are bound in a relationship with them, not just for the pleasurable beauty or fragrance they may provide as we come and go from our home or hang out in the yard, and not just for the other creatures they help sustain (from pollinators to birds). We're also elementally bound together by the shared, interdependent, natural cycles of air — the exchange of carbon dioxide and oxygen — and water, the stuff of life as we know it.

When water is rationed or in short supply, when rain is a rare event, when we constantly hear dire stories about falling reservoirs and depleted aquifers, we worry. We should worry. Water is precious and vulnerable to human demands as well as forces that feel beyond our control, like weather patterns and macro-climate change.

And yet, having an attractive yard isn't a foolish wish, nor is it a luxury. Your yard is part of your home and part of the big picture of the larger landscape.

Rather than giving up, adapt. Become a good steward. This chapter gives you a brief overview of what you can do. Find out how to conserve water, how to better deliver it to wisely chosen plants, and how to keep it all healthy and beautiful.

Defining Low-Water Landscaping

Low-water landscaping is using less water, more efficiently.

Sustaining home landscaping on less water isn't mysterious. Many excellent techniques and ideas come from farming and agriculture. And of course research is continuing.

Certain water-conserving ideas from agriculture translate well to smaller and more intimate settings, whether you only have a courtyard or balcony, or you're trying to maintain a half-acre or more around your home. Also other gardeners have developed clever, effective ways to successfully nurture many plants with less water.

This book is here to help. I explore low-tech watering aids and ideas in Chapter 3 and delve into various irrigation systems you may wish to consider in Chapter 5.

REMEMBER

You don't need to reinvent the wheel, so to speak. Plenty of trial and error and research, worldwide and over many centuries, has yielded innovative and practical ways to install and care for plants.

Here I begin by taking a closer look at where you can reduce water use and how. Not every suggestion will apply — but many will! Conserving is a matter of examining every opportunity.

Seeing where it makes sense to implement

There are many places and times where saving water can (and should) be possible. These include the following:

>> Where getting water to your yard and plants is difficult or complex

>> Where the water supply is expensive/where water bills just keep going up and up

>> Where the water source is uncertain: unreliable, depleted, or drying up

>> Where rainfall is unpredictable, sparse, or briefly seasonal

>> Where water rationing is mandated and enforced

>> Where the landscaping you do have is suffering from lack of water

>> When you don't have time, funds, or the energy to fuss over your yard

>> When you're ready for a change to more responsible and creative landscaping

Understanding why being water-wise is important

Global climate–change weather models suggest that severe droughts may not be occasional anomalies to endure but become the norm — sobering news. Therefore confronting the situation and being proactive about your water use is imperative.

REMEMBER

Should things improve or monsoon rains be generous, well, the good habits and practices you develop ought to stay in place anyway. Wasting water is a careless habit; conserving water shows respect for life itself, starting with the plants and creatures inhabiting your yard and also respect for your neighbors and neighborhood, your municipality, and your bioregion.

Leveraging your water sources

Part of water-wise gardening is gathering all the water you can and sometimes storing it to use with care later — in other words, maximizing your supply. You may be surprised by some of these useful ideas (check out Chapter 2 for starters):

>> Start monitoring how much water your garden needs and uses.

>> Install one or more rain barrels.

>> Collect and store water in a cistern or tank.

>> Use gray water. *Gray water* isn't all of your household water, but rather the sources of relatively clean consumption, such as sinks, showers, bathtubs, and even the washing machine (not the toilet or utility sink). Some municipalities regulate the use of gray water and, of course, you don't want to use certain soaps or cleaning agents, which would make the re-used water unsafe or unsuitable for your plants or soil.

>> Route or reroute drainage from your roof. Study and route or reroute drainage out in your yard (see Chapter 16).

>> Put in a *rain garden,* a garden area set up in a low area where rain pools or where you can divert your rain gutters (details in Chapter 16).

>> Find out whether your municipality has *reclaimed* water, which is water that has been treated but isn't meant for drinking/not potable. They may be using it to irrigate city parks and other public places, but it may also be possible to access it for your personal landscape.

Eliminating wasteful watering practices

A series of seemingly minor changes in your watering habits can help. Here are a few suggestions:

>> **Prevent runoff.** Don't overwater, don't water too long, and help water soak in so plants can use it. It begins with good soil, actually; read and heed Chapters 4 and 16.

>> **Create watering basins around individual plants.** Chapter 3 explains how to make one, with a helpful illustration.

>> **Create water-need zones by grouping plants with similar needs together so you can water them together.** More in Chapters 3 and 10.

>> **Water when chance of evaporation is lowest.** A full explanation and discussion — including myth-busting — is in Chapter 3.

>> **Hold water in the ground around your plants by mulching.** It's cheap, it's easy, and it's tremendously effective. Consult Chapter 15.

REMEMBER

Just to get on the Mulch Soapbox for a moment: Anyone can mulch their plants and everyone, especially those needing to conserve water, should! Mulch has profound benefits. Mulch prevents evaporation, which is huge because most plant roots are fairly close to the soil surface. Mulched plants need water less frequently and stay fresh-looking longer after a watering. Mulch also helps keep weeds at bay, and weeds are notorious for stealing water and nutrients from your desired plants.

>> **Choose watering gear wisely.** Replace old-model sprinklers and sprinkler systems with some amazingly efficient new technology. A wide range of items and networks deliver water directly to the roots of your plants (and not to the sidewalk and gutter!). Review your options in Chapters 3 and 5.

TIP

Like to grow and display plants in containers, but you've definitely noticed that they're more water-intensive than plants in the ground? Good news: You can get the needed water to potted plants without waste or worry. Among the options are clever self-watering pots and water-holding crystals added to potting soil. See Chapters 15 and 17 for more details.

Replacing Impractical Plants with Practical Ones

If you're honest with yourself, you already know that your yard — including but not limited to your lawn — has some plants that aren't doing so well these days. Not enough water is obviously their problem. They're getting to be too much trouble and expense to maintain.

To be blunt, the solution is obvious. Out with the old, in with the new! I want to reassure you that not only can you make changes, but you can also embrace changes by making smart and creative choices that will look great. Keep reading for some general suggestions.

Getting rid of your lawn

Taking out your grass feels like the end of an era . . . because it's the end of an era. Green lawns suck up a lot of resources, mainly water but also fertilizer and perhaps weedkillers (all of which can be harmful to wildlife, your environs, and groundwater) — not to mention all your own effort and sweat in mowing and clipping. And what's the point if water is limited and no matter how hard you try, it doesn't look as lush as you want?

Completely removing your lawn isn't as hard as you might think. Lawn grass isn't deep-rooted, and you can dig it up and peel it away like a thick old carpet. You can also get rid of a lawn by tarping, solarizing the area, or undertaking sheet or "lasagna" mulching. Chapter 11 provides full instructions, details, and tips.

REMEMBER

After the deed is done and you've removed your grass, you'll have a clean slate, an area of open space, presumably in full sun and in full view of you and your neighbors. This is a brand-new landscaping opportunity! Yes, look at this transition as pivoting to a new and better way — because it is.

While you're contemplating your next steps, don't leave bare, exposed ground. Weeds — those hardiest and most resilient of all plants, even in dire drought conditions — will invade. The saying "Nature abhors a vacuum" is never truer than when a spot is freshly cleared. Just cover over the area until you're ready to re-landscape and replant (see Chapter 11 for a rundown of effective temporary barriers).

Considering lawn alternatives

You have a lot of options for alternatives, depending on the size of the space, your budget, and your energy. I recommend not only that you study the more in-depth discussion in Chapter 12, but also do a little (fun and inspiring) research by looking at how others in your neighborhood and region have dealt with lawn replacement.

Meanwhile, the following can jump-start your thinking:

>> **Put in a native drought-tolerant grass or grass blend.** True, your lawn won't look like a golf green, but it may serve as a pretty and quite water-wise new installation. A plus: These types of grasses look more harmonious and natural, rather than out of place.

>> **Consider ornamental grasses.** Unlike turf grasses, ornamental grasses are clump-formers, so they tend to be taller and need to be planted more closely if you're still wanting broad coverage. You can clip or mow to maintain a desired height.

>> **Install a meadow.** Full disclosure — installing a meadow takes soil preparation, careful selection of a balance of flowering plants and native grasses, and some regular maintenance to keep it looking nice. It's gardening; you can't just sprinkle a can of meadow mix and be done. However, the results can be gorgeous and gratifying, and the area definitely will consume very little water once established.

Some municipalities and homeowner associations are still reluctant to allow or approve of meadow gardens, particularly in front yards or areas clearly visible from the street.

>> **Put in a groundcover.** Plenty of plants certainly can fill in and cover up a broad area and look terrific. Some introduce different shades of green and other colors (and/or seasonal color changes, which can be lovely) to your home landscape. Chapter 7 has an annotated list of carpeters to consider.

THINK OUTSIDE THE GRASS BOX

Other ideas for an area once devoted to a lawn go beyond what you may have originally imagined. What about these solutions?

- **Lay down a base of gravel and rocks.** But do it right. Make sure water can get through and weeds are minimized. Explore different colors, sizes, and textures. Place larger rocks so they look natural and perhaps also serve a practical purpose, such as sheltering small plants vulnerable to wind. Chapter 14 can give you the ideas and information you need to proceed, including attractive planting suggestions.

- **Put in a terrace, patio, or deck.** In the case of a terrace or patio, instead of a slab, explore the new permeable options that allow you to tuck in low-growers like creeping thyme between pavers and also help filter water through your landscape rather than letting it run off. Check out Chapter 16.

- **Take a fresh look at artificial turf.** Don't scoff — cruddy ole Astroturf is a thing of the past. Artificial turf has experienced a major boom in recent years, thanks to new materials, technologies, options, and installation savvy. Consult Chapter 13 for more details. Such a lawn won't use water at all, except perhaps for an occasional rinse-off!

TIP

Don't be succulents-averse. There are more options than you may realize, and mixing and matching can also supply impressive, beautiful, and effective coverage.

Checking Out Suitable Ornamental Plants

A brave new world of exciting ornamental plants (grown for beauty and decoration) is available for low-water settings. In fact, never before in the history of gardening has there been such a broad selection of appropriate choices! The chapters in Part 2 are full of descriptive lists of water-wise plants. The lengths of the lists and the information, I hope, will be an eye-opener.

REMEMBER

Newly installed plants, of any kind, need and deserve a good start, especially ones billed as drought-tolerant. Once planted properly — see the guidance in Chapter 10 — they'll need extra water for at least their first year to help their root systems get established. After that, count on them to become much more self-sufficient.

Before looking at — and falling for — individual plants, get oriented. These sections describe the many different kinds and then delve into ways to tell if any given plant that catches your fancy will be a good choice for your low-water landscape.

Looking at the different types

The following are the general categories. Rest assured you can find many choices within each type that do well in low-water settings:

>> **Perennials:** These plants bloom year after year, often increasing in size or spreading out. Many are flowering, and you can pick ones to have colorful gardens at different times of the growing year.

>> **Annuals:** Although these plants live for only one growing season (hence the name), they deliver a lot of color and many are truly tough, standing up to heat and drought.

>> **Succulents:** Sure, these are a dry-garden cliché, but let me reassure you that your choices are endless. Get away from the ordinary and have fun!

>> **Shrubs:** Some bushes are good for hedges, some work well all on their own. Some have attractive needles or leaves, some change color with the seasons. Some flower and fruit. They always bring substance and heft to any home landscape.

>> **Trees:** They provide shade and beauty. The trick is to select ones appropriate to your climate and of a size that works for your yard.

>> **Vines:** Don't forget vines, which can grow quickly and drape over fences and other supports to add beauty of foliage and flower — at eye level or even higher. Some also produce fruit or attractive seedpods.

TIP

Ideally, you want some of everything in order to create a diverse home landscape. Variety keeps your yard interesting in all seasons.

Identifying appropriate plants

Any good plant nursery or garden center has a lot to offer, but you can't always be sure that everything is water-wise. Fortunately, recognizing the features of dryland plants isn't difficult when you start shopping around.

Succulent leaves and stems are such an obvious sign of drought-tolerance that I'm not going to call them out in the following lists. These plants have evolved to hold water and use it as needed; they're supremely appropriate for low-water landscapes. In fact, many don't need any supplemental water after they're established in your yard. Hard to beat!

When shopping or viewing plants in any setting, check the leaves. Look for:

» **Waxy coating:** The covering helps seal in and conserve water. Although many plants have coated leaves, dryland ones have especially obvious coatings — you can tell by touching or running a finger across one (sometimes a bit of the whitish powdery coating will come off on your finger).

» **Leathery texture:** Tough and/or thicker leaves are a sign that the plant isn't holding a lot of water, but neither does it have as much to lose.

» **Silver or gray color:** Lighter-colored leaves protect themselves and their plant from intense hot sun by reflecting back the light rather than absorbing it.

» **A coating of fuzz:** This is actually made up of many tiny, short hairs, which serve to slow water loss. The hairs also help to shield the leaf from direct sunlight.

» **Narrow and small leaves:** Plants transpire water through tiny openings in their leaves called *stomata*. Narrow and small leaves have less real estate available for stomata. Less stomata means less water loss!

Also check the stems. Look for:

» **Compact growth:** Watch for leaves that are held close to the stem, parallel or at a narrow angle (rather than splayed outward like an open hand). They still get necessary sunlight but are less vulnerable to drying out quickly.

» **Fuzz:** Like the fuzz that covers some leaf surfaces (see the previous bulleted list), these tiny hairs put the brakes on water loss and also shelter the stem surface from direct, drying sunlight.

» **Spines:** You may have heard that spines discourage animals from eating plants that bear them, and that's true, but they do more: Like the tiny hairs of fuzz, they reduce water loss and offer a little shade. (In the case of cacti, water may condense on the spines and eventually trickle down the ground, hopefully offering a bit of moisture to the plant's root system.)

COMPARING NATIVES VERSUS NONNATIVES

You may think that gardening with native plants results in a yard that looks a lot like an unkempt local or regional wild, natural area. What's the point, you ask? Don't people want their home landscapes to be more beautiful? Don't many gardeners want their yards to stand out? And don't they also want them to reflect their own taste as well as their wishes for enclosure and sanctuary?

There's no doubt that growing native plants makes practical sense. Native plants are well-adapted to local climate, weather patterns, and soils. They're naturally tough and thus allow a low-maintenance landscape. They're accustomed to getting by on low water and staying alive.

The chapters in Part 2 offer specifics. Here are some general guidelines:

- **If your concern is that native plants are too rangy, sprawling, casual, or sloppy, fret not!** Many savvy gardeners and horticulturists have been sorting through the many different species for quite some time and have spent their attention on the best ones, the ones that are suitable for home gardens — focusing on manageable size, tidy growth habit, best/prettiest foliage and flowers, longest bloom time, and so on. A lot of work has been done and continues to be done. The native plants offered for sale at local and regional nurseries and area plant sales meet these standards.

- **You can have it all — tough and beautiful native plants.** Another ongoing process is the improvement of native plants. Occasionally a rogue or random yellow-flowered plant will produce some irresistible red flowers (for example, coreopsis), someone will notice and take a cutting and, before too long, the red-flowered one is on offer. Horticulturists also have fiddled with and selected for longer bloom times, larger and more flowers, and smaller-size plants, which show up for sale as *cultivars* (cultivated varieties) or *nativars* (specifically, cultivated varieties of native plants).

- **Are nonnative low-water plants less preferable?** Some believe gardeners should stick to growing native plants because they best support local ecosystems, including beleaguered native butterflies, pollinators, and birds. That's an assumption. Low-water plants from other parts of the world (such as Mexico, Australia, the Mediterranean, and South Africa) make attractive garden plants and often the local insect and wildlife population adapts. Research is ongoing. ***Conclusion:*** There's nothing wrong with planting some natives and some nonnatives.

- **What if you want to support your local ecosystem?** I recommend approaching this concern on a case-by-case basis, or rather plant-by-plant. Research each plant you choose, no matter the origins; a good nursery staffer ought to be able to reassure you both on a plant's qualities and habits and on its benefits to native creatures . . . or point you to alternatives.

Exploring Beauty and Color Tricks

"But I don't like desert-dot landscaping," you say? Take heart. You can avoid clichés in many ways and have a great-looking yard that uses minimal water. These sections give you an overview.

Building up your yard from the ground up

When redoing a yard or an area, you can tackle two projects first and foremost. These aren't really beauty tricks, but the results can be dramatic enough that you and your neighbors might think so! Either or both of the following will result in a major boost for whatever you install next (healthy, happy plants lead to a gorgeous home landscape, it's as simple as that!):

>> **Install an in-ground irrigation system.** This project tends to involve a lot of digging and disruption, so plant when you're done. Consult Chapter 5 to get a handle on what's involved.

>> **Improve the soil.** If plants and landscaping projects have struggled or failed in your yard in the past, it may be high time to stop and start over.

Dig out and replace terrible or depleted soil, or at least improve what you have by adding organic matter (turn to Chapter 4 for details). This could be a game-changing step on your way to a successful new landscape, one that uses less water (because the improved soil holds moisture so much better) and is beautiful (because the plants are thriving). Consider it before you do anything else!

Exploring dry-design ideas

Look, really look, at what others have done. Begin right now by turning to the color insert in the center of this book and flipping through the images.

Then, next time you're online or on Instagram or Pinterest, run some searches and feast your eyes. Also take the time to go into a bookstore, the shop attached to a botanic garden, or even just the racks at your local home-and-landscape center, stand there and browse colorful books and magazines — buy a few, bring them home, and study the many good ideas.

This sort of exploration is necessary, nourishing, fun — and inspirational!

HOW TO GET A LUSH LOOK

To get an appealing, filled-in, lush look with low-water plants, choose plants with care. Start by cruising through the long lists in Part 2. Here are a couple general suggestions:

- **Aim for a balance of colors.** You want variety, but not a total mishmash. Do this by choosing and emphasizing colors you like and are compatible with each other. Different shades of green foliage can tie it all together.

- **Plant plenty!** You want to cover open ground without crowding. Intermixing makes all the difference — surround a small tree or shrub with flowers (see the photo in the color insert for a great example) or have an ornamental grass arise from a carpet of groundcovering sedums.

WARNING

Beware the fool's paradise of an "instant landscape." This is when a bunch of larger plants are brought in and planted close together to give a mature and finished look. The satisfaction and pleasure don't last. It won't be long until the plants start crowding each other, or some start to dominate and overrun the others. The health and good looks of all of them start to falter. You'll end up having to prune often and/or take out some plants — a lot of extra work and expense, most unfortunate.

Borrowing ideas from nature

The natural world is the original testing ground for what survives and what thrives, no matter what your soil and climate challenges. Here's a sampling of that wisdom that you can use in your own yard (Chapter 10 has much more information):

» **Capitalize on microclimates in your yard.** A *microclimate* is a hyper-local situation, differing somewhat from its immediate surroundings. The shelter of a large rock, wall, or courtyard offers you the chance to grow plants that need extra protection, either because they dry out faster or get damaged or toppled on windy days. You can make little nooks or vignettes in such spots.

» **Leverage strength in numbers.** Plants grown in close proximity can not only present an attractive composition but can also help protect one another from everything from being stepped or nibbled on to collectively raising the local humidity for mutual benefit. Check out Chapter 3 for additional details.

» **Have color going on at all times.** Flowering plants cycle in and out of bloom. You can maximize color by choosing plants that bloom over a long period, but planning for changes is fun and gratifying. Study the lists in Part 2 and make wish lists according to colors and seasons.

TIP

Don't forget foliage color! Succulents, in particular, offer a wonderful array of colors, everything from rosy red to sage green to powdery blue to burnished gold. Check on leaf colors for ornamental grasses as well as for some perennials and shrubs. Some plants have *variegated* leaves (leaves of more than one color); others change hues with the seasons.

» **Play with texture.** Nature abounds in variety, and that's absolutely true when it comes to the leaf and plant textures of low-water plants — shiny, smooth, rough, fluffy, brushy, quilted, spiky, and so on. When you fill your landscape with a range of textures, the eye travels, delighted and intrigued.

Chapter **2**

Conserving and Harvesting Water

A s more and more people confront and worry about the scarcity of precious water, remember that farmers and gardeners in other cultures and, indeed, throughout history have found ways to conserve and collect it. These days modern technology also plays a helping role. This chapter looks at how this inge-nuity applies to maintaining your home landscape.

You'll come away with good ideas to try, and I hope you can responsibly sustain and nurture the plantings in your yard for beauty, food, or both.

Understanding Water

To fully comprehend water, think of the *water cycle* (see Figure 2-1). Water is con-stantly in motion, through the earth, into waterways natural and man-made, and up into the air as vapor, only to regroup and fall back to the earth as rain (or sleet or snow). Somewhere. The planet as whole sustains a finite amount of water.

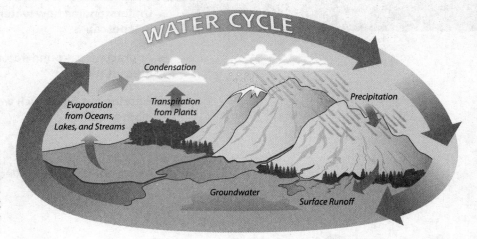

WATER CYCLE

Condensation

Evaporation from Oceans, Lakes, and Streams

Transpiration from Plants

Precipitation

Groundwater

Surface Runoff

FIGURE 2-1: Water, in various forms, is constantly cycling through the environment.

Source: https://gpm.nasa.gov/education/water-cycle

If the area where you live has dry cycles or is increasingly dry, that means there is less water "within the regional system" to work with. Bear with me here: The following sections discuss the public water supply's issues, which *is* applicable to how people manage their home landscapes.

Explaining evaporation

Evaporation is the (invisible to one's eyes) loss of water to air as it converts to water vapor. Evaporation isn't a small matter! In dry climates, with low humidity, it happens faster and more dramatically. Massive amounts of water are lost to the air.

Like sweat, evaporation is a cooling process, which would be some small comfort if it weren't for the fact that replenishment is such a challenge. For the human body or a plant, replenishment is a matter of the delivery of more water to keep oneself or the plant comfortable and alive. When water leaves the reservoirs, lakes, rivers, and man-made impoundments, the vapor may end up as rainfall very far away — unfortunately, it often does. That is, it doesn't necessarily cycle locally.

Take the situation with Lake Mead, for example, which provides water for Las Vegas and several other cities. The annual rainfall in that general region is a paltry 4 or fewer inches, and Lake Mead has an evaporation rate estimated at nearly more than 6 vertical feet per year. Multiplying this rate by the surface area of Lake Mead gives a volume of 1.04 million acre-feet/year lost to evaporation! Meanwhile, the entire state of Nevada is (currently — this figure could change in the uncertain future) is allowed to remove 300,000 acre-feet per year from the

Colorado River. In other words, astoundingly, the amount of water lost to evaporation from Lake Mead is more than three times larger than what Nevada is allowed to remove from the Colorado River. Sobering to contemplate, to say the least.

Preventing evaporation

The Catch-22 of the public water supplies is that the holding reservoirs like Lake Mead are wide open to the air — evaporation is inevitable. Can anything be done to stop or at least mitigate the loss?

You may live near or have heard about how Los Angeles back in 2015 acted to prevent evaporation by dumping millions of black plastic floating shade balls onto the surfaces of their reservoirs. It worked well, but it was expensive. Other municipalities have experimented with using floating covers where practical to prevent or slow evaporation. Oily surfactants, in a very thin layer, can also slow or stop evaporation from the surface of water bodies, but they're hard to apply evenly and may present water-quality problems.

Meanwhile, those who manage public water understand the importance of doing everything in their power to keep water within a regional watershed. Treated wastewater is routed back to the regional reservoir(s). If only the "budget" came out even (same amount of water in and out); that's the goal, of course, but in practice, it doesn't always work out that way. Lake Mead continues to experience a net loss, despite a variety of efforts aimed at evening things out, which isn't good news.

Looking at what you can do to reduce evaporation

Here I discuss the problems of evaporation and what you can discover in the context of your home landscape. On the far smaller scale of a home landscape, the following are the important takeaways you can consider and reflect upon (indeed, these are the essence of water conservation):

>> **Don't store water in broad, open areas.** Enclosed and out of the hot sun is best. Consider a rain barrel or cistern.

>> **When you store water, cover the surface of the storage container to mitigate or prevent evaporation.** A fitted plastic or plywood cover works; if necessary, secure it in place with clamps or a bungie cord.

>> **Cover plants to absorb heat and lower evaporation.** Put plenty of mulch over your planted areas. Shade trees or shade structures shelter in-ground or potted plants. Shade cloth protects vulnerable plants (refer to Chapter 16).

>> **Keep water cycling hyperlocally.** Literally, to the extent you can, aim to make your own yard a contained or conservative system — hoard, keep, use, reuse, and don't let it get away. Doing so definitely can lower your water use and water bill.

The section, "Collecting and Storing Water," later in this chapter provides more help.

Differentiating between drought-resistant and drought-tolerant

Speaking of landscape plants in the context of water use, choosing ones that can get by on less water is paramount. Here I discuss how they do this.

Plants take up water through their root systems and then the water travels through the plant. A well-hydrated plant has sturdy stems and firm leaves, and if water remains sufficient, the ability to produce buds, flowers, and fruit/seeds. But the water doesn't stay — more water is constantly needed to sustain the growth and production. (A water-stressed plant grows slowly or not at all.)

Water exits plants through the undersides of leaves, through tiny pores called *stomata*. Water departs invisibly, as water vapor. This is called *transpiration* — the plant version of evaporation.

In a nutshell, here is the difference between two types of dry-climate plants:

>> **Drought-resistant plant:** This type of plant can close its stomata and thereby lose less water; a drought-resistant plant controls its transpiration rate, notching it down during dry times to conserve water within itself. Many plants, particularly native plants, are drought-resistant.

>> **Drought-tolerant plant:** This kind of plant is adapted to low or, at times, no water. It's drought-resistant all the time, not just in response to a crisis drought or dry spell. These plants are the toughest of the tough.

For information on and lists of such plants, turn to Part 2.

Knowing Where Your Water Comes from

In order not to take anything water-related for granted or operate under misconceptions, understanding water sources — and the associated threats and challenges — is important. The following sections briefly explain the main ones.

Eyeing issues with primary sources

Where water comes from and how it's collected and used is, actually, rife with issues and sometimes controversy. Here's a quick overview:

Groundwater

To generalize and simplify, the earth holds freshwater deep in the ground (underneath the layers of topsoil, subsoil, and rock — refer to Chapter 4 for more about those layers). This water is called *groundwater*, and the under-earth lakes are called *aquifers*. Sometimes water travels or bubbles to the surface via springs.

Here are some of the challenging issues that groundwater faces:

>> **Overdrilling:** "Too many straws in the milkshake" is a good way to cast a serious problem. Too many wells being drilled into an aquifer depletes the amount available to everyone (or to a minority — witness how irrigation for agriculture in the West depleted the Navajo Nation's water supply). Wells are dug or drilled ever-deeper, but is drilling deeper really a solution?

>> **Pollution:** All manner of substances and materials are considered pollutants — anything from fuel and solvents to cleaning products to pesticides and weedkillers. Such things contaminate groundwater and, at least for drinking purposes, people must find a way to clean it to make it safe for consumption. (If not, people get sick, land is contaminated, and/or the water can't be used.)

>> **No reliability:** Springs fluctuate or may go dry seasonally or for long periods in response to groundwater levels; that is, their flow isn't guaranteed to be dependable.

Precipitation

Precipitation brings evaporated water back down to earth, directly in rainfall and in a more-delayed delivery with snowfall (that is, people wait for spring's annual snowmelt to bring that water down to lower areas). It goes into lakes (man-made and natural), streams, and rivers. Its arrival recharges aquifers, although some eventually runs out to sea.

Here are some of the challenges of dealing with precipitation:

>> **Runoff:** This water often runs off before it can be used.

>> **Collection:** Collecting it is logical but raises the issue of: who owns the rainwater? Colorado restricts residential rainwater harvesting on the grounds that the state government owns and needs to control (gather and distribute) the water that falls from the sky and homeowners must not divert too much of it to their own use.

>> **Snowpack:** As for areas that depend on melted snowpack, they may be disappointed and in trouble if there's a light winter.

Rivers, lakes, and streams

Water naturally collects and moves through nature's own drainage and collection basins — rivers, lakes, and streams. The volume and stability of these sources is subject, of course, to forces beyond human control, including rainfall and underground supply. A plus is that water that moves naturally through soil and rocks gets naturally filtered.

Here are myriad and vexing challenges:

>> **Water-use rights:** Often these sources are part of larger and complex systems, and upstream and downstream rights are debated, negotiated, and argued over. The needs of agriculture and cities conflict as they compete for water from the same sources.

>> **Pollution and its sources:** Identifying and mitigating pollution and contamination can be complex — runoff from agriculture is a particularly serious problem.

>> **Consequences of diversions:** Humans have proven capable of altering even large features; witness how diversions for irrigation destroyed the now-dried up, once-enormous Aral Sea located on the border between Kazakhstan and Uzbekistan (one of the greatest ecological disasters of modern times).

Looking at how water is accessed

You turn on your home's faucets, your home's hose, and/or your home's irrigation system. But where does that water come from? These sections explain that question and how you can plan to use that water.

WATER, WATER, EVERYWHERE, AND NOT A DROP TO DRINK

Pictures from space show that the Earth is a blue planet, three-quarters of which is covered by water. That should be heartening to know, especially as humanity confronts water shortages, but the reality is that almost all of that water isn't freshwater, available for sustaining life on land (drinking and irrigating). In fact, 97 percent is saltwater, 2 percent is frozen in the polar ice caps — which are currently losing some of that mass and melting. The remaining 1 percent is what land dwellers (humans, animals, terrestrial plant life) depend upon to live. A pretty meager number!

No wonder the world has so much water stress. Population growth — more humans are alive on this planet than at any time in history — and the pressures of climate change combine to make this limited water in great demand. Conservation, creativity, and innovation are scant hopes (desalinization of seawater still isn't widespread or, many feel, a realistic, cost-effective option). It's incumbent on every person to wisely consume what water they're able to access.

Municipal tap (potable) water

If you live in a town or city, your drinking (*potable*) water supply — via pipes under the street and into your home — comes from a shared water supply. That's made possible by often-complex networks of reservoirs, treatment plants, and sewage facilities, served by pumping stations, aqueducts, holding tanks, and water towers, and maintained and monitored by crews of professionals with a variety of responsibilities.

Unfortunately in many places, this infrastructure is aging and needs to be upgraded and replaced (if only there were sufficient funds). You're probably aware of the dangers of lead pipes and tainted drinking water (Flint, Michigan still isn't fixed). Also challenging is the fact that older systems waste water, mainly because of leaks throughout the system, including in difficult-to-identify or hard-to-access spots.

Given the safety standards that drinking water is supposed to meet, realizing that a portion never makes it to your faucets is sobering. If your community is struggling with solving this daunting problem, you're well aware; at the very least we, the end-consumers of potable water, can do is conserve it and not compound the loss and waste issues. Fix all leaks in your home and yard!

Municipal reclaimed (purple-pipe) water

Water can be captured and recycled, but not treated all the way up to drinking-water quality. The city of Tucson, Arizona, is a pioneer in this regard. A waste treatment plant called *Agua Nueva* (Spanish for "new water") collects and treats household water, everything but flushed-toilet water — sink, tubs and showers, washing machines, dishwashers — and cleans it using various filters, chemicals, and microorganisms. That water is then sent back out for public use in pipes that have been painted purple. This reclaimed water irrigates many things in the city, including parks, school campuses, and residential landscapes. The aquifer water is reserved for drinking water, a different treatment and delivery infrastructure.

Tucson isn't alone. Other communities have their versions. In fact, the purple (or magenta) pipes are dubbed "Irvine Purple" for the community in southern California. CalTrans in California also irrigates highway-side landscaping with reclaimed water — and posts signs saying so, partly I imagine to pat themselves on the back but also partly to head off "what? Water is in short supply and they're irrigating the freeway oleanders?!" outrage.

WATER-BILL WAKE-UP CALL!

No surprise that an in-demand resource is both highly regulated and not at all free! Indeed in many areas now water districts have boards of directors to oversee the supply, management, delivery, and price/rates. Membership on these boards is often an elected position — all I say about that is, yes, it becomes political.

Anyone whose property is connected to a municipal water system gets a bill, usually monthly. Billing units are HCF or CCF (hundred cubic feet/centum cubic feet, same thing), which translates to 748 gallons of water. There's often a minimum base charge, and when you exceed that — as many do — you're billed accordingly. Water districts set it progressively so that big water users really get slammed. Restrictions, bans, and fines are also deployed.

A close look at your bill shows not only your consumption for the past month, but also your own usage in the past and sometimes even how you're doing compared to neighbors. All of this information is to induce you to pay attention! I consider that it's like monitoring my car's gas mileage in these times of high prices — merely paying attention certainly inspires you to conserve.

Getting a whopper water bill is a horrible feeling, but it's also a wake-up call. As you explore and put into practice some of the ideas in this chapter and book, keep an eye on your HCFs. You can always make that number come down.

If your community has this system in place, use purple-pipe water to irrigate your home landscape. If it doesn't, perhaps you can advocate for it. My guess is that the cities of the future, large and small, will all have to find a way to go this route eventually.

Well water

Before water and sewer systems became widely available, water came from wells. Some rural areas where it's simply not possible or cost-effective to deal with water in these ways still get water from wells. And waste went into seepage pits or larger-capacity septic fields and septic tanks.

Having a well serving your home and landscape isn't always a guarantee of a steady or consistent water supply, as many people have learned the hard way. Sometimes a well runs dry and the remedy is to deepen it or dig a new, deeper one, perhaps a distance away (and sufficiently far from where waste is going).

But a new or deeper well isn't always a solution or a long-term fix. If the aquifer is depleted, if there is too much demand on it, then you're back to the "too many straws in the milkshake" problem that I discuss in the section, "Groundwater," earlier in this chapter.

Ideally, simple, small, and seemingly independent wells are a low-tech and manageable source compared to the energy, effort, and infrastructure it takes to deliver water to a resident of a big city. But returning everyone to well water clearly isn't an option. Also monitoring and managing well-water quality, even with testing and filters simple or sophisticated, is also a common problem. Toxins, agricultural runoff, and salts are the tip of the iceberg. These are reasons why rural residents, as civilization creeps out into their areas, are often willing to tap into the modern, treated, water supply infrastructure should it be offered.

Checking on Your Landscape's Water Use

Monitoring and managing your consumption is important to do, but discovering what your actual needs are takes investigating as well, which these sections explain.

Confirming soil moisture

How much water are your plants getting? How much do they need? The answers to these questions vary, but I can get you started on figuring out what's going on in your yard.

Using the good ole finger test

Don't rely on what you see or think you see. In fact, if you've mulched like I urge (see Chapter 15 for full details), you can't tell because that mulch layer is blocking your view.

TIP

The easiest way to check is to stick your finger in your garden ground near a plant or planting, past the mulch layer, right down into the soil. Plunge your index finger to your second knuckle and then pull it back out. Your finger can tell you:

>> Is it clean and dry? Water is needed in that spot.

>> Is soil clinging to your finger? No water is needed at this time.

I know that this test is primitive. But you'd be surprised at how accurate it is. Give it a try.

Trying slightly more sophisticated tests

Simple soil-moisture tests before and after watering will give a clearer picture. Repeat until you're satisfied that water is getting to the level you want it — that it's soaking in deeply enough. Try these:

>> **Utilize a probe.** A slightly more sophisticated variation is to use a probe. That is, plunge a stick, dowel rod, or even a piece of rebar into the ground near any plants you're wondering or concerned about. If it emerges clean, the area is too dry; if it emerges fairly coated with soil, all is well for the time being.

>> **Dig down.** Seeing how deeply the water is soaking in — with your own eyes — is eye-opening. To do this, get down on your hands and knees with a trowel and dig down in a planted area. Do this both before and after a water delivery, taking care to avoid root systems (carefully replace the soil afterward). Soaked soil is darker.

Working with the ideal guideline

The most common reference point is to give your actively growing landscape plants an inch a week of supplemental water if rainfall doesn't supply it — or make up the difference.

That number can go down if you put in plants that need less water. If your area is often quite dry, give priority to succulents and native plants. Flip to Part 2 for specifics.

REMEMBER

That number is higher when you're caring for newly installed plants; baby plants always need extra irrigation to help them get their roots under them. After their root systems are established, you can dial back the water deliveries.

You may be wondering, what exactly does an inch a week mean, and how do I find out whether that's what my plants are getting? Well, I'm here to help:

>> **The hypothetical ideal:** An inch of water per square foot per week is the ideal and, in theory, that's approximately one plant — one pepper plant in your vegetable garden or one penstemon plant in your flowerbed, just for examples.

>> **The calculation:** Here's a little bit of math for the hypothetical example: 12 inches × 12 inches × 1 inch is the volume of ground per plant (30.5 cm × 30.5 cm × 2.5 cm). How much water does it take to saturate 144 cubic inches (366 cubic cm) of soil?

>> **The handy converter:** You don't have to do the rest of the math to arrive at the ideal amount of water needed here. Use a converter:

- **English (inches):** www.asknumbers.com/cubic-inches-to-gallons.aspx

- **Metric (centimeters):** www.gallonstoliters.com/

The answer is a rather shocking 0.6 gallons (2.3 liters) of water per plant per week.

To figure out how much ideal water you'd need to supply in the absence of rain in planted beds, then figure out their volume (length × width × 1 inch/2.5 cm) and plug that figure into one of the above calculators. Actively growing plants receiving this much water will thrive.

Measuring rainfall

Knowledge is power. Being empowered to detect wished-for rainfall — when it's arriving and how much falls — is helpful so you can adjust your watering plans and thereby not water needlessly. Looking outside or checking your local forecast, or both, is the easy way. (A reminder that incoming rain also offers the opportunity to capture water; I discuss rain barrels and other ways to collect water in the section, "Collecting and Storing Water," later in this chapter.)

Technology offers more nimble and precise ways to monitor, including the following.

Rain gauge

A range of different products is available. The simplest, most inexpensive gadgets are plastic tubes with an internal floating marker and measurements (inches, cms, or both). Just as with an outdoor thermometer, you want one that's easy to read from a distance: a large and colorful floating marker and large, legible markings going up the side. Securely mount it on a fence or post where you can easily view it from indoors. Some models involve plunging a pointed stake into garden ground.

A little fancier is a digital gauge (battery-powered), readable from indoors. It comes with an outdoor bucket that transmits data to it and self-empties afterward. Features vary, so pick one that supplies only the info you expect to need and use and program it accordingly. (Some store historical data, a nice feature if you're interested in discovering and responding to weather patterns.)

You can spend more and get something bigger and more decorative, if you wish — functional yard art. I'm referring to whimsical-looking items based on old-fashioned rain-measuring gadgets. A common configuration is where rain is collected in a glass vial; the weight activates a float-and-lever system, which responds to show the rainfall amount on a large decorative/visible-from-afar display. Search online for "decorative Jeffersonian-era rain gauge" and you'll find several mail-order sources.

Rain sensors

You can mount these small gadgets on your home's gutters and sync them to your in-ground irrigation system; they can even override or shut down the system if it's delivering water when rain arrives unexpectedly or exceeds original projections. Some are wired, some are wireless. They operate using sensitive internal hygroscopic discs.

TIP

Install a rain sensor where rain won't be blocked — for example, in a spot that's not obstructed by a roof overhang, tree branches, or anything else that might interfere.

Phone/email alerts

Match up your devices (phone or computer) to weather apps. Certain irrigation systems bypass your involvement altogether, providing the option of connecting via Wi-Fi/Bluetooth to such apps and responding by altering their output.

RECOGNIZING SIGNS OF WATER STRESS IN YOUR PLANTS

If you're watching your plants carefully, they indicate how they're doing and whether they're getting enough water. I know you'll coddle them when they're first planted, but don't abandon them after their first year or two in your landscape. Visit often and observe.

Signs that plants are water-stressed:

- Wilting and drooping
- Slow or stopped growth
- Curled leaves
- Sunburned leaves
- Foliage that loses its usual color, fading to unhealthy-looking bluish or grayish hues
- New leaves that are too small
- Dropped/aborted leaves, buds, and/or fruit
- Failure to revive in cooler evening hours and/or after a water delivery
- Attacks by insect pests and/or signs of plant diseases

Early detection of water stress and, whenever possible, good soaking deliveries of water (and mulch, if it's been depleted) can bring such plants back from the brink. Needless to say, if you aren't on the case or miss the signs, water-stressed plants falter and die.

Signs of overwatering can look similar and throw you off. Those signs can include drooping leaves, leaves that lack color and luster, and yellowing leaves.

Collecting and Storing Water

Various ways to grab and save precious water are available and worth looking into because water collection is easy, convenient, affordable . . . and smart. The two main options are rain barrels and cisterns. You may hear these projects referred to as *rainwater harvesting*.

The main source of water is rainwater routed from your home's gutter system, so you want good gutter coverage of your rooflines, complete with screens or filters. Make a practice of cleaning out the gutters yearly, ideally in a dry season (because it's easier). Other possible sources include runoff from other impervious hardscape in your home landscape, such as an elevated patio or deck where you can route and collect that runoff.

WARNING

Before proceeding, find out if your area has limitations — that is, limits on how much water you can collect from your own home and landscape. Colorado's regulations are a case in point (refer to the section, "Precipitation," earlier in this chapter where I discuss them). Presently most homeowners in that state are limited to a maximum of two rain barrels with a combined maximum storage capacity of 110 gallons. Permitting may apply.

Another thing to check locally is whether tax incentives, rebates, or discounted suppliers are options. Many municipalities offer them in order to encourage water conservation and stormwater control in their community.

Rain barrels

Not all rain barrels are created equal — they're usually made of some kind of heavy-duty plastic; some are larger, some are smaller. Colors and styles as well as capacity varies. Household barrels are typically 50 gallons (though larger ones are available). They range in price from about $100 to $400. Look around at what your neighbors are using and shop around locally and online to locate the many choices.

REMEMBER

Unless your area is fortunate enough to receive regular rainfall (uncertain or unlikely, to be honest, for most households in water-scarce areas), rainwater collection isn't a dependable or year-round source of water for your home landscape. Consider it supplemental and, of course, make the most of it.

TIP

You get what you pay for. The best rain barrels are made of UV-resistant resin, with seamless rotational molding and spin weld fittings. They aren't cheap, but they're long-lasting and work beautifully.

Or you may choose to make your own. Use a large, clean, sturdy plastic barrel and install a lid (with an opening for the incoming gutter water) and spigot. Heed the following information — features that good, purchased rain barrels should also have. Figure 2-2 shows a good example of a rain barrel.

WARNING

Recycled barrels may be tempting, but you must find out what the original use was; solvents, oils, and farm chemicals are all no-no's. Old garbage cans may be leaky or not strong enough to support a full volume of water without buckling.

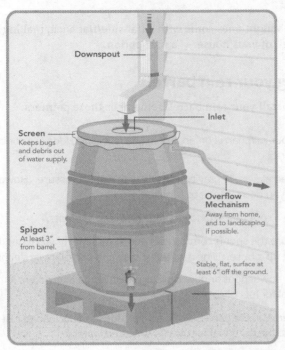

Downspout

Inlet

Screen
Keeps bugs
and debris out
of water supply.

**Overflow
Mechanism**
Away from home,
and to landscaping
if possible.

Spigot
At least 3"
from barrel.

Stable, flat, surface at
least 6" off the ground.

FIGURE 2-2:
Your rain barrel
should have
certain key
features,
especially a
secure lid and an
access spigot.

*Source: https://lincolnstormwater.org/
residents/rain-barrels/*

Seeking certain features

Rain barrels work best when they have the following practical features:

>> **A sealable lid:** A securely fitted lid keeps out debris, bugs (including mosquito larvae, definitely unwelcome), and animals (including birds and snakes). Screening may not be sufficient because pollen and dust can still get through (and if the water will be directed into an irrigation system, tiny materials like those items can clog emitters). Use a solid lid such as a board, piece of metal, or plastic.

A good, nonflimsy, secured cover is also a safety matter, if you have a curious outdoor cat on the premises or small children playing outdoors.

>> **Outlet spigot:** It needs to sit low-down on the side of the barrel. Otherwise water sits below it and becomes stagnant.

>> **Overflow pipe:** When a barrel gets really full, it will overflow. A pipe inserted near the top can carry off excess water — it should be long enough to be routed to a nearby plant or bed. Thus no water is lost or wasted!

>> **Sturdy construction and fittings:** These prevent leaks.

Some store-bought ones come with a flat side/flat back, making it easier to wedge against a wall of your house — a nice option.

Installing your rain barrel

When you install your rain barrel, remember these pointers:

>> Place your rain barrel on an ample and level spot, ideally a concrete pad or pavers.

>> If you can elevate it, gravity will help with water pressure. (However, not too high — you don't want it to topple.)

>> Site it in a spot that's handy to your garden and plants.

>> Make sure the spot is comfortable and accessible *for you* (checking on it, hooking up a hose, filling a watering can, and occasionally cleaning it).

>> Route a downspout or downspouts into it; add a filter/filters if there's the potential for lots of debris.

>> Consider multiple barrels because if all downspouts lead to just one barrel you have the potential for overflow/wasted water.

Using the water from your rain barrel

When you're ready to use the water in your barrel in your yard, keep the following in mind:

>> You can hook up a hose to the spigot.

>> You can simply fill a watering can at the spigot and make repeated trips into the garden or to your potted plant collection.

>> You can even hook up an inground irrigation system to it (refer to Chapter 5 for information).

WARNING

Don't hook up a soaker hose to a rain barrel's spigot. There isn't enough water pressure for the soaker hose to operate effectively, particularly at its farthest reaches.

Maintaining your rain barrel

Clean out your rain barrel and perhaps replace the spigot, and any filters, once or twice a year. Otherwise silt may build up in the bottom, and/or the interior may get a stinky film.

SUPPLEMENTAL WATER FOR YOUR RAIN BARREL

What if there's a period of no rain? Your rain barrel stands empty and unused, which is unfortunate.

You can supply it with household water, then. Collect kitchen-sink water, veggie-rinsing water, bathtub/shower water, even dehumidifier water. Avoid water that has particles in it or soaps that may contain microbeads. Use pitchers or buckets in the house, and once they're full, make a delivery to the rain barrel, replacing the lid afterward.

If your winters have freezing weather, completely empty the barrel beforehand. Freezing water in a spigot can ruin it, and residual water in a frozen barrel expands and can damage it. Store it in a garage, shed, or barn over the winter months.

WARNING

Water that runs off your roof, into your gutters, and then into your rain barrel is untreated and may pick up chemicals and debris from your roofing material. It may also be contaminated by anything from bird droppings to microbes, or contain impurities absorbed from the air, such as arsenic and mercury. Even if you have filters in place or flush off the first few collected gallons, *don't drink it.* Only use this water on your plants and lawn!

Cisterns and tanks

Cisterns are large tanks for storing as much as 20,000 gallons (75,708 liters) of water. Although farmers and market gardeners as well as public parks and gardens may use such things, residential homeowners can stockpile water for later use, too. A homeowner-size one is around 10 × 20 feet and 3 feet deep (3 x 6.1 × 0.9 m), with a capacity of around 4,000 gallons (15,141 liters).

Check with your local authorities to see if cistern use is permitted or regulated in any way. Areas with severe water restrictions ban these.

If you do get the green light, new challenges lie ahead, including location, materials, cost, delivery, and setup. You also want to consider how you can protect it from heat and sun (overheated water or algae growth being the problems) and what types of filters and pumps to use, if any. If you're determined to proceed, consult the supplier — whether a home-improvement store or an ag-supply outlet.

Other ideas

Water directed from downspouts from your roof, or an upper deck or balcony area, and routed directly into your garden can bring needed water to your plants — assuming it rains. Although this isn't a viable year-round watering strategy, it's safe and legal.

You may want to consider a rain garden. Chapter 16 discusses rain gardens in greater detail.

Another option is a relatively new technology called *rain walls.* They're basically slender vertical water-storage tanks, made of strong, UV-stabilized, food-grade plastic. Pioneered in Australia, they come in building blocks and are thus stackable or can be set up as interlocking forms. You can fit one or more into a very narrow side yard, for example, or make a fence or wall out of several or many. Installation is straightforward. Check out www.rainwaterhog.com.

Using Gray Water: A Good Idea?

Gray water (sometimes spelled "grey") may be another source of water you can collect and give to your landscape plants. *Gray water* is water from inside your home, basically anything but toilet-flushed water bound for the sewer or septic tank. Also avoid collecting utility-sink water. Gray water is wastewater from household sinks, showers and tubs, and laundry.

Utilizing it is indeed water-wise. You've paid for it once if you get your water from your municipality, yet you're using it twice (for those with well water, similar point: you're using it twice). Thus you're conserving water and conserving energy. By not sending this wastewater into the sewer or your septic tank, you're lightening their load, too.

There may be incentives to use it, or there may be restrictions. Check your city, county, or state websites and/or confirm with phone calls before proceeding.

Here are the best ways to get it into your garden, where it's needed:

>> **Collect in buckets and pitchers.** Leave them in the tub and sinks at all times so everyone in the household gets in the habit of dumping gray water in them.

>> **Route directly.** An outflow pipe from the kitchen sink or washing machine goes straight out to the yard.

LOOKING IN A CRYSTAL BALL — THE FUTURE OF WATER

We aren't living in a time of plenty. Even though this book was conceived as being directed to residents of the arid West — a broad area, to be sure — people in other regions probably will be needing this information in the future. Humans and our endeavors, including maintaining our home landscapes, consume a lot of water. Anything you can do to reduce and reuse is not just for the sake of the planet — it's also in your own best interest.

Getting in the habit of conserving water in our own backyards has an important advantage: It makes us more sensitive to and participatory in our surroundings. Gardeners can lead the way.

TIP

An on-off valve is a good idea, for those days when you run three loads of wash, which may be too much water for your plants, especially if you're growing drought-tolerant natives.

» **Rig an irrigation system, complete with storage tank, filters, and outgoing lines.** This sort of thing takes some expertise, and some municipalities don't allow DIY installations; you must hire a trained and licensed professional to install it.

WARNING

Because people use soap products in all of these areas, and some soaps are harmful to the environment (to soils, to plants, and to groundwater), find out what's allowed and what's best. Basically you want to favor soap products that don't contain microbeads, phosphates, salts, boron, or oils. You may have to change brands in order to collect maximum gray water. Also use common sense: don't reuse household water that contains bleach or cleaning products, or laundry water that rinsed diapers or a mechanic's work clothes.

Out of an abundance of caution, don't use gray water on certain plants, including anything you'll eat — for example, salad greens and melons. However, watering tomato and pepper plants, berry plants, and trees (including fruit and nut trees) with gray water is considered okay.

IN THIS CHAPTER

» **Making the switch to smarter watering**

» **Implementing efficient water delivery**

» **Looking at low-tech tricks and techniques that help**

Chapter **3**

Waste Not, Want Not: Watering Strategically

Water is basic. With few exceptions, home landscapes and gardens everywhere need water. However, succeeding with meeting plant moisture needs in areas with little rain, seasonal extremes, and/or increasing water restrictions is undeniably challenging.

REMEMBER

I can't help but point out that most people overwater — without realizing it. Established plants, especially, require far less water than new arrivals and baby plants. Keep your eyes on this prize: Your water-wise landscape will use less and less water as the years go by.

At any rate, you don't need to duplicate what other people have already mastered. All sorts of techniques, tricks, materials, and gadgets are available to help, leveraging both the most current technology as well as ancient practices. This chapter is full of empowering ideas to help you water more strategically. Waste not, want not, here you go!

Recognizing the Purpose of Watering

Providing water to plants sustains them and also powers growth — which in turn powers beauty and food.

Where the water supply is scant, unreliable, or unpredictable, plants adapt. That is, native plants adapt. A number need little or no water for long periods. But they still need *some*, particularly those chosen to enhance and beautify home landscapes.

Turning to native plants, or comparable ones from similar climates, is logical. (Making appropriate matches between climate, region, and your own yard and plants is what Part 2 is all about.) But providing some water, sometimes, is still going to be part of the picture for nearly every gardener.

The good news is, you can change or fine-tune ways to manage and deliver water so your plants get what they need — with little or no waste.

WASH NOT — SUBSTITUTIONS FOR CLEANING

Many people can remember a time when they, their neighbors, or their parents routinely used water more heedlessly for tasks that can be managed without water. The low-hanging fruit of water management is to stop doing these wasteful things. Here are two classic examples:

- **Car washing:** Water running off your car and down the driveway into the gutter may inspire glares from neighbors or even, in some communities, a citation or fine. If you really must clean your vehicle, try a commercial car wash, which can consume less water by using fast, high-pressure water delivery. Or wash using a single bucket, sponge, rags, and good old elbow grease.

- **Sidewalk, patio, and driveway cleaning:** Treat yourself to a quality broom and you may be pleasantly surprised at how efficient these traditional chores become (I favor a stiff-bristled push broom). If your area experiences the occasional sudden, intense rainstorm or a period (winter) of rainfall, go out soon after with the broom and use the free washing water to clean up and help direct water toward plants.

  I know some tidy people prefer to clean debris, leaves, dirt, strayed mulch, and so forth with a leaf blower, but most models require fossil fuel and are noisy. Sweeping is good exercise.

There is — assuming decent or improved soil — moisture below in the ground or toward the bottom of a container. Water supplied from above, by you in some fashion or by all-too-infrequent rainfall, ideally makes its way down until there's no intervening dry zone. Basically water "meets in the middle," not only answering to gravity but also leveraging soil structure that moves water between pores. *Evenly saturated ground* is the ideal because it's consumption-efficient and offers optimal growing conditions for plant roots.

Transitioning to Low-Water Use

Cutting back dramatically on your water use doesn't have to be a cold-turkey situation. The following sections establish compelling reasons to do this (more than you may have realized!) and then discuss ways to ease into water reduction, including a glance at how professional landscapers cut back on their water use.

Eying the pros and cons

Good reasons to use less water include the following:

>> Lowering your water bill

>> Avoiding citations and fines

>> Spending less time and less money on watering

>> Taking better care of the environment and being a better citizen

>> Reducing strain on the water supply

>> Freeing up more water for human and animal use/survival

>> Minimizing harmful pollution

Here are some reasons you may be reluctant to cut back:

>> You've invested money and time in your plants, particularly your lawn.

>> You like the look of your landscape even though you know it guzzles too much water.

>> Low-water landscaping doesn't feel like gardening (this entire book, I hope, persuades you otherwise!).

Phasing in

Rome wasn't built in a day, right? You can approach landscape water conservation in steps, assuming your water source isn't in a state of crisis.

TIP

Cut back where it's easiest, first. Work your way through the following list in whatever order makes the most sense for you and your home landscape:

>> **Water consistently.** This sounds obvious, but too often people fall into a pattern of crisis management, responding to distressed plants by pouring on the water. Peaks and valleys of water deliveries are stressful for many plants. Just assume that your plants need evenly moist soil when actively growing and supply it routinely. The result is that you'll use less water overall. Also you'll find that it takes less time to maintain an even moisture level.

>> **Find and fix leaks.** If you have an irrigation system or even if you just use a hose, check that everything is functioning correctly. Replace any broken and worn parts — even a dripping faucet. Perhaps it needs a new washer. Rubber ones dry out, crack, and stop doing a good job, adding up to a lot of wasted water.

>> **Pull weeds.** Seriously! They can be real water hogs, greedily usurping water that your desirable plants need or will benefit from.

>> **Fertilize less.** Fertilizing inspires lusher growth, and lusher growth consumes more water.

>> **Alter your watering schedules.** Consult the section, "Figuring Out When to Water," later in this chapter.

>> **Mulch your plants.** Mulch isn't hard to apply and is a true game-changer, helping keep moisture in the ground while also suppressing those greedy weeds. Chapter 15 has lots of options and information about how best to mulch.

>> **Prune with care.** Taking branches from your trees and shrubs inspires water loss from the pruned plant and also reduces shade. The best time to prune is when your plants are dormant in later winter (in mild climates) or early spring (as growth ramps up).

Doing what the professionals do

Professional landscapers, including the ones who service places like parks, business or school campuses, and golf courses, tend to have a mandate to "do more with less." That is, they're required to use as little water (and other resources) as possible but still keep the place they're responsible for looking great. How about you borrow some of their techniques?

Here's a quick overview of what I mean:

>> **Consider frequency.** Watering often but shallowly only encourages shallow root growth. Watering is also time-intensive. Therefore, while you want to water consistently, it's also important to water less often.

>> **Focus on depth.** Watering deeply is almost always the best. The roots go down where it's cooler and damper, and the plants will be better sustained as a result. Deeply watered plants are stronger plants.

>> **Attend the watering.** Standing there requires time, which may be in short supply, and patience, which sometimes runs out. And yet activating an irrigation system, setting up a sprinkler, or setting a hose at a trickle at the base of a tree or shrub isn't a walk-away project.

Knowledge is power. Find a balance between delivering the needed water and checking up on its progress — the attentiveness you invest now will pay off in allowing you to walk away for at least a spell later. You can see what's going on.

Strategizing Your Watering Plan

Most home landscapes have a variety of terrain and plants. Hence, one-size-fits-all watering won't work. You can water efficiently in a surprising number of different ways. You have to be observant and analytical when you put some or all of these practical ideas into practice. Trust me, you'll marvel at their effectiveness.

Grouping plants in water-need zones

Creating a watering plan starts with where you group plants in your landscape according to their water needs. In other words, put like with like.

The most dramatic rookie error is plunking in colorful annuals among drought-tolerant perennials, particularly when you're waiting for those perennials to get established and bulk out. Most colorful annuals are shallow-rooted and dry/wilt quickly, crying out for water. But the perennials don't benefit from frequent, shallow water deliveries. Nobody wins!

A discrepancy can also happen when, for example, you place a water-appreciating plant like irises near a plant that doesn't require a lot of water like ceanothus. Summer water delivered to the bed sustains the irises but may be fatal to the shrub. One plant gets underwatered and one gets overwatered — a lose-lose for both plants.

TIP

The good news is that these situations are easy to fix. Create plant communities, basically, grouping ones with similar needs together so you can water them together. Everybody wins.

TIP

If you need some guidance, browse the plant-selection chapters in Part 2 and draw up lists (you'll be selecting for other characteristics, too, such as flower colors or bloom times, or foliage hues), and then cross-check your scheme wherever you buy the plants. Keep these other tips in mind:

>> **Place thirstier plants closer to the water source.** Picture your landscaping as ever-expanding circles. The ones closest to your hose, or right under your nose outside the front door or just off the patio, ideally should have accessible water close at hand — whether the hose or a rain barrel.

>> **Let the farther-away plants be tougher, more independent plants.** The native shrubs, perennials, and succulents can go out by the back fence or in distant corners of your landscape. Am I recommending "out of sight, out of mind"? Yes, essentially.

>> **If you install a drip irrigation system, the controls will offer watering zones.** Although you can customize water delivery (faster emitters or more emitters are put in the root zones of thirstier plants), keeping the landscaping and its water deliveries simple has its merits. Chapter 5 discusses the ins and outs of drip irrigation.

This scheme prioritizes the near plants over the more-distant ones. The thinking is, you'll see and spend more time in the company of the near ones, coming and going from your house or spending time on a patio or porch. You'll remember to give them water first, or to choose to irrigate them if water is scarce.

Watering individual plants versus watering broad areas

If you look out over your present landscape or consider your dream one, you may be rolling your eyes and groaning, imagining all the work and effort it would take to water plants one by one. Bear with me here. You have options, which I discuss here.

REMEMBER

Watering ground that has no plant roots in it — whether an expanse of gravel or nice, improved soil — is wasteful. (If you're using drip irrigation, use poly tubing or a hose to skip areas that don't need watering.)

Solo watering, using a basin

The most water-efficient way to water individual plants is, yes, individually. You can tailor the delivery to the plant's needs, by its age/maturity, and by season.

When your delivery method is hand-watering (hose or watering can), you can simplify the job and make the irrigation efficient by creating a basin.

REMEMBER

A *basin* is a raised circle created around an individual plant — literally a barricade to prevent runoff (refer to Figure 3-1). Creating a basin around each and every incoming plant on planting day is a good habit and practical. Some of the native soil from the excavation hole can be pressed (literally!) into service to make a low mounded circle that you may have to shore up occasionally as time goes by. Or you can create one out of rocks, or use both soil and rocks.

FIGURE 3-1:
A basin prevents waste by directing the water right where it needs to go, down into the root system.

© John Wiley & Sons, Inc.

A basin should be right over the root zone. Think ahead and make it bigger/wider than the young plant. Incoming water thus soaks right in where it's needed instead of running off.

TIP

The easiest way to determine the size of a basin is to create it around the drip line of the incoming plant. The *drip line* is the farthest extent of the foliage or the plant's canopy or overall bulk. It's pretty simple to do with most perennials, shrubs, and herbs. A few feet/a meter out will be fine for an incoming tree.

Watering more broadly

There is a time and a place for watering broad areas that aren't chockablock with plants. You usually only do it temporarily — at the outset of a new planting — with the idea that you'll use less water and the area will become more self-sufficient once it's established. Here are some examples:

>> A new food garden or raised bed full of seedlings

>> A hedge of shrubs or a line of edging plants, where your goal and hope is that they'll all grow to approximately the same height and/or width

>> A newly seeded lawn (yes, even if it's a drought-tolerant or native grass or grass blend)

>> An area devoted to a groundcover, wildflower meadow bed, cover crop, or several small plants that are meant to grow together

Ways to water such areas and projects efficiently include using a soaker hose or a sprinkler or installing an in-ground drip system *before* planting.

Planting in blocks versus planting in rows

In an ornamental garden, planting in *blocks* — that is, arraying plants in groupings — looks better and lusher, or at least it gives the illusion of more lushness or plenty. I'm not saying that you should avoid planting flowers or other ornamental plants in rows or lines; if you have enough water and the patience, those too can fill in and look full after a while.

TIP

In a kitchen garden where you're raising vegetables and perhaps some herbs as well, planting in blocks is practical. These plants tend to need more water, particularly if you anticipate a tasty, succulent harvest, and grouping them together is a more efficient use of limited water.

Planting in blocks rather than rows has the added advantages of strength in numbers. Local humidity, however minimal, is helpful to the plants. And they may physically help each other, that is, offer some shade at certain times of day, with taller, bulkier plants reducing stress and evaporation for their near neighbors.

Watering in two intervals

Water soaks in better to already-damp ground; you can use this simple fact to water more efficiently. Provide water to a plant or an area for a short period, say, 15 minutes, and then turn it off. Return in 15 minutes and repeat.

I'm not suggesting that you stick to this exact timetable, but rather you visit twice to assure yourself that the first delivery has a good chance to soak in. Different plants, different areas, and different times of year will cause the intervals and amounts of water to vary. This start-stop method is particularly suited where you're observing runoff, or if you know that your soil is heavy clay, which is slower to absorb water.

The down-time interval doesn't have to be idle or wasted time for you. Instead, move on to another plant or area and soak that and then circle back to each. As for how long the down-time period should be, you're going to have to watch and tailor to your situation. The moment the first watering starts to run off, that's your cue to stop and wait.

If you have an irrigation system with a timer, just program it to deliver half the water first . . . pause . . . and then finish a bit later.

TIP

When rain is in the forecast and needed because your landscape is thirsty, go out and give the planting beds a light soaking beforehand. Few garden sights are as heartbreaking as a flash-storm passing through and all the water running off and escaping, but this idea also applies even when the natural precipitation is but a disappointing little sprinkling. Capture what you can.

Deciding how deeply to water

Determining how deeply to water varies, depending on where you live, your soil, your plants, the time of year, and so on, but here are some general guidelines. Start with the following and then fine-tune over time as you monitor your plants and water supply (Chapter 2 explains saturated soil in greater detail):

>> **Perennials:** Aim for the deepest extent of their root systems, usually between 6 and 18 inches (15.2 and 45.7 cm).

>> **Groundcovers and small shrubs:** Strive for at least 12 inches (30.5 cm) deep.

>> **Bigger shrubs and dwarf trees:** Aim for 12 to 18 inches (30.5 to 45.7 cm) deep.

>> **Trees (ornamental and fruit):** Go for between 2 and 3 feet (0.6 and 0.9 m) deep.

>> **Vegetable and herb plants:** If they're in raised beds, saturate to the bottom (12 to 18 inches/30.5 to 45.7 cm). If they're in the ground, aim for that same figure as well.

Figuring Out When to Water

Become attentive to the timing of water delivery in your home landscape. Altering your older, wasteful habits and switching to more prudent timing can make a big difference.

REMEMBER

Don't forget that the age/maturity of a plant is an important factor. Ideally your established plants only need water in the absence of rainfall.

WARNING

The worst thing you can do is water in the heat of the day. More heat equals more evaporation. If the day is dry, or dry and windy, evaporation only increases. You can literally lose 30 to 50 percent of the water you're trying to give your landscape by watering in such conditions. Just don't!

Watering your landscape plants can and should be optimized. That way, they get the irrigation they need, when they need it — and waste is greatly reduced or eliminated. Consider the following information.

Comparing morning watering and evening watering

Invariably morning and evening are calmer times to water when the air tends to be stiller and drift is minimized or not a factor. Watering at dawn or dusk or in darkness also conserves water because drying sunlight isn't a factor.

Gardeners are often cautioned not to water in the evening hours because then the yard is damp overnight and fungal diseases and mold can afflict damp plants or the surface of mulch. That's certainly a possibility where evenings and overnight are humid, but if your climate is dry, don't worry — go ahead and water in the evening if that works for you.

All that said, early morning is ideal. Moisture delivered to your plants before dawn will send them into the day hydrated. If you're not an early riser, then program a timer for however you water to take care of this task while you sleep.

Watering through the seasons

Landscape plants don't need the same amount of moisture year-round. You must adapt your watering regimen, whatever it is, to the seasons. However, a typical and prudent plan is to reduce water in fall and ramp up in spring. Keep the following in mind:

REMEMBER

>> **Follow natural plant-growth cycles.** Plants grow actively in spring, may maintain or slow down in summer (depending on how hot and dry your climate is), and grow some more in fall before beginning to slow down and/or go dormant for the winter. Their highest need is when they're actively growing — if there's rainfall, wonderful; if there's not, or not enough, you must supplement.

>> **Provide consistent irrigation when a plant is flowering or ripening fruit.** Those things are hard work for a plant. Sufficient, ample water yields the best (and tastiest) results.

>> **Water less during the fall and winter.** Plants use less water in cooler shoulder seasons, by some calculations, 40 to 50 percent less. Plants may consume a lot of water in the peak of summer, if you're willing and able to supply more water then. (If you aren't or can't, choose plants adapted to drier summer conditions — see Part 2.)

Touring Low-Tech Watering Aids

Before there was widespread ornamental gardening, agriculture the world over had become sophisticated. In climates with challenges of heat and drought, farmers deployed ingenuity to sustain food crops.

The following sections are techniques and materials pioneered by innovative farmers in places like the Middle East, dry Africa, Pakistan, and Mainland China — interesting, clever, and perhaps worth trying in your own home landscape.

For more elaborate, modern/technologically advanced watering systems, flip to Chapter 5. The following are simpler, lower-tech ideas.

Deploying buried clay pots

Olla is the traditional name for this ancient and useful item; it's thought to have originated in China thousands of years ago. An *olla* is simply a clay or terra-cotta pot buried in the garden ground up to its neck near a needy plant. Water is decanted in and then seeps out slowly and steadily into the surrounding soil, nurturing the adjacent plant roots. This is a great method for watering plants sparingly but evenly in very dry areas.

To discourage bugs, slugs, snails, and other small critters, to keep out debris, and to prevent evaporation, be sure to cover the aboveground opening with a snug lid or even just a tile or rock. Leave a lip above the surface so you can find it. Cover it to help keep out dirt and debris. I usually simply plunk on the base (the drainage saucer) that came with the pot. Figure 3-2 shows an example.

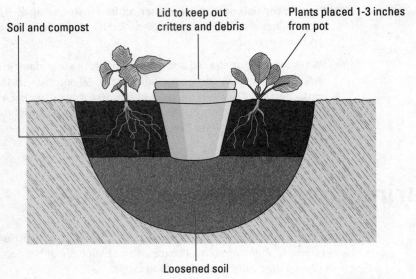

Soil and compost

Lid to keep out critters and debris

Plants placed 1-3 inches from pot

Loosened soil

© John Wiley & Sons, Inc.

TIP

If you use a regular clay pot (as opposed to a traditional narrow-necked olla), be sure to plug the drainage hole in the bottom, ideally with a rubber stopper. The water should only be seeping out through the walls. The exception is a season or more into the life of a thriving shrub or tree; in that case, you can try removing the stopper in later years so water can get down even deeper into the ground, where you want the roots to go.

Most DIYers can make an entire watering system based on this technique, connecting a network of buried clay pots to a common water source using flexible piping. These suggestions can help you with this method:

>> **Best pots for the job:** You want to use an unglazed porous pot — terra-cotta is usually fine. Results will vary according to factors such as the composition and hardness of the clay and the thickness of the pot's walls.

>> **Installation:** Leave about an inch (2.5 cm) showing, to keep out dirt and runoff and also so you can easily find it again and refill it with water with ease.

Install one before or at planting time, so you aren't disturbing or harming plant roots. You can put one within inches/cms of a freshly planted seedling, but you're going to have to install one farther away if you're aiming to hydrate a plant with a larger or established rootball.

>> **Effectiveness:** Experiment and install one or a few and see how it goes. If you're determined to maximize the benefits, run a few tests to find out how fast and how far the water drains into your particular soil. Getting the best results — including using far less water and perhaps only topping off an olla once a week during the growing season — requires some more trial and error.

To encourage the water to move out into the surrounding ground, wet that ground slightly.

Try different types of clay pots as well as different sizes. Use larger pots for plants with bigger root systems. And because those pots can hold more water, you may not need to refill every week.

>> **Spacing of multiple ollas:** Intervals of 2 to 3 feet (0.6 to 0.9 m) work in many garden beds, though your results may vary depending on your soil and the types of plants you're irrigating. Make sure to place them closer together in sandy, quick-draining soil and farther apart in clay, heavy soil.

>> **Alternatives and variations:** Upend a bottle or jug of water into a clay or other porous container. It won't look beautiful in operation, granted, but you'll be able to see how fast the water is being used.

Trying bottle-drip irrigation

Another good way to get water efficiently into a root system is to bury or place a perforated bottle close by. This method works best for watering individual plants.

Take an old plastic jug or water or soda bottle, poke it full of holes, and bury it in your garden ground. Pour water in the exposed end; it will gradually disperse in the root zone of the nearby plant or plants.

This method is great to use when you're going on vacation in order to keep your plants alive while you're away. But you don't have to be going anywhere; it's useful during any dry spell or even as a general practice when your plants are actively growing.

Experiment with these variations:

>> Keep the cap and puncture it once or twice. Fill the bottle, replace the cap, and bury head-down.

>> Create holes in the lower part of a plastic jug or bottle and set it (temporarily) adjacent to the plants you wish to water gradually — right on the surface of the ground next to them.

TIP

An easy way to puncture holes in plastic is with a small nail — it's basically a homemade-irrigation-system pilot hole.

Putting in wicking systems

Perhaps you're acquainted with *capillary mats,* which are commonly used in greenhouses and even in those little inexpensive seed-starter kits so popular for getting vegetable and flower seedlings going. Underlaying the growing flats or pots, the material holds moisture from a water-filled tray below it. The soil mix above it absorbs the moisture slowly from the mat.

TIP

Take your cue from the commercial capillary mats and don't use pure cotton or T-shirt fabric. A material that is synthetic and polyester-based has the advantage of lasting longer and being less prone to mold. Nylon or parachute cord, as well as some kinds of rope, can also work. (Check the effectiveness with an easy test — add food coloring to the water and check the progress.)

You can use a similar principle with your outdoor plants. Place one end of a strip of absorbent fabric or rope at or near the bottom of a bucket or reservoir of water and run the other end into the soil. Use an ample piece so that it doesn't stretch tight; it should lay easily in place at both ends. You can thread a length of wider-diameter vinyl tubing along part of its length (the middle, not the ends), which protects exposed fabric or rope and can make the length more maneuverable.

Put a water bucket on the ground near to a plant and run the absorbent cloth into the ground close to or within the root system. Gravity will help, that is, if the water is traveling downhill, wicking works faster. (For watering potted plants in low-water situations, consult Chapter 17.)

Pushing in pipes

This is a simple and primitive idea you can try with modern materials. Push a length of pipe into the ground, deep enough to be in the root zone of the plant or plants you wish to irrigate. Secure it into place by packing soil in around it; you want it to stay firmly vertical.

The pipe acts like a straw — that is, you'll pour water in the top and the water will travel down to and disperse in the root zone.

You can use metal, plastic, clay, or ceramic piping, it really doesn't matter. Start out using half-inch to 1-inch (1.3 to 2.5 cm) diameter; either size works for most situations. The piping doesn't need to be perforated — in fact, tiny holes in its length can clog up.

Here are a few cautions:

>> Take care not to harm root zones. Install the pipe at the same time that you install the plant.

>> To keep dirt, debris, and even small critters from getting into and clogging the pipe, cap it when not in use or at least cover the top with secured screening.

>> Keep the end above the soil surface a bit so you can easily spot it and to prevent debris from getting in.

>> If you're watering food plants with this method, check that the piping material doesn't leach or shed toxins into the ground.

Burying porous pipes

This method allows you to deliver water to a bigger area; in fact, agriculture has used it in places as diverse as central France, Pakistan, and arid parts of Africa where water is precious. Trenches are dug, the porous clay pipes are laid down, and then they're buried (in rows or grids) — with an exposed access point or points for water delivery. The crop plants, fruit trees, or ornamental plants are installed after the system is in place.

However, in practice, this method turns out to be tricky. Making water delivery even from one end of a planting bed or field to the other is difficult, harder still the longer a pipe or pipe network extends. If joints aren't well-sealed, there will be leaks and/or roots will invade. Sections can be heavy and awkward to maneuver. Also, over time, clay pipes crack, break, or simply disintegrate.

Alternative, more durable materials may work better, such as permeable concrete or old sewer pipe. Research is being done on this, so keep your eyes open. If the materials and logistical problems can be solved or mitigated, porous underground piping could become important in the future of home landscaping.

Drainage projects sometimes use perforated PVC or HDPE pipes, laid at angles or horizontally under the ground, sometimes embedded or laid upon gravel. These pipes may also serve your watering projects, acting essentially as underground drip irrigation (check Chapter 5).

Avoiding Watering of Foliage

Watering leaves, the foliage of your growing plants, sometimes happens, sometimes accidentally. That is, you run a sprinkler or spray a hose over a plant or planted bed and the water lands on the leaves. Although you may figure that the water will run or drip off and soak into the ground anyway, this is a wasteful method, so don't do it!

Why not? Two reasons:

>> **Risk of burn:** You aren't cooling off hot plants by watering leaves — quite the contrary. Water droplets on leaves can act like lenses and magnify the heat of the sun beating down, causing stress and even damage. Yes, this can happen naturally, after a cloudburst or downpour of rain followed by sunshine, but there's no reason for you to — pardon the pun — magnify the possibility.

>> **Risk of disease:** Water on leaves can harbor, promote, and move plant diseases around, whether miniscule organisms or fungal spores. Rose foliage is especially vulnerable (you'll see black or brown spots), but other plants are also affected. You're asking for trouble if you wet leaves late in the day and they stay damp overnight.

'Tis true, misting leaves of certain plants can be beneficial and help keep them hydrated. Foliar misting is mainly a way to care for tropical plants and houseplants that need or prosper in high humidity. But tropical plants and houseplants that like high humidity are poor plant choices in arid, water-scarce climates.

It's always best — most beneficial, most efficient, and water-wise — to deliver water to your plant's roots, not to their leaves.

Hand-Watering: Bonding with Your Plants

Even if you have a large yard to maintain, or even if you've invested in in-ground and automatic watering systems, I think there is always a time and a place for hand-watering. Certain plants at certain times benefit from individual attention: for example, the calamondin tree is ripening fruit; the newly planted flowers are flagging in the blazing sun; the new row of boxwoods are still babies and hot weather is arriving.

Answer the call — step in with extra water. Visit with your plants and see how they're doing, an intimacy you miss when watering is less in demand or being done automatically. After all, your plants aren't merely décor. You're in a relationship with them!

The two main ways of hand-watering are using a hose and using some sort of watering can. It's worth taking a fresh look at each of these methods to remind you of their advantages as well as best practices. Also both have variations that are worth remembering and may persuade you to go out and get some new, improved gear.

Using hoses

Even where water is scarce, a hose is indispensable for all manner of gardening and yard-maintenance projects as well as for spot-watering. Here are the main kinds:

TIP

» **Traditional garden hose:** You get what you pay for. Poor-quality hoses kink, break down in sunlight, can become stinky, and end up having to be discarded. Treat yourself to a quality hose. Longer is better, just because of extended reach.

Hoses made of PVC (vinyl) have come under increased scrutiny because they contain and deliver to your soil and plants contaminants, including lead and phthalate plasticizers. Instead shop for a polyurethane hose (these are often labeled "drinking-water safe" and/or "non-PVC").

» **Soaker or leaky hose:** These types of hoses dribble out water slowly, evenly, and steadily. Again, buy a good-quality one. Wend them through a newly planted area, a vegetable patch, or around the base of shrubs and trees. Black ones are barely visible. Keep an eye on it, though, unless you have it on a timer — runoff happens when you're not looking. (For information about employing one or more soaker hoses as a simple drip system, refer to Chapter 5.)

» **Accessories/extras:** Watering wands deliver water gently so it can soak in better. Bubbler attachments also deliver modest amounts of water and may come in handy (they're less wasteful than sprinklers). Hose-end sprayers allow you to add fertilizer (according to label directions) while watering.

All of these items screw right on to the end of a hose, with or without an adaptor. Check out what's available in your area's well-stocked garden-supply store or look online; you may find things that make hose-watering easier, more efficient, and more pleasurable for you and the plants.

Using watering cans

This time-honored method of delivering water to plants is old school, but I love it. A watering can allows you to put the water exactly where it's needed, straight to the roots (okay, you may have to bend down a bit). It also enables you to slow down and monitor your plants one by one. Besides helping you be more attentive to a given plant's water needs, you may also notice early signs of pests or disease — or spot swelling flower buds!

A visit with a watering can is also a good way to deliver diluted fertilizer — if you fertilize (for a full discussion, turn to Chapter 10). Put the fertilizer in the can first and then add water so it mixes in well. Follow the directions on the label regarding dilution rates — or deliver half-strength twice as often.

Some watering cans are attractive, even beautiful, either in design or color or both, making them a nice garden accessory. But my favorites are durable galvanized steel cans, complete with a perforated rose at the end of the spot. These allow you to shower plants lightly but evenly. Just don't get a really big one; although you can visit more plants or stay longer, you may stagger under the weight of a full can.

Tackling Special Watering Challenges

No two home landscapes are the same, but all seem to pose an occasional or ongoing watering challenge. Here are the most common ones, along with suggested remedies.

Watering a slope

You may have a slope or embankment on your property, or perhaps your whole yard is sloped. Built-in challenges like this — even in climates that aren't dry — include erosion and runoff. Access can also be a major headache as you scramble up and down that slope, hassling with keeping it landscaped. And when conditions are also hot and dry, the situation becomes even more difficult.

If you face this problem, try one or more of these ideas:

>> **Plant a low-maintenance groundcover.** The effort you invest in planting and nurturing it should pay off later, in a year or two or three, when at last it fills in and holds soil and water. Consult Chapter 12 for plant suggestions.

TIP

One good thing about growing plants on a hillside or slope: The drainage is good. Make the best of it. Put plants that like excellent drainage to the upper parts and those that benefit from extra water near or at the base. (Check out the extensive plant lists in Part 2.)

>> **Irrigate it with soaker hoses.** They water slowly and allow moisture to sink in deeply.

>> **Install drip irrigation or pay a professional to tackle what could be a difficult project.** Consult Chapter 5 for more details about drip irrigation.

>> **Help plants on the slope individually.** Refer to the section, "Solo watering, using a basin," earlier in this chapter. Basins on slopes, however, need a higher downhill side to trap the irrigation water in place (and lower or no uphill side).

>> **Convert the hillside to terraces.** Admittedly this is a big and potentially expensive project (especially if you hire help, though bear in mind that the pros can do it a lot faster and perhaps better than someone who has no experience).

>> **Install a swale.** A *swale* is a digging-and-land-contouring project that looks like a ditch with closed ends. Basically it catches and holds landscape water so it can't run off and instead absorbs into the ground. (You can find more information in Chapter 16.)

Accessing a distant water source

Running a hose or soaker hose all the way across your lot isn't convenient. Not to mention you may experience a loss of water pressure, the farther away you try to extend a hose.

WARNING

Another reason not to run a long line out to a distant corner: The water that remains sitting in it between uses really heats up. You don't want to deliver scalding water to plants. Even though you could drain it (string it down a slope) between uses, doing so is a hassle. (And if you're in an area where winters freeze, you'd also have to drain the full length and perhaps store it away until spring — another major chore.)

Here are some potential solutions to watering plants far away from a water source:

>> Put in an underground water line, with an access spigot (so, you'll have more than one). Have a contractor who does outdoor plumbing assess, discuss, and provide an estimate.

>> Put a rain barrel or water tank in the distant spot. (Refer to Chapter 2 for more on rain barrels.)

>> Take multiple trips with a watering can.

TIP

Consider taking out water-needy plants that are far from your water source and therefore a pain in the neck to water. Replace them with more independent, drought-tolerant selections — or a shed (storage shed, she shed, or potting shed) or hardscape such as a patio or gravel pad.

Coping with clay soil

Clay soil is composed of fine particles. Although it has the advantage of holding nutrients and moisture, it drains poorly. To help clay ground drain better and thus perhaps widen your landscaping possibilities, including plant choices, here are a couple things you can try:

>> Dig in organic matter.

>> Improve drainage by installing trenches, gravel beds, dry wells, and/or perforated piping. A good landscape contractor can advise you.

You can find more details and information in Chapter 4.

Dealing with standing water

Although not a common problem in dry, water-poor regions, puddling happens after a cloudburst or during a spate of fall or winter rains. If it happens after you water, the issue is overwatering, so reduce watering.

Most likely the real problem is compacted soil that can't absorb water. The solution is to improve the soil's ability to absorb water by adding organic matter such as compost and/or to incorporate some sand. Emergency medical care is a matter of tossing a shovelful of gravel into every puddle.

Other remedies include the following:

>> **Check your home's gutter system.** Look to see whether water can be redirected, perhaps into a dry well or a rain garden? (Read about rain gardens in Chapter 16.)

>> **Install drainage.** A good landscape contractor can advise you.

Chapter 4

Making Soil Your Ally

There is an undeniable link between decent soil, water, and thriving plants. Here I begin by figuring out what sort of soil you have and move on to improving it for better water efficiency and the good of your plants. I also look at a few other ways to leverage soil's help to physically conserve water.

Few parts of landscaping are as important, and as potentially heartbreaking, as soil quality. I once visited my brother in Los Angeles after hearing about his struggles. "I picked a sunny spot and put in appropriate plants, like you said," he related, "and I did water them," he added a bit defensively. He ticked off his choices: rosemary, salvia, bougainvillea, blanket flower, penstemon, parsley. "One by one, they've all died," he said, aggrieved. He walked me up the driveway and indicated the bed in front of his house.

I knelt and picked up a handful of the dirt, which sifted loosely through my fingers. Dry gravely urban grit. The consistency of cheap kitty litter. What water he supplied ran right through. That "soil" delivered no sustenance and was basically holding the plants erect for the short duration of their doomed lives.

If dry gravely kitty-litter grit is your nemesis, this chapter comes to your soil's rescue. However, soil situations have other kinds of challenges. Some people struggle with dense clay or silt. Some move into a new housing tract and discover that all the topsoil was either scraped away during construction or was densely compacted. In many arid areas, soil pH is alkaline, that is, higher than the ideal so often cited in gardening circles of between 6.0 and 7.0.

Answers and remedies for all these situations are ahead. The first and most important thing to understand is, soil is alive. Discover how to nurture it and gardening successes follow.

Understanding Soil Composition

Soil is alive, so what does that even mean?

The ground under your feet didn't just happen. It's made up of many things, but primarily of organic materials including decomposing plants, leaves, and roots, as well as the bodies and waste of animals large and small, from coyotes to birds.

Many creatures make their home in the soil and contribute to its content as well as its texture (aeration, at least) — think of earthworms, but also beetles, ants, other small insects, plus a host of even smaller creatures and fungi, microbes, bacteria, and more. Just to help you picture how full of life soil can be: A teaspoon contains millions of microscopically tiny bacteria.

Soil is also made up of some inorganic materials, namely decomposed rocks and minerals.

All of these ingredients blend, mix, and build up over time, aided by digging and burrowing creatures, freeze-thaw cycles, and roots moving in and around and water passing through. It all adds up to a complex, wondrous recipe for supporting life.

REMEMBER

Gardeners often think we're feeding our plants when we add organic materials to garden ground, but in reality, we're feeding the soil and the creatures in it. When we do this for our soil, it can in turn better nurture our plants.

These sections take a closer look at what's down there. I then discuss how to care for and feed your soil — basic information I had neglected to explain to my frustrated brother in the story in this chapter's introduction!

Going deep into topsoil and subsoil

Soil is typically layered. Plunge a shovel in and here is what you usually find (see Figure 4-1):

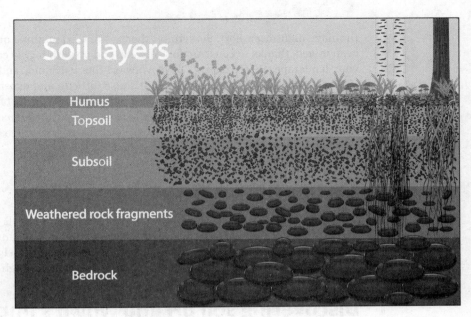

FIGURE 4-1:
The different
layers of soil.

Soil layers

Humus
Topsoil
Subsoil
Weathered rock fragments
Bedrock

>> **Humus:** *Humus* refers to organic, broken-down plant materials right on the ground's surface — decomposition that's mostly complete. Examples of humus include grass clippings (dried, not fresh) and mature forest soil. Humus is dark in color, black to brown, with a spongy texture, and it retains water well.

>> **Topsoil:** Ideally what you want to grow your plants in is *topsoil.* This is the uppermost soil layer, just under the humus layer (if any). Being at and close to the surface, it contains more organic matter than subsoil. More organic content means topsoil tends to be darker-colored and lighter-textured than what lies below.

It may be a foot deep, a few inches (30.5 cm to less than 15 or 20 cm) deep, or — in the case of scraped-over new subdivisions — almost nonexistent.

>> **Subsoil:** Under the topsoil is another, lighter-colored layer, called the *subsoil.* It tends to be less active, though of course some earthworms and deep roots make it down there — and they'll find and bring up moisture, minerals, and nutrients. Subsoil also tends to be harder, more resistant to your shovel, and slow-draining.

The subsoil layer may be quite deep, up to several feet (m) deep.

>> **Weathered rock fragments and bedrock:** Below the subsoil is generally rock(s). Plant roots stop there, and you won't be able to go any deeper.

WARNING

Drainage nightmare alert: Sometimes the topsoil is so minimal or the layers have been mixed, thanks to construction. You can end up with highly compacted soil in your landscape. Water doesn't go downward like it should, and it can even go sideways. That isn't just unfortunate, it's also difficult and expensive to remedy. Solutions include removing and replacing the terrible soil or installing subsurface drainage — your call. If you can't face the trouble and expense, consider avoiding the problem and putting in raised beds. Read the nearby sidebar about dealing with compacted soil.

Testing holding capacity

The easiest way to find out which way your soil tends is to handle it. Pick an ordinary day during a period of stable weather, go out, and grab a handful of soil from a spot where you want to grow plants. A handful of clay forms a ball, like a ball of dough. A handful of sand doesn't hold together and runs through your fingers.

Discovering soil pH and why it's important

You may or may not need a soil test, depending on your *soil's pH*, which refers to how acid or alkaline the soil in your yard is.

Most soils actually aren't extreme, that isn't overly acidic (sour) or overly alkaline (sweet), though in many low-water areas, the scales tip toward alkaline more often than not. The reason you want your garden soil to be midway between 1.0 and 14.0, around the area between 6.0 and 7.0, is that the life in the soil — notably beneficial bacteria — is optimized at the midway range.

ANOTHER WAY TO TEST YOUR SOIL

Here's a different way you can test your soil. Just stick to these steps:

1. **Dig a hole, about a foot deep and wide (30.5 cm).**

2. **Fill it to the top with water and let it drain.**

3. **Refill, and using a ruler or stick, monitor how fast it drains.**

A healthy drainage rate for growing many plants is an inch an hour. Much slower than that indicates your soil tends toward clay. Much faster indicates your soil tends toward sand.

Some plants do like very acidic soil and others prefer highly alkaline, but most are in the middle. My advice is to strive for good, healthy soil and don't worry overmuch.

The following sections discuss what's involved with soil testing and what you can do (remedy soil pH or leave it).

Getting your soil tested

However, if you have reason to believe your soil is especially alkaline — a possibility, of course, in warmer, drier climates — you can get it tested. Inexpensive kits are available where gardening supplies are sold, but you'll get more precise results and receive practical recommendations about how to alter it if you have your soil tested professionally. Search online and/or make some calls to find out if a nearby Cooperative Extension office or if private labs in your area offer this service. It does cost a little money, but it may be worth it to you.

For the test, you take several small soil samples around your property, mix them, and send in the requested amount in a small, plastic, sealable baggie or container. Follow all directions carefully and fill out all forms completely (including your planting goals so they can tailor their recommendations). Mail in and await the report.

Altering soil pH

If you find out that your soil is alkaline, higher than 7.0, and you want to nudge it down a bit, the recommendations that came back with your soil test will guide you. When you send in the paperwork, make sure to note what sorts of plants you want to grow so the advice is appropriate.

A high-pH soil level means your soil has higher calcium, magnesium, and sodium levels and that your plants will have a harder time absorbing other, necessary nutrients. You can dig in some or all of the following amendments to lower your soil's pH:

>> **Ground rock sulfur:** Cheapest alternative, but slower-acting.

>> **Aluminum sulfate (sulfur + ammonium):** Faster-acting but you'll need more.

>> **Ferrous sulfate (sulfur + iron):** The iron component, if recommended by your soil test, boosts plants that suffer from yellowing foliage and weak growth.

When adding amendments, avoid over-concentrations by mixing them with compost and then digging the blend into your soil.

How much to add depends on the results of your soil test and your planting goals for the area you're improving. A good, thorough soil test will advise you. Bagged amendments, available wherever gardening supplies are sold, list the application rates on charts.

Other ways to lower soil pH include the following:

>> Digging in peat moss (which is acidic, but requires dampening . . . and, it's not an easily renewable resource, so even though it continues to be widely available, I hesitate to recommend it these days).

>> Digging in composted wood chips or even aged sawdust (if you can get them, they're cheap and organic; just make sure they don't have any contaminants).

More than likely your soil isn't overly acidic (such soil is far more common in places like New England), so I don't delve into those details here except to say that the soil–test results will guide your remedial actions — you typically dig in lime (powdered or granulated) and/or wood ashes to raise a low pH.

Leaving soil pH as is

If your soil is alkaline — 7.0 or higher — instead of trying to change it, I suggest seeking out plants, native and/or otherwise, that thrive in this kind of soil. Here are a few suggestions (refer to Part 2 for more details about each):

>> **Flowers:** California poppies, coneflower, lavender, phlox, red valerian, yarrow, zinnia

>> **Veggies:** Asparagus, beets, cabbage, cauliflower, celery, cucumber, okra

>> **Herbs:** Borage, oregano, parsley, rosemary

The struggle is real: Recognizing types of soil

Soil varies a lot, from region to region, and even from neighborhood to neighborhood. At the extremes are clay and sand and, as you will see, there are advantages and disadvantages. Many soils are in between — the idealized middle is loosely called *loam*. But even so, you may find yours tends toward one or the other.

Getting rid of lousy soil isn't a simple, nor often a practical, remedy. Instead, I encourage you to work with what you have to make steady, incremental, important improvements. Refer to the section, "Enhancing/Making Improved Soil," later in this chapter for more details.

Clay, heavy soil

>> Drains poorly — holds water and nutrients longer, is fertile

>> Dries out slowly — hold water better in hot, dry conditions

>> Is made up of tiny, mineral-rich particles that cling together

>> Feels slick when wet, hard and lumpy when dry

>> Can be difficult for roots to penetrate and is poorly aerated

Meanwhile, sandy, light soil

>> Drains quickly and well, taking nutrients away from roots

>> Dries out quickly — roots will be aerated (which they need) but drier (which can be stressful)

>> Is made up of larger particles — easier for roots to penetrate

>> Feels gritty and dry

>> Warms up quickly in late winter to spring, jump-starting plant growth

TECHNICAL STUFF

Some areas of the arid West and Southwest have *caliche*, a natural formation of calcium carbonate in desert-type soils. It appears as light-colored lumps in your yard; the worst-case scenario is a solid layer of it. The soil has been literally cemented together and roots can't penetrate, water can't pass through, and salts accumulate. Among your options: break it apart, dig it up, or create drainage holes in it. If you suspect caliche in your yard, seek local, seasoned advice about dealing with it from your gardening neighbors, from a landscaping service, or from a staffer wherever you buy plants.

DEALING WITH COMPACTED SOIL

Compacted soil is hard, dense, and dry, with few or no available air spaces. It's probably low in organic matter.

Here are signs that you have compacted soil on your property:

- During digging and planting projects your shovel or trowel has a hard time penetrating

- Water runs right off or sinks in slowly

(continued)

(continued)

This problem has various causes:

- You inherited compacted soil when your home or subdivision was built. Heavy equipment may have scraped all, most, or all of the topsoil, plus the very weight of such machinery bears down on the ground.

- If you live in an area of cold winters, freeze-thaw cycles can contribute to compacted soil.

- The area is heavily trafficked (places where you, other people, your pet, a wheelbarrow, cart, or ATV traverse frequently).

- Something heavy has literally crushed and crunched the soil (trash bins, a vehicle).

Here's what you can do with compacted soil:

- Remove all the struggling plants. Discard them, move them to a better spot, or pot them.

- Mix in decomposed organic material to a depth of 6 inches (15.2 cm) or so, or the depth of root systems of plants you want to have in that spot. Breaking up the hard ground will be hard work — it may help to dampen it before digging. Cover and "let meld" (mix-settle-break down a bit) for a few weeks, months, or a season; this allows time for soil organisms to get good work done — decompose organic matter further and create air spaces.

- Improve the soil by planting a cover crop in the fall, such as rye, letting it grow all winter, and tilling it under the following spring.

- Rope, fence off, or define the area with edging, and route foot traffic around or away from the area.

- Continue to improve the soil by adding more organic matter in the months and years to come.

If all else fails or these remedies don't appeal to you, consider installing raised beds, planters, or an array of pots atop compacted ground. You can fill them with good soil for the plants you want to grow. Chapter 17 can guide you.

Enhancing/Making Improved Soil

The single best thing you can do for your soil is add organic matter. You may not achieve rich, friable loam, but you can certainly improve the soil you have. When you do, your plants will use water more efficiently, access nutrients, and prosper.

Soil-replenishment work is also ongoing (like laundry or hand-washing your dishes — you'll get on top of it but have to return to it again and again). It's as important a part of maintaining a landscape as putting in and caring for plants. Indeed, no pun intended, soil work is foundational.

You may wonder why even bother with soil improvement when existing ground is already organically based. Because chances are your soil isn't ideal (nice rich loam that is positioned between sand and clay, with a neutral pH) and because you want to give your plants nicer growing conditions than found in nature — they'll prosper and they'll look better!

Plant roots take up necessary nutrients in water. Thus, sufficient water must be available to them. Here are the main goals, the wish list:

>> **Aerated soil:** The goal is soil with spaces for air and water to pass through. Roots also depend on oxygen to function properly.

>> **Good soil structure:** You want absorbent soil that conducts water sufficiently to nurture roots, neither too dry nor too soggy.

>> **Fertile soil:** The goal is nutritious soil, which nurtures plants as well as creatures living in the ground. That ideally means a balance of nitrogen, phosphorus, and potassium, as well as a smattering of other elements called *micronutrients* (such as magnesium, zinc, sulfur, and more). Sound familiar? Fertilizer sold for gardens offers these micronutrients — but good, nurtured soil has them.

Drum roll — you can bring sandy soil as well as clay soil into this realm with the very same remedy: organic matter. Keep reading for more details.

Appreciating the need for organic matter

Organic matter, to quote author Steven Frowine's definition in *Gardening Basics For Dummies*, is "once-living material that releases nutrients as it decays." Its presence in soil is key to the health and success of all sorts of plants.

The following is an overview of the various kinds of soil you may have and a few words about what organic matter can do:

>> **Sandy soil:** Water passes through too quickly, leaving many plants thirsty. Continually adding water may not be an option; at best, doing so is wasteful. Sandy soil benefits from the addition of organic matter, which helps it become more absorbent, more retentive.

>> **Clay soil:** Holds water too long, causing plants to struggle (less air) and roots to rot. Clay soil benefits from the addition of organic matter, which helps aerate it and allow roots to take up what they need.

>> **Intermediate soil:** Receives organic matter on a regular basis, nurturing healthier plants and, over time, improving. This is a commitment on your part!

>> **Loam soil:** It's a roughly equal mix of silt and sand, with some clay. Loam soil is highly esteemed by gardeners and landscapers because a great many plants, ornamental and edible, thrive in loam's plant-friendly texture and nutrient-loaded environment. (You can purchase it by the truckload for your yard, if you want, if it's available, and if you can afford it.) Yes, it holds water well; water soaks in nice and evenly.

WARNING

Buyers of delivered truckloads of soil, beware. Sometimes you get chopped-up weeds or (hard to see, but unfortunately present and ready to sprout) weed seeds. Ask specifically for loam (not topsoil — too vague) and be prepared to pay more for a quality product.

Compost, on the other hand, is something people make by encouraging organic matter to break down. It's not nearly completely decomposed, like humus is. Refer to the section, "Composting 101 — Making your own," for more information.

Recognizing the types of organic matter

Many types of materials help boost your soil's organic matter and bring you the benefits of water absorption and plant health. You may use any of the following, depending on what's available to you and within your budget (nor do you have to choose just one; it's fine to use several or use different ones at different times):

>> Homemade compost

>> Bagged aged compost or humus

>> Bagged dehydrated and aged livestock manure

>> Aged sawdust (fresh depletes soil nitrogen, so let it rot before using)

>> Shredded or ground-up composted bark

>> Composted, chopped-up fall leaves (*leaf mold*)

>> Dried, decomposed grass clippings (assuming they don't contain any fertilizer or weedkillers)

>> Mushroom soil

Adding organic matter

You can add organic matter to your home landscape at any time. Certainly you should do this when you're clearing out a new gardening-bed area, but you can also add it to every planting hole, going forward.

TIP

I don't recommend creating areas of 100 percent organic amendments, which is not only a big project but also an expensive one. Rather, add organics to your native soil, mixing them together (like cake batter!). In this way, you'll make improved and fertile new homes for the plants you choose. Native plants, in particular, don't need a rich diet.

Just follow these steps when adding organic material:

1. **Decide what you're going to get and how much.**

Have it ready near the planting area.

2. **Prepare the planting area.**

    If it's a full bed, dig it to a depth of 6 or so inches (15.2 cm), which suits the root systems of many plants (more or less, depending on what you will plant). If it's an individual plant coming in, dig an ample hole, wider than the incoming root system and a bit deeper. Remove weeds, rocks, and debris.

3. **Add the amendment(s).**

    If it's a full bed, spread the material to a depth of an inch or two (2.5 to 5 cm). If it's just a planting hole, sprinkle it in about halfway up. If your soil is sandy, use even more.

4. **Mix thoroughly with the native soil.**

    Work it in. Use a garden fork, your hands, a shovel, or rake, whatever is easiest for you.

5. **Plant immediately.**

    If you can't, cover the area with a tarp (corners anchored!) so weeds can't invade.

TIP

Another option and a current gardening trend: You can essentially jump-start your soil to build more of its own humus by purchasing and incorporating mycorrhizal fungi. Typically sold in bags, often labeled as "landscape inoculant," it isn't cheap. You can order online or from a garden supplier; expect to pay around $150 for a 10-pound bag.

Composting 101 — Making your own

Don't buy compost when you can make your own, which is easy to do.

Compost is especially beneficial as a steady, dependable source of organic matter. Growing plants in a hot, dry climate is challenging enough; making your own compost is one powerful, proactive step you can take to improve your garden soil. In the long run, you'll save water and money.

Composting turns yard waste and kitchen scraps into crumbly soil-like material gardeners refer to as *black gold.* Dug into your garden or new planting holes, it has many benefits, including enhancing your soil's structure, health, and water-holding capacity.

To make your own compost, follow these easy steps:

1. **Pick a good location.**

    Choose a spot away from your neighbors and your own back door (because of organic smells, though if you follow these directions, they're never as bad as you feared). Don't choose a shady corner because warm sunshine speeds decomposition. Don't choose a hard-to-access spot because you'll be making many trips.

2. **Select a bin.**

   Research has shown that something around 3 by 3 feet (0.9 by 0.9 m) works best. Make one out of wire mesh or cinder blocks or simply buy one. Those basic black heavy-plastic bins work great.

3. **Get set up.**

   Lay some branches or cut-to-fit dried cornstalks in a layer on the open bottom right on top of the native soil to allow a bit of air in.

4. **Start making deliveries.**

   Put in "green" organic materials: kitchen scraps, grass clippings, spent crops, and yard waste. Make a habit of chopping up or mashing bigger pieces to speed things along.

WARNING

   Never add to compost: oil, meats, bones, pet waste, plastic, and ashes. These don't break down quickly if at all and make your pile smelly.

TIP

   Sprinkle in a bucket of garden soil now and then, which introduces *worker microorganisms* (minute organisms that do decomposing work) to the pile. Compost activators, available at garden suppliers, also help, but this trick makes them unnecessary.

5. **Layer.**

   A general rule is one part green/nitrogen materials to three parts brown/carbon. So toss in handfuls of brown material after every delivery. Suitable brown materials include straw (not hay, which harbors weed seeds), shredded, dried fall leaves, bark, and chopped twigs.

6. **Keep it damp.**

   Decomposition slows to a crawl if a pile is too dry. But neither should it be soggy. Add water with the hose or a watering can to maintain your compost pile like a damp sponge.

7. **Stir it up!**

   Getting air into the pile hastens decomposition. I like to use the handle from an old broken hoe; it's long and strong enough. But any sturdy stick will do. Poke and stir about once a week during the growing season.

REMEMBER

   If you skip watering and stirring, your pile will still make compost, just much more slowly. A *cold* compost pile may take a full year to decompose into usable material.

TECHNICAL
STUFF

You'll notice warmth, or even steam rising off your pile at times. That's a sign that microbes are at work decomposing your deliveries and no cause for alarm. In fact, a temperature between 135 and 155 degrees F (57 and 68 degrees C) is both normal and desirable as the heat kills harmful organisms and pathogens. *Hot* compost is productive — you can get usable humus in a matter of weeks or months.

Eyeing the basics of biochar

Another way to boost soil fertility is to add biochar, using a technique that is both ancient (used in the Amazon basin by indigenous people for centuries!) and more recently trendy. *Biochar* is basically charcoal — not ashes — made from burnt plants and plant parts such as branches and twigs that's then added to your garden ground. Here I take a closer look at biochar and explain how you can make your own.

Seeing how biochar works

Compounds in the charcoal form loose chemical bonds with water-soluble nutrients (including but not limited to nitrogen, phosphorus, magnesium, and calcium), efficiently helping to retain them in the soil. Produced and deployed correctly, biochar can be a game-changer in areas where rainwater and irrigation usually wash away nutrients in the soil.

Unlike the much-smaller bits of ash, larger pieces of charcoal offer holes, cracks, and crevices that microorganisms in the soil can cling to rather than being rinsed away. Biochar can help better plant growth — sometimes impressively.

REMEMBER

Adding biochar to poor-quality soil isn't a silver bullet. It only helps when you combine it with compost and organic fertilizers.

Making biochar — The how-to

The object is to make a controlled, contained fire out of flammable plant materials. Follow these steps to make your own biochar:

1. **Gather woody brush.**

   Use branches, twigs, prunings, and bramble canes, but also perhaps some spent plants or even weeds to get the fire going — basically items you won't be composting.

2. **Dig a trench or pile everything into a metal barrel.**

   Either way, a minimum depth of 10 to 12 inches (25.4 to 30.5 cm) works well.

3. **Start the fire.**

   Use your campfire skills, and light a match to a small pile of twigs or kindling, adding more as needed. After it's burning, monitor the fire constantly and don't walk away to do other things. Have some soil, of any quality, on hand to help control the flames.

WARNING

   Fire safety for this project is key! Check with your municipality to make sure burning is allowed and if so, when; get a permit if required. Take every precaution, including having emergency flame-dousing water ready (a hose or several buckets) and a safe, cleared perimeter. Do the work on a windless day.

4. **The fire begins hot; tamp it down by reducing air (oxygen).**

5. **Watch the smoke.**

   White smoke occurs first and is mostly water vapor; fragrant yellowish-brownish smoke, which is burning sugars and resins, follows it. Near the end of the process, the smoke will thin and turn grayish blue.

6. **Dump soil over the fire (at least an inch, 2.5 cm).**

   Let everything smolder at a much lower temperature for several hours before completely putting out the fire with water or more soil.

   Allow the remains to sit a few days before using (let them dry out if you doused them with water).

GETTING BIOCHAR ELSEWHERE

You may be daunted by the process of making your own biochar or your municipality may strictly forbid residential fires for any reason. You can acquire biochar from other sources and mix into your garden soil. Always, only gather from cold, finished fires. Here are some other sources:

- **Partially burned campfire wood:** If you or a neighbor have a fire pit, or if by chance you have access to the fire pits at a campground or picnic area, grab some partially burned wood there.

- **Chimney, chimenea, and wood-stove remains:** These may also suit, so long as you're gathering discernable (not disintegrated) wood chunks and charcoalized bits.

- **Wood-burning grill wood:** Assuming the hamburger cookout didn't use all the lump hardwood charcoal, grab some of that.

Avoid: Any source that may have been adulterated with additives, such as burnt treated lumber, burnt painted fencing or deck boards, or BBQ briquettes treated with paraffin or petroleum products.

TIP

If possible, dig a trench right where you intend to plant after the entire process is complete. Then you won't have to move the charcoal bits — they'll be right where you need them, ready to be mixed with soil and/or other amendments.

Caring for Your Soil — The Best Practices

The following are a few more things you can do to help sustain and nurture your landscaping (and some things you probably shouldn't do!). The object is to *work with* your soil.

Mulching

Mulching is a wonderful landscaping practice. It holds soil in place, helping to prevent erosion. If you've worked hard to improve your soil, you want to hang onto it!

Mulching also helps hold in soil moisture, slowing and preventing evaporation in the soil's upper layers (where most plant roots reside). Mulch has the ability to mitigate temperature extremes so your plants can be more resilient. Chapter 15 has the full details of mulching.

Weeding unwelcome plants

One definition of a weed is "a plant that's out of place." It may in fact be something most people consider a weed, such as purslane, pigweed, or bur clover. Maybe the seeds stirred up in your soil, maybe birds, other wildlife, or Mother Nature (water or wind) brought in the interlopers. Maybe some bindweed snuck in as a hitchhiker in the pot of a perennial or shrub you planted.

Unwanted plants are more than unsightly. They're also opportunists and robbers — they suck up soil nutrients and moisture that your desirable plants could use. Pluck them out, the younger/smaller the better. Weeding is always easiest after a rain or irrigation, and you should always try to get unwanted plants out by the roots. Then mulch around your garden plants to discourage the weeds from returning.

WARNING

Dispose of weeds safely. Even though some gardeners add weeds to their compost piles, hoping the heat will kill any seeds and any viable roots or root bits, I wouldn't gamble on that possibility. You may be tempted to toss weeds over the fence into the non-gardening neighbor's yard, but you'll be sorry later because they can mount a return (not to mention your neighbor may not send you holiday cards again). You also may be tempted to add weeds and weed bits to your municipal green bin or mulch collection, but doing that just runs the risk of passing the weed problems on to somebody else. The best way to get rid of weeds is to throw those unwanted plants in the trash.

Fertilizing

Fertilizing feeds the soil, delivers missing or low-level nutrients to the soil, and benefits plant growth that way. However, fertilizing isn't advisable in low-water, arid situations.

Fertilizers can negatively impact mycorrhizal fungi and beneficial microbes in the soil — an unintended consequence and potentially quite unfortunate, as current, ongoing research continues to demonstrate the amazing role these unseen organisms play in helping move nutrients and water through soil.

Also, heavily fertilized plants tend to put on a lot of lush growth. Lush growth consumes and demands more water. Lush growth can also attract insect pests.

An exception is plants grown in containers, from raised beds to pots and urns to hanging baskets. Chapter 17 discusses their care, including how and when to fertilize.

Cultivating and tilling — not so fast

Getting out or renting a tiller or digging deeply and vigorously forking over soil are familiar landscaping activities. But they aren't necessarily needed — or good. I have a radical suggestion. Don't cultivate, don't till. Less work now, less weeding later.

The action of turning over soil brings lots of weed seeds to the surface. As soon as they're closer to the surface and get a little light and air and water, they germinate. Some weed seeds can lay dormant in the soil for years, waiting for the moment you come along and awaken them. Also the tines of a tiller chop up and bring up bits of roots and rhizomes of weeds, and those start growing — many weeds are really good at regenerating from the smallest bits. Best to let sleeping dogs lie.

You can prepare soil for planting and kill off weeds so they won't mar your landscaping plans and compete with your garden plants for water and nutrients in other ways, including tarping and solarizing. Turn to Chapter 11 for details.

You can still dig in the soil and turn it over. You can still mix in organic matter as recommended and described in the section, "Enhancing/Making Improved Soil," earlier in this chapter, in a full bed or in individual planting holes. Just don't go to all the trouble of chopping up and stirring up large areas.

Exploring the Soil-Water Relationship in Your Landscape

Water works with soil, and soil works with water, especially soil improved with organic matter. There are different ways to observe, and alter, what water is already doing in your own home landscape. I start with the micro and move on to the macro, checking out some ways to tinker and improve.

REMEMBER

The water always obeys gravity (flows downhill) and always tries to take the path of least resistance.

Eyeballing

Nothing can substitute sitting on the ground (I know, not always easy to get back up!) and observing what is happening from the plants'-eye level. Try this before you irrigate and after — you'll discover what's really happening, not what you *think* is happening! Here are some guidelines:

>> **Test the soil informally.** Poke your finger into a plant's root area to find out how deep water is soaking in.

>> **Check whether the soil is generally damp or dry.** Soil is darker when wet. Surface water or water that only soaks in an inch (2.5 cm) or less is only helping surface roots. Better yet, dig down — carefully, to avoid damaging the roots, not too close — and look around.

These simple tests can lead you to water longer, slower, and more deeply so that the root systems not only receive water but also are encouraged to grow more deeply into the ground to access water as it drains down — desirable, of course, so they'll be more tolerant of dry spells.

Leveraging the relationship

A horticulture teacher once told me, "plants don't work any harder than they have to." By that, I believe she meant that if your watering habits or irrigation system mainly supplies water at the surface of the soil, the roots will stay there — they won't venture deeper.

But where water is precious, this isn't good. Moisture levels farther down in the soil are bound to be higher — water tends to sink in, right? Also water deeper in the ground is far less subject to drying due to exposure to air and wind. Water deeper in the ground isn't going to evaporate away. It's a good and cooler place for roots to go.

REMEDIATING CONTAMINATED SOIL

If you have reason to believe your soil is contaminated — by, say, paint, gasoline, wood-preserving chemicals, pesticides, or solvents, to name the main horrors — don't attempt to do anything about it until you get a soil test. When you send off the sample, be sure to note your suspicions and observations. Await results and recommendations.

Definitely don't cultivate or water a potentially contaminated area (water can carry toxins into groundwater, compounding or spreading the problem). The following are also wise:

- **Don't grow food in the spot.** Plant roots may survive in contaminated soil, but edible plants can take up and hold toxins. It's not worth the risk. If it's your best spot (sunny and open), consider covering it over and setting raised beds on the site instead.

  Some plants actually thrive in and take up toxins from the soil. They can then be harvested (and if the problem is heavy metals, sometimes those compounds can be recovered by burning the plants at season's end). Research on this novel solution continues, but the applications are mainly for industry and Superfund sites, not for ordinary yards.

- **Mitigate and improve.** Introducing lots of organic matter to the site can dilute and reduce the toxins and their effects, especially if you keep after it over many consecutive growing seasons.

- **Dispose.** Digging up contaminated soil can be risky. Again, the test results will guide you, including suggesting how and where to dispose of bad soil.

Remember: Toxins in your landscape's soil aren't easy, nor perhaps even safe or within your power, to mitigate or clean up. Cover the area over with non-plant items, such as trash or recycling bins, a patio, or an elevated deck, and don't meddle.

Assuming you've engaged in some soil improvement, the addition of organic matter, your soil will hold water better and the "go deeper" wish for root systems will work out. Water slowly and deeply!

TIP

After inaugurating slower, deeper watering, check how it's going — after at least a few weeks of active growth (in spring or, in milder-climate areas, fall). Dig down with a trowel near a plant and observe darker, damper soil and longer, deeper roots. Pat everything back into place, stand up, and cheer!

Mitigating Drainage and Runoff Issues

The following sections discuss the larger macro water issues in your landscape. This takes a different kind of observation — no sitting down on this job. Instead, patrol your yard after watering (not during — one thing at a time, please). Also go out and walk around after a rainfall, including after a major winter cloudburst.

Identifying site challenges

No home landscape is perfectly flat, and you're bound to see some variations on the paths and patterns of water in your yard. (Actually, perfectly flat isn't necessarily desirable — it can have runoff problems, too!) Look in particular for answers to these questions:

>> Where do channels form?

>> Is water running off and away from plants?

>> Is water ending up on the driveway, sidewalk, patio, and being wasted?

>> Is the slope of your land the only issue, or are there obstructions that route water such as large rocks, a patio or terrace, or larger plants?

>> Is water pooling in certain spots? Do you want it to/is that a good thing?

>> Where is gutter water going after a rain?

>> Is water entering your yard from an adjacent property? Where, and is this desirable?

>> Is mulch being moved around and washed away from where you originally placed it?

Figuring out remedies

Not everything happening with water flow in your yard is undesirable or a problem to be fixed. But if you identify a situation or area you want to fix or improve, soil and by extension, topography can help. Here are some suggested remedies:

>> Move plants to better spots for them, rather than struggling to alter their current site.

>> Create basins around thirstier plants to encourage water to soak in right where needed.

>> Dig swales or create little hillocks to make the scene not only more attractive, varied, or interesting, but also to route water to where it's most needed.

>> Stop water from carrying away mulch by digging a simple drainage-diversion channel with a trowel. Check your work! The easy way is right away, with a hose (even though it means running some water, which you may be reluctant to waste). The hard way is to wait for the next cloudburst and go out afterward and see what happened, and make improvements as needed.

If more-major earthworks seem like a good idea, flip to Chapter 16 and read about trenches, swales, basins, and berms.

Helping plants by manipulating soil

In your yard, as in nature, where a plant is growing may be to its benefit. Sometimes it's a matter of a smart siting decision, sometimes you can tamper to good effect. The following are some instances when you can create better planting spots for certain plants.

Plants that need good drainage

Some low-water plants absolutely require good drainage; they don't tolerate slow-moving or standing water. You have these options for keeping them happy:

>> At minimum, check if they're in the path of runoff and either move them to a better spot or guide runoff away from them.

>> Make special planting areas for them — mounds or berms — and plant them at or near the top. These can be created out of or incorporate plentiful gravel and rocks. You're trying to strike the sweet spot between good drainage and stability, which may take some tinkering to get right!

>> Include a larger rock or two to help anchor or hold up a mound or berm. Rocks also help keep the root zones a touch cooler; it's not terribly significant, but every little bit helps, eh?

Mounds and berms made solely out of soil tend to wear down and slump over time. Incorporating gravel helps prolong their useful life.

>> Grow them in pots or raised beds that are filled with fast-draining soil mix. The addition of sand or materials like pumice, perlite, or crushed rocks helps.

>> Customize their planting holes. Again, putting in sand or materials like pumice, perlite or crushed rocks will help.

Plants that need more water

For thirstier plants, you can take these actions to make their lives easier:

>> **Contour and shape and mound the soil** so rainwater or excess irrigation water collects where plants are located. Deliberately create such a set-up prior to planting. But you may also be able to fool with soil contours to the benefit of existing plants in your landscape.

Use your hands, a trowel, or a shovel, to do minor earthworks projects like this. Shore up plain soil by adding gravel or rocks. Remember that over time, such mounds do sink and erode, so if the arrangement is working, maintain it.

>> **Plant in a lower spot.** Because water moves downhill, it stands to reason that there will be more soil moisture at the bottom of a slope. That's the spot to put those plants that need more. Refer to Chapter 3.

Chapter **5**

Watering with Irrigation Systems

Welcome to the plumbing chapter, low-water landscapers. Various types of irrigation systems distribute water efficiently to your plants — whether you intend to do so for your entire yard, just one bed, or even some raised beds. Here I look at basic drip-irrigation set-ups, which are networks of tubing, emitters, and valves that snake through your landscaping. I also check out some water-efficient sprinklers.

The good news is you can do most of this yourself. I provide basic overviews, but I encourage you to also go find and watch some YouTube videos of people walking through the installation process step-by-step. Viewing how it's done and how it all works is really helpful. I also offer advice about getting a contractor to do it for you if you just aren't handy, don't want to attempt these projects, or envision a larger and more sophisticated installation.

The goal, as ever, is to get water where it's needed, effectively and consistently — without leaks, without overwatering, without underwatering. You can customize a good system to your particular yard and needs. You'll not only save water, but you'll also save time! And perhaps most persuasive: even after you buy the supplies (and/or hire help), the investment will repay itself many times over in savings on your water bill.

Because plants don't grow at the same rate year-round, the way you water has to adapt. Peak demand may be summer, or it may be spring, depending on your climate. Plants use less water in cooler months, and a rainy spell or season will allow you to stop or greatly reduce irrigating. Therefore the more control you have, the more efficiently you'll water.

Considering Outgoing Line Items

Before you get to the irrigation system, pause with me for a few minutes at your water source — your outdoor spigot. You can and should install several things there first, particularly if your irrigation project encompasses most or all of your yard or will serve more than one planted area. Although none of these items are strictly mandatory, all are helpful and ultimately will make your system run much better.

Consider installing a Y-shaped hose-splitter (or *manifold*) at your water source, right at your outdoor bib or spigot (or, if you want, one that splits three or four ways). Then you can put in your irrigation system but also still have a way to hook up a good old garden hose or fill a watering can, both of which will still come in handy from time to time. Get one with on-off manual valves for each and every outlet (*gated Ys*) just for an extra measure of control and to prevent drips and wasted water.

If you're replacing an existing sprinkler system, then likely your water source is a valve (not a spigot), with a control box/timer already present. If so, you may be able to skip this section and consider the project an upgrade or retrofit. (If you aren't sure, consult with a contractor.)

The following small but practical and important parts are available wherever irrigation gear is sold and are simply screwed onto the line before you even get to the lines going out to your yard. None are large or expensive, and installation is pretty much just a matter of screwing things together after you make sure of compatible size (half-inch or three-quarter-inch, 1.3 to 1.9 cm, diameters are standard sizes).

Installing a timer

A good timer for however you water your landscape is, honestly, optional, but I highly recommend investing in one (or more, as needed). A timer gives you control of the situation — a useful, welcome control.

Regarding how to program a timer, you can purchase complex ones and simple ones, but, no worries, they all come with instructions.

Some timers are battery-operated, whereas others are solar-powered. It's up to you which one you choose. Note that battery-operated ones are pretty efficient; you probably only have to replace the batteries once a year.

A timer goes on right at your water source, your outdoor faucet/spigot for your hose, or hose bib. It screws directly into the outlet faucet. If by chance the timer doesn't fit, you can install an adapter made for this purpose (available wherever irrigation parts are sold) so the water source and the timer are securely connected.

REMEMBER

Technically the tap is always on, but water doesn't flow unless you've set it to do so.

TIP

Take a look at how many zones a timer can handle. One is baseline and may be all you need. Others can handle two, three, or more outgoing lines. These are the places where you attach (press then screw on) piping going out into your yard. Alternatively, you can create the option for more than one zone by simply attaching a fitting that splits into two or more outlets.

Timers sold for outdoor irrigation aren't expensive. You can spend as little as $30 to $50, and as much as a couple hundred bucks. Weigh your options and your budget, but in the end you'll be glad you spent the money.

Although a timer can connect to Wi-Fi or be Bluetooth-enabled, is this necessary? The setup doesn't really need an extra layer of technology to work well. On the other hand, I'm willing to admit that the Wi-Fi feature that links your timer to a local weather forecast would be pretty handy (canceling or reducing a scheduled watering when rain is coming, for instance). Clearly some sort of rain sensor option is practical.

Installing a backflow preventer

A *backflow preventer* keeps water from going back up into your household water system, which you don't want. Contamination or water problems inside your home could ensue. Better safe than sorry. Look carefully when shopping (or going over all this with your contractor); it may be already part of the installation package or you may have to add it.

Installing a filter

A *filter* keeps any grit and debris that manages to get into the system from slowing things down and/or fouling the works. You can find various kinds at various prices; talk this over with the supplier and get their advice. Some filters will need to be cleaned or replaced from time to time. The important thing is that the filter does its job while keeping the water flowing cleanly.

You screw the filter into the outgoing line, after ("south of" or below) the timer if any. There are different sizes for different-size outgoing lines, that is, you can get a 0.5-inch one or a 0.75-inch one and so on.

Installing a pressure regulator

A *pressure regulator* regulates the pressure within your irrigation system; 25 psi (pounds per square inch) is standard. Because most household water systems are between 40 and 60 psi, this gadget basically lowers the pressure to become appropriate for landscape irrigation. It's not an expensive part (in the neighborhood of $50).

Place it on the outflow side of a timer or any valves in your system, following the backflow preventer and filter.

Although you don't need one, a pressure regulator is a smart addition to a drip system because drip systems don't need high water pressure — they operate at a lower pressure than your household water system. With one in place, your drip system will work better and not waste water.

Adding a hose adaptor

After you add all the previous items of your drip-irrigation system you arrive at a most important order of business: attaching the poly tubing. In contracting lingo, a hose adaptor is "female," and you want one that fits whatever diameter of poly tubing you'll be using (again, usually either half-inch or three-quarter-inch) — connecting to a "male" garden-hose thread.

A *hose adapter* connects all these water-source items to the main line of poly tubing, so you can finally get underway with the water-delivery part of the project.

Installing a water hammer arrestor

An optional accessory, a *water hammer arrestor* is worthwhile because when water shuts off abruptly, it absorbs the jolt or pressure surge (announced by a hammer-like noise). The T-shaped gadget is basically a shock absorber.

It screws right on to the side of many timers; if you want this accessory, either buy them together or make sure your timer has a spot for one and buy it separately (be sure to check for compatible size, 0.75-inch or 0.5-inch, 1.9 or 1.3 cm).

Installing In-Ground Drip Irrigation

These days, in-ground systems are the clear favorite for efficient irrigation of home landscapes, superseding the inefficient, unwieldy in-ground metal sprinkler-head systems of the past.

Note that some municipalities offer attractive tax incentives or rebates for homeowners who install drip systems. Check your City Hall's website or give them a quick call to find out whether these apply to your project.

Time of year you install generally isn't an issue, although bear in mind your own comfort and don't undertake the project on a hot summer day.

TIP

Installation is always easier if the plants aren't yet in place, such as when you're setting up a new planting area. You can trample around at will, without risk of stepping or sitting on the plants as you work. If the plants are already in place, just work more carefully.

These sections take a closer look at how they work and what's involved. You need a good grip on this information even if you don't plan to install anything yourself but rather to hire a contractor. Don't worry — I proceed slowly and try not to get overly technical.

SIMPLE SOAKER HOSE ALTERNATIVE

Using a soaker hose is the easiest and simplest alternative, suitable if your project isn't large, say, just one bed or a large, raised bed. Follow these easy steps:

1. **Run a regular half-inch line to the area first.**
2. **Attach it to the supply line before arraying the soaker hose throughout the bed.**
3. **Use an adaptor if needed to securely connect the two.**

Most soaker hoses come with a built-in water-pressure reducer, but if not or if you'd rather control the pressure yourself, install a pressure regulator at the water source or a ball valve on a gated Y. (Water pressure will vary anyhow due to all sorts of variables, including the diameter and the length of the tubing, any bends along the way, and elevation gain or loss.)

The beauty of this setup is also its downside: It soaks an entire bed rather than individual plants.

Understanding why it's a big advancement

These systems are composed of various types of heavy-duty plastics. They're reliable, efficient, and built to last. Nothing gets unintentionally bashed, knocked askew, bent, or kicked over. Nothing rusts or weathers. Emitters don't get moved around or lost. Lines don't clog, overload, or burst.

Unlike the sprinkler systems of decades past, the water never sprays or spews through the air, so waste and evaporation are greatly minimized. Instead water goes directly into the soil adjacent to or below the plants that need it.

Grasping what's involved

These systems are made of flexible black polyethylene (sometimes referred to as *poly* or *flex* for short) tubing that connects to your water source and conveys the water to your plants. The water delivery can be highly targeted, which is both wonderful for your plants and good for your water bill.

Solid (not perforated) half-inch poly tubing is commonly used to carry the water from the source to the garden bed, between beds, or across areas where irrigation isn't needed. Thus water isn't wasted on hardscape areas or areas of bare dirt or decorative mulch. (Alternatively, if your project isn't big and to save money, use a common half-inch/1.3 cm diameter garden hose.)

How exactly the water is delivered to your plants after it gets into the yard varies. You can get in-line tubing with emitters already in it, dripping water at regular intervals. Or you can install emitters yourself — of various kinds/delivery rates — by punching holes at intervals of your choosing. The emitter can go right in the hole or you can extend the reach by putting in a line with an emitter on it.

You can lay lines, rows, webs, grids, or circles, depending on your needs and the flexibility of the materials you invest in and the needs of your different plants.

All is possible and customizable with valves, barbed elbows for handling corners/ turns, and end-caps, all the right size for the tubing diameter you're using.

Because irrigation lines aren't especially attractive and because you don't want anyone or anything to catch on or trip over them, irrigation systems are covered or buried. These further conserve water by preventing evaporation and also by making sure water is released to roots and not the ground surface. What's not to love?

Shopping for drip-irrigation supplies

Particularly if you live in an area where many other people are using drip irriga-tion, a local nursery may actually stock everything you need. Also try a local hard-ware store. The staff at smaller, local places is often quite knowledgeable and helpful, and can help you pick out what you need, which isn't always true at the big-box stores.

Alternatively, you can shop online, even on Amazon. Do take care to shop places that serve ordinary homeowners and small landscaping firms, not big farms, greenhouse operations, or big agriculture.

TIP

Two well-established, well-regarded specialists that carry a wide range of gear are

>> www.dripdepot.com

>> www.urbanfarmerstore.com

Here are some recommended tools for this work:

>> **Needle-nose pliers:** They're good for both plugging in emitters and *goof plugs* (small black plastic items to shove into unwanted holes or holes you regret

TIP

making in the poly tubing) and prying or tugging them out, either in main lines or slender emitter lines.

Make sure you have goof plugs on hand. The fat end plugs a hole in the main poly tubing; the skinnier end can go right into the slender brown irrigation tubing. Presto, mistake fixed, potential leak plugged!

» **Garden pruners, scissors, or a cutting tool (with an embedded razor):** Any of these will neatly slice through the lines as needed. Keep 'em sharp!

» **A poker for making neat holes in poly tubes:** These are small, super-useful, and available wherever supplies for these projects are sold. They're just a short handle attached to a sharp pointed end (more substantial than a nail; meant for making a quarter-inch hole usually).

TIP

While you're shopping for tubing and accessories, be sure to get some *couplers*, wonderful little parts that easily allow you to connect tubing to other tubing. They're handy when you run out of tubing and need to extend/add more. They're also a lifesaver when you cut tubing and then realize you cut too short! Just shove in tubing on both ends and carry on.

Considering depth

How deep you should bury your system varies, depending on how much foot traf-fic the area gets and how to get the water to plant roots most efficiently.

TAMING THE LINES

If, as you run the lines out into your yard, they won't lay flat or they kink, you can control them:

- Set the rolls of black poly out in the hot sun for a few hours before you start to work, which softens them and makes them more cooperative.

- To hold the lines where you want them, secure them by pressing 6-inch (15.2-cm) landscape staples at intervals (every 4 or 5 feet, 1.2 or 1.5 m, is a general rule), gen-tly tapping them into place with a mallet or rock.

Burying the lines, instead or additionally, also helps secure them.

Bear in mind that main supply lines are black or dark-colored, which helps hide them from view but also absorbs heat (the brown irrigation lines are more easily disguised by similar-colored bark mulch). You don't want heated water going to your plants, so that's another practical reason to bury the lines out of sight. Growing plants can eventually shield and hide the lines.

You have two options, and you don't have to stick to just one throughout your entire landscape. Instead, do what makes the most sense for the situation. You can bury lines:

>> **In a shallow trench:** Create/dig the trench after you've laid the line down, not before, so the trench is right where you need it. Be careful so you don't ding or cut into the waiting tubing. You may elect to only bury the parts that are the most visible. You can cover over with lawn, soil, gravel, and/or mulch.

>> **Deep in the ground:** Ideally dig about 4 to 5 inches (10.1 to 12.7 cm) or more. However, digging this deep is another kettle of fish altogether! Even deeper burial of irrigation lines, whether plain delivery poly and/or ones with emitters, protects them from aboveground damage (including UV light), but doing so isn't advisable where the ground gets saturated or freezes.

Some installers excavate, lay down landscape fabric (garden plastic that lets air and water pass through but thwart weeds), add gravel, lay down the lines, and pour on still more gravel. It makes for a very stable installation. If the plants above all this prefer to grow in soil, lay down 4 to 6 inches (10.1 to 15.2 cm) or whatever the root systems will require. The water and the roots will meet underground as intended!

When you're digging, protect the root systems of plants that are attacked by tunneling pests like gophers and voles by encasing the roots in wire cages.

Contemplating irrigating options

This section moves into the realm of tubing called *drip tubing* (some call it *spaghetti tubing* because it's so slender), which is more flexible than the black poly main lines, is often brown in color and comes in different diameters but is most commonly quarter-inch microtubing. It's easily connected to the black poly main lines. Check out the nearby sidebar that discusses tips for installing it.

If you've calculated the size of the area you want to irrigate, you may be able to purchase a kit. These kits come with all the necessary parts, a few spares, and written directions with explanatory drawings or photos.

REMEMBER

Don't forget that, even when you've made drought-tolerant plant choices, some plants benefit from more water — generally speaking, bigger plants need more water and smaller ones need less. So if you have a mixed bed or varied landscape, customizable drip irrigation will be more sensible.

The following are your options:

>> **In-line drip systems:** Drip tubing tends to be a half- or quarter-inch (1.3 to 0.6 cm) in diameter and the embedded emitters are standard at 12- to 18-inch (30.5 to 45.7 cm) intervals.

These lines are excellent for mixed landscape beds, planted curb strips, and even laying into large, raised beds.

>> **Mesh driplines:** These are, as the name implies, a network or netting-like system of lines with emitters already installed. You simply lay them on or in the planting bed and then connect to the water supply. Handle them with care so the lines aren't kinked.

>> **Special driplines:** These are circular quarter-inch lines for placing around the perimeter of the root systems of shrubs and trees as well as larger perennial plants including ornamental grasses. Some models are nearly circular but have a small gap, so you can slip it around the base of a larger, established plant (without having to try to pull it down from above, which may not even be possible!).

If a plant is a bit too far from the main line, you can send out a side line (spur) to it, using a coupler poked into the main line and microtubing with an emitter out to that plant's root zone.

>> **Customized lines:** If you want to determine where emitters and lines go, going with a customized line isn't only possible but also surprisingly intuitive and easy. You just run line out into your planted beds and install the slender brown tubing and emitters wherever you want.

Understanding emitter options

Regardless of the manufacturer, emitters are standardized for certain water-delivery rates and color-coded so you know their output potential. Half of the emitter, the colored half or cap, will be showing when installed, whereas the other half — the end that goes into the poked hole in the water-supply tubing — is black and barbed so it can seat securely in the tube.

If you're having trouble deciding which option to use, do one of the following:

>> Talk with the supplier and get their advice.

>> Try a few different ones and work to determine which ones your plants prefer, fine-tuning as you discover what works best.

>> Install more than one emitter per plant (rather than trying to figure out the color codes/different types and rates).

Here are the standard sorts of emitters and the situations to which they're best-suited:

>> **Fast delivery:** Fast emitters are ideal for sandy, quick-draining ground or soil with some loam content. For example, a gallon (128 ounces) per hour, black, or two gallons (256 ounces) per hour, red. If you ever needed or could afford to deliver 5 gallons per hour, that's a tan emitter.

>> **Medium delivery:** It's good for average or organic-matter-amended ground or soil with some clay content. A half-gallon (64 ounces) per emitter per hour. Blue.

>> **Slow delivery:** It's best for heavy clay soil. Very low flow, less than 40 ounces of water per emitter per hour. Usually just plain black.

You can find intermediate options between these extremes.

Hooking up emitters

You can connect an emitter to the main poly water supply tubing before running it up to the soil surface or out to a plant's root system in four different ways. You'll need a supply of emitters, the basic tools I recommend in the section "Shopping for drip-irrigation supplies," earlier in this chapter and also (slender, brown, flexible) drip tubing. The four ways are as follows:

>> **Inject the emitter right into the main tube.** This option has a low risk of clogging and is easy to clean if a problem occurs.

>> **Install the emitter partway up the outgoing line.** Insert a quarter-inch barb, add a piece of line, add the emitter, and then add more line.

>> **Install a valve at the main line.** You can put a tiny ball valve at the main line, add a piece of line, put in the emitter, and then add more line if you want. This option has the advantage that you can turn the water on and off right at the main line, such as when a plant dies and you don't want water to flow out of there anymore. Of course, you can also pull out everything and insert a goof plug.

>> **Install the emitter at the top.** Insert a quarter-inch barb into the main water-supply poly tubing, add a piece of line, and top with the emitter. This option potentially puts the emitter above, at, or near the soil surface, which is popular because you can watch the water dripping out. But this configuration has a significant downside: dirt, sediment, or debris can get into the emitter and clog it.

Getting good coverage on a planting bed

The goal of getting good coverage on your beds depends on a lot of variables — your plants, their size/age, the soil you're growing them in, and so on. You have two main options:

>> **Run a line up and back the length of a bed (see Figure 5-1a).** It's simple, logical, and distributes water fairly evenly.

>> **Lay lines in even curves or S-turns (see Figure 5-1b).** Doing so takes more line but delivers water more thoroughly. It's a good approach in larger beds or where you're growing plants that require more water in order to prosper, such as veggies.

The simplest way to array irrigation lines is straight up and down (a). A curved layout takes more line but delivers water more thoroughly (b).

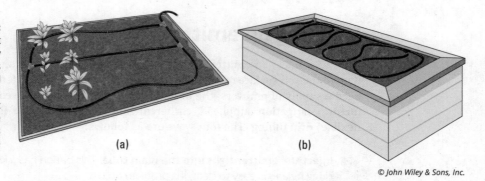

(a)   (b)

© John Wiley & Sons, Inc.

TIP

Don't rely on how water delivery appears on the surface to judge if water is soaking in evenly — it can be misleading, with gaps that don't exist underneath. Investigate by poking in a finger and/or digging down and looking (refer to Chapter 3).

DIY INSTALLATION — TIPS TO MAKE YOUR JOB EASIER

Here are some ways to make drip irrigation installation easier and more efficient — good advice and handy tricks from those who've done this work:

- If lines of black poly tubing or slender brown drip tubing give you any trouble as you try to push them into adaptors along the way, soften the stubborn ends by dipping them for a minute or so in a mug of boiling hot water.

- For cheaper or simpler connectors that lack a rubber washer, you can install them securely and prevent leaks by wrapping the screw surfaces in the same inexpensive but effective Teflon tape that indoor plumbers use.

- If you notice a difference in diameter between the main supply poly line and the drip tubing, don't worry. Simply install (push or screw on securely) barbed adaptors, Ts, and elbows, made for this purpose.

  Remember: Sometimes the cheap ones disengage or blow right off when water is coursing through your system, particularly when you've put in a reducing one (one that moves water from a larger diameter to a smaller diameter). Secure them in place with inexpensive clamps and tighten. A better but more pricey remedy is to buy better adaptors and links — you get what you pay for. Good-quality ones are more secure, more heavy duty, and may be labeled "perma-lock."

- To deliver water evenly, so that near areas get approximately as much water as distant areas, insert some Y-fittings along the length. Partially close the nearest gate and leave the far-off one wide open. Doing so evens the water pressure down the length of the line. Even delivery is important if you have a row of the same kind of plant (say, a hedge or raspberry bushes) and want even growth all the way down the line.

- The intervals between emitters vary with soil types. Because sandy soil soaks up water quickly (drains faster), space your emitters more closely. With clay soil, they can be farther apart.

- Watch some instructional YouTube videos if you're a visual person.

Hiring and supervising a contractor

If you aren't enthused about, unable to install a system, or your project is large and daunting, by all means hire someone. Seasoned professionals always work faster and more efficiently — they don't have a learning curve!

As with any other contractor-hiring situation, seek recommendations, read reviews, ask around, and make sure that whomever you engage understands your project and expectations. Get signed estimates, check insurance, and do your due diligence.

When you hire somebody else to install your drip-irrigation system, they may offer a service contract, which perhaps is worth considering, particularly if you're unable to maintain it for whatever reason. Otherwise, get the information you need to use and do the maintenance yourself.

REMEMBER

Find out whether the equipment, supplies, and cost of installation qualify for a tax incentive or rebate in your area. If so, make sure you get documentation. Clarify this *before proceeding*; your water district may require that one of their staff come out and inspect the before and after situation.

Maintaining Watering Systems

The beauty of simple drip-irrigation systems is that they're so forgiving. They're generally not hard to maintain or, if necessary, repair. As with household plumbing projects, you can usually do minor work yourself and call in the pros if something more major baffles you or goes awry.

All that said, you can't kick back after installation. You must monitor the system and its many parts. Fortunately, you put it in in order to nurture your plantings and you're keeping an eye on them too. These sections walk you through what you need to monitor.

Keeping up with routine maintenance

Here are the basics for routine maintenance:

>> **Do a visual inspection at least weekly during the seasons the system is in use.** You're looking for signs of leaks or wear such as cracks in the main line poly or dripline tubing.

>> **Sniff!** Crud such as bacteria or algae may build up in the lines and your nose may detect a funky or rotten smell. Flushing the lines helps with plain water. (A chlorine bleach rinse may be suggested when this happens with indoor plumbing, but you don't want to subject plants to bleach.)

If your lines are out of sight underground, gravel, or mulch, detecting leaks is obviously trickier. Here are two cues to be attentive to:

- Plants don't appear to be getting the water they need and show distress by wilting or growing slower than expected.

- A bigger water bill — surprise!

>> **Check the filter(s) on the main line and clean or replace them as necessary.** Always buy extra filters and keep them around.

>> **Check the emitters.** Make sure they're operating correctly. Clogs are sometimes due to debris or dirt getting in, and you can flush out the clog with water. If your water leaves mineral deposits or salts, emitters will be vulnerable to being clogged by the residue. The remedy is flushing with something acidic like vinegar (and then flushing the acid out with plain water). Consult the place where you purchased your supplies for guidance; they can sell you safe, effective flushing products and explain how to deploy them while protecting yourself and your growing plants. If flushing out doesn't work, replace the affected piece(s).

In the arid West, hard water (water that is high in dissolved minerals, especially calcium and magnesium) eventually clogs inline emitters, often in a year or two. Rinsing and cleaning might clear out the deposits, but it's probably easiest just to replace the emitters. They aren't expensive, after all.

Fixing leaks

You can repair leaks in the following ways (remember to always shut off water to the trouble spot before undertaking any repair):

>> Splice in fresh tubing.

>> Replace faulty emitters.

>> Use goof plugs.

>> Patch the spot with epoxy or pipe-sealing tape. Frankly, this is the least-desirable option simply because water pressure can render a patch job short-lived or ineffective.

If leak detection and repair is beyond you, turn off the water as close to the problem spot as possible and call in outside help.

Watching your plants and adjusting

Young plants need more water when they're getting established. You can reduce water deliveries in a year or two. Keep the following tips in mind as you check on your plants:

>> **Provide more water when your plants are producing fruits and flowers.** Plants need and use more water then. In the case of fruit, consistent water is the key to a tasty harvest. Tick up watering a bit when buds are forming (for flowers) or baby fruit appears (for good, edible fruit later).

>> **Tinker with the amount and frequency of irrigation and you may discover that many of your plants can get by on even less water than you projected.** Part of this is due to the success of your system — when the water soaks in deeply, the roots will grow more deeply and the plants will become more self-sufficient.

REMEMBER

>> **Experiment with how often you need to water.** The frequency of when to water is based on your yard's conditions, what plants you grow, and your climate. One hour every three days? Fifteen minutes on and fifteen minutes off for two hours, once a week? It depends! Don't take shots in the dark, though. Ask other irrigation-system users in your neighborhood or town for advice.

Readying a system for winter

When preparing for colder weather, make sure your system is free of water. You never want water to freeze within your system, which can damage parts and lines. Remember these pointers:

>> **Reduce water deliveries as the growing season winds down.** You don't want fresh new growth happening when winter is coming; cold weather can damage new growth. If your winters are milder but you get rains, at least power down your system or shut it off for the duration.

>> **Remove and store.** In late fall before a freeze, take everything off the hose spigot, manifold, timer, and all — and store it all in a cool, dry place indoors until next spring.

>> **Empty the system of water.** Unscrew the endcaps/plugs and drain or blow the water out (with an air compressor).

Your contractor (if you hired help) or the folks from wherever you bought your supplies may provide further instruction and cautions.

Considering Sprinklers

Sprinklers have gotten a lot of bad press in areas where water is in short supply. Among the reasons: They may be hard to regulate and water is wasted, running off on sidewalks and driveways, and, because water is traveling through the air, it's subject to evaporation.

However, that's old news. The latest technology in sprinkler systems may persuade you to reconsider. Here's a quick overview, but I encourage you to go online or to a well-stocked garden supplier and take a closer look at what is offered these days. You may be impressed!

If you decide to go this route, take care with installation, use, and maintenance to minimize water loss.

Eyeing in-ground sprinklers

A sprinkler that sends forth water too quickly, that is, emits too much water too fast, is wasteful simply because the soil (or lawn or landscaped bed) can't absorb the moisture and excess runs off. Highly efficient pop-up sprinklers, the latest technology, can deliver needed water far better and potentially lower your water bill by as much as 30 percent — clearly worth considering.

TIP

Also, some municipalities incentivize these sprinklers, either by offering the systems and the parts to residents at a reduced price or offering tax breaks or rebates. Check with your water district.

The modern adjustable nozzles are also great; you can tinker with arc and radius to customize to your particular watering situation, either by hand or with a small tool that's included with your purchase.

You have lots of choices in efficient nozzles. Shop with care so you get a quality product that delivers what your landscape needs. In particular, seek the range you need; determine how far you want water to travel: 10, 20, or 50 feet (3, 6.1, or 15.2 m)?

TIP

If your property already has an in-ground sprinkler system, rather than tear it out, check to see if you can just take off the old heads and replace them with new, more efficient ones. (This is the outdoor equivalent of replacing your shower head indoors.)

Nozzles are available in two main options:

>> Water comes out as a stream (technically, in bigger drops). This may at first seem counterintuitive, but this design is far more effective at getting water where it's aimed than the misting types of sprinklers (which wind can toss off course and which evaporate faster).

>> Water also comes out more slowly and evenly. This better allows it to soak in, which means you'll probably have to run it for longer (another counterintuitive thought).

Looking at temporary sprinklers

Portable or movable sprinklers have always been popular for spot-watering and temporary watering situations, such as delivering water to a freshly sown lawn, a newly planted flowerbed, or a young vegetable garden. And don't forget that the kids and dog love to run through them on hot days.

However, these days people want efficiency and little or no waste. The main culprits are speed of delivery and coverage area, and people want to have the ability to adjust those settings to the situation.

If you get one of these sprinklers — many variations are available — look for these features:

>> **Portability:** Do you have to drag it around, or is it on wheels? How agile are those wheels? Can they turn easily as needed?

>> **Stability:** Heavier rigs don't jump around or tip over, though you may be able to stake down a lightweight one if you have to.

>> **Automatic shut-off:** This handy feature allows you to prevent waste. You can connect it to a timer.

>> **Accessibility:** Look to see whether you have access to the nozzle head and whether the sieve is cleanable, just in case grit gets in.

>> **Durability:** Metal is preferable to plastic because it holds up better over time and doesn't break easily or break down. Galvanized steel is most resistant to corrosion.

TIP

Try never to leave one of these unattended. Waste happens when you wander away or aren't monitoring water delivery. At minimum, be present for its first run and make necessary adjustments.

2
Making Smart Plant Choices

Take a closer look at flowering perennials and annuals.

Find out about the amazing diversity of succulents.

Consider the best low-water shrubs, vines, and trees.

Check out your options for growing food plants.

Get a handle on basic planting and care of low-water plants.

Chapter **6**

Choosing Flowers

I f you're operating under the assumption that a low-water landscape will be limiting or dull, this chapter is for you. Prepare to be amazed, and enticed, by the many choices you have in the realm of colorful flowers.

The plain truth is that gardeners love flowers; indeed, your main wish may be a garden and yard overflowing with colorful blooms. Certainly enough so that the main impression people get when they stop by is abundant color. Perhaps you'll even have some blooms to spare for homegrown bouquets for yourself or to give way to those visitors.

Instead of looking jealously at the lush gardens of England or wetter places like the Northeast or Pacific Northwest, recalibrate your expectations and goals to flowers that will thrive for you.

This chapter doesn't include the justly popular and practical plants for drier gardens, succulents, many of which produce flowers. Check out Chapter 7 if you're interested in succulents.

TIP

Garden color is more than a matter of flowers. Often you can bring out the best in your plant selections if you incorporate other sources of color that contrast with or complement the flower show. This includes integrating colorful foliage as well as including garden ornaments, furnishings, and backdrops such as brightly painted walls and fences. Check the color insert to see examples.

Selecting and Planting Perennials

Perennials are long-lived herbaceous plants (unlike *annuals,* which only last one year; I discuss annuals in the section, "Avoiding Commitments with Annuals," later in this chapter). *Herbaceous* just means "no woody stem"; plants with woody stems, of course, are trees, shrubs, and many vines. All in good time — I explain them in greater detail in Chapter 8.

Perennials are a diverse group, many grown not only for their flowers but also for their foliage that helps keep the show in your yard attractive even when they aren't in full bloom. Read the descriptions carefully in this section, keeping an eye out for features and colors that you want.

REMEMBER

You have to have a little faith when you plant perennials. Unless you have access to a nursery or garden center that sells big plants, the usual way is to start with small plants. With good growing conditions and good care, they won't stay small, so make sure you allow them space to expand and reach their potential mature size.

Perennials are an investment, because — assuming they establish well in your yard — they're in it for the long haul. They'll bloom reliably year after year. Not indefinitely, though; plants, like all other living things, have lifespans, but certainly for years to come.

TIP

How will you know if a perennial can be grown or will survive where you live? Some people refer to USDA Hardiness Zones (most dry-climate areas are in Zones 7 to 11) or the more detailed, Western-informed Sunset Zones pioneered by *Sunset Magazine.* You can find all about those in *Gardening Basics For Dummies* or *Landscaping For Dummies.* You can also head to https://plianthardiness.ars.usda.gov/.

TIP

Here's an easier suggestion: If a flower is sold at a locally owned garden center or plant sale in your area, it's probably going to do fine for you — after all, those sources don't want unhappy customers. Shop local, it's bound to be safe!

Getting down to the root

Some perennials touted in the following sections grow from heftier root systems, including *rhizomes* (creeping rootstocks) as well as *tubers* (enlarged roots) or *corms* and *bulbs* (similar to tubers but often bigger, and often clasped with fleshy scales not unlike an onion if you were to try to pry them apart for a closer look). It makes sense that certain dryland plants evolved to develop these — the more-substantial underground structures help plants hold and conserve precious food and water.

SUMMERTIME AND THE LIVING ISN'T EASY

As you peruse the lists and descriptions of plants in this chapter, consider the time and duration of normal flowering for each perennial. Maybe you prefer your yard's peak glory to be springtime, but having flowers on view in summer, autumn, and/or winter would also be nice. Unfortunately, you may not get your wish in summer because of the following:

- **Gone but not forgotten:** In areas where summers are punishingly hot and dry, some perennials will slow down or *go dormant.* That is, their topgrowth disappears from sight although their roots remain alive, waiting to resurge when growing conditions improve.

- **The summer pause:** Many suitable perennials are in the habit of blooming lustily in spring, slowing down during the heat-stressful summer months, and getting their mojo back in the fall. Not surprisingly, this preference for the shoulder seasons is a response to better opportunities for water and friendlier temperatures.

TIP

Before you buy any plant, check the roots because they're so critical to a plant's chances of survival. Plants with healthy roots succeed, whereas those with dried-out, soggy and rotten, or pest-ridden ones struggle. Sometimes pot-grown perennials have unfortunately become *pot-bound* and should be avoided (roots are questing out the bottom and there's almost no soil; such plants have trouble growing well even when transplanted into a good spot in your garden).

Some tubers, corms, and bulbs reproduce by *offsets,* small baby plants developing off the original root system or bulb itself.

Generally speaking, perennials are available in these three ways (you can find more information on how to shop, select, and plant them in Chapter 10):

>> **Bareroot:** Literally, you can see the roots. These perennials are offered not potted, but (often) wrapped in damp newspaper or paper towels; their vulnerable little roots may be additionally protected with moisture-conserving plastic wrap or a baggie. There will be only a little *topgrowth,* or foliage, above the roots because it has been trimmed short. Handle with care and plant correctly, and these plants will do fine.

>> **Container-grown:** More common, more expensive, and more impressive-looking are pot-grown perennials. Some come in small pint or quart nursery pots, whereas others are growing in a gallon-size pot or larger. Topgrowth and perhaps even a few flowering stalks or buds are evident, but give equal attention to the quality of the root system. Check the roots before buying if at all possible.

>> **Divisions:** Because perennials are outgrowing their space or because they need to be *revitalized* (flowering has slowed down over the years, for example), the plants are dug up and divided into smaller sections suitable for replanting — each piece with a balance of roots and topgrowth. If you're at a plant sale or nursery, you may spot perennials for sale in this form. Buying divisions is a good bet; you're getting a mature plant that should take to its new home in your yard with vigor.

Going native

Most popular perennials for low-water settings are native to a drier landscape somewhere — the Mediterranean Coast and mountains, central France, Portugal, Greece, California, Colorado, Chile, Mexico, Australia, and so on. The nursery industry is well aware that these perennials are successful in other similar areas and you have many splendid choices. You may not even have thought about inquiring about or looking into a plant's origins — especially if the plant performs well in your climate and delivers beauty to your garden.

However, plants that originate in your state or region tend to do the best simply because they're already regionally adapted to the area's weather, seasons, and soil.

Native plants are also adapted to native wildlife — everything from birds to insects to small mammals. This means they tend to be nibbled less and are less likely to succumb to plant diseases; they're naturally healthier. Being native can also mean that the plants are well-behaved, not invasive, as local creatures keep their growth in check.

REMEMBER

When you choose a native plant for your home landscape, you're helping your immediate area's ecosystem. Increasingly habitat is being lost, and birds and animals can't get the foods or shelter they depend upon for survival. Plants from distant places don't support them as well. You as a gardener have the ability to help or hurt your environs. Who wants to contribute to or create an ecological desert by leaving out native plants? I flag native perennials in the following lists.

WARNING

A number of the plants I recommend for your low-water garden are native plants that you may see growing wild — at a nature preserve or state park or even just along a favorite hiking or biking trail. *Don't dig them up* and bring them home for a few reasons:

>> **You're causing undue stress to the plant.** You usually notice them when they're flowering, and transplanting any plant when it's blooming is quite stressful for it. This is especially true of dryland natives.

» **You're tearing them away from a place where they prosper.** Setting aside the ethics of plundering natural areas (poaching), this is a bad idea from a practical standpoint. The soil in wild or uncultivated spots is too different from garden ground, and transplanted plants inevitably perish.

» **You're disturbing the local ecosystem.** Native plants are an integrated part of their habitat, nurturing insects, birds, and animals and in turn being nurtured by the soil and soil organisms (including mycorrhizal fungi) they've grown in all their life.

Avoid the temptation to get free plants by uprooting them. Instead buy small plants from a nursery or native-plant sale. Or, purchase or gather seeds for planting in your yard — granted, growing them from seed takes longer but frequently produces stronger plants in the long run.

Loving the sun

In the lists that follow, I provide each perennial's common name, followed by the scientific name, which is helpful for clarification. Many perennials nurseries provide both names.

Here are my top choices for low-water, drought-tolerant perennials for areas that get plentiful sunshine, listed by when their blooming time generally begins. Be sure to check the color insert to see a few favorites pictured.

Spring-blooming favorites

Spring flowers are such a wonderful sight! These are my top choices:

» **African daisy,** *Arctotis.* Hot colors! These South African beauties come in hot pink, orange (look for one called 'Pumpkin Pie'), yellow, scarlet, as well as white and multicolors. Foliage is silver-gray. Like to form broad patches, so you can fill large areas of your yard, including under trees and other taller plants. Pests and problems are rare. Flowers up to 4 inches (10.1 cm) across; plants grow about a foot high (30.5 cm) and sprawl to the sides.

» **Bearded iris,** *Iris × germanica.* Big gorgeous flowers in solid colors and stunning color combinations; some are even rebloomers. The leaves are large green or gray-green blades. Flowers tend to be big, 5 to 6 inches (12.7 to 15.2 cm), while the plants get about 3 feet (1 m) high.

» **Blackbird spurge,** *Euphorbia* 'Blackbird'. This unusual selection has purple-to-black foliage on red stems, a striking sight. The small flower bracts (an inch or less; 2.5 cm or less) are lime-green, as they are with many other euphorbias. The plants get no more than 2 feet (0.6 m) tall.

» **Bulbinella,** *Bulbinella nutans* or *B. robusta.* Little star-shaped flowers of sunny yellow appear in clusters early in the season, covering the plant. Foliage is slightly fleshy, grassy-looking, bright cheerful green, and stays about a foot high (30.5 cm) but spreads to form nice colonies. Blooms on 3-foot (0.9 m) stems.

» **California buttercup,** *Ranunculus californicus.* Native. Unlike some of its relatives, this buttercup can get by on no summer water. Plants range from 1 to 2 feet tall and wide (0.3 to 0.6 m). The small buttercups (1 inch, 2.5 cm, or less) are borne on leafless stalks that rise above the green foliage.

» **Camas,** *Camassia.* Native. A bulbous plant that sends forth spectacular spires in many shades of purple (you can even find white ones at some nurseries), with contrasting yellow stamens. Untroubled by pests, disease, rodents, or deer. Gets between 2 and 3 feet (0.6 to 0.9 m) tall.

» **Cluster lily,** *Brodiaea.* Native. In shades of blue, pink, white, lilac, or purple, these tubular flowers, carried in small clusters, are pretty. Narrow, grassy foliage in mounds. A little extra spring water encourages better blooming. Entire plant varies from 4 to 16 inches (10.1 to 40.6 cm) tall.

» **Firecracker penstemon,** *Penstemon eatonii.* Native. Spikes of bright red flowers. Dark green foliage. Blooms early — late winter to early spring in mild-winter areas. A plant can get up to 4 feet (1.2 m) tall and half as wide.

» **Foothill penstemon,** *Penstemon heterophyllus.* Native. This one's flowers are blue, light purple, and sometimes even rosy. Expect the plant to grow a bit shorter than other penstemons, about 3 feet (0.9 m) tall and wide.

» **Germander,** *Teucrium* species. The spikes of little flowers are in the pink to purple range and are abundant when the plants are established. Most have gray-green leaves, which are pleasantly fragrant (a sagelike scent) and grow thickly. Plants are wider than tall, generally 1 to 2 (0.3 to 0.6 m) high and twice as wide, so they're good for massing.

» **Gold coin,** *Pallenis maritima.* Handsome yellow daisies (darker in the centers) cover a tough, spreading plant that grows 12 inches (30 cm) high and about 18 inches (45 cm) wide.

» **Heuchera,** *Heuchera* species and cultivars. Native. A lot of these are available these days, but not all are suitable for a drier garden. Look for the following:

  - *H. sanguinea* has handsome mottled leaves and wands of tiny hot pink to ruby-red flowers; it goes only about 1 to 2 feet (0.3 to 0.6 m) high and wide.

  - *H. elegans* is smaller and has pink-and-white flowers.

  - The hybrid 'Santa Ana Cardinal' is worth seeking out if you want red flowers.

» **Hill Country penstemon,** *Penstemon triflorus.* Native. Showy 2-inch (5 cm) pink flowers in clusters of two or three are the reason to grow this one; they're marked with white and darker pink. Green leaves sometimes have a coppery hue. Up to 2 feet (0.6 m) tall and wide.

» **Horned poppy,** *Glaucium flavum.* Branched stems present a profusion of golden yellow poppies. Blue-gray foliage. Just 2 feet (0.6 m) tall.

» **Hot Lips sage,** *Salvia microphylla* 'Hot Lips'. So exuberant and full-growing that some people mistake it for a shrub, this perennial sage is studded with bicolor white-and-hot-pink to scarlet flowers that draw hummingbirds, butterflies, and pollinators. Reaches 4 feet (1.2 m) or more high and wide.

» **Hummingbird sage,** *Salvia spathacea.* Native. Magenta flowers draw crowds of hummingbirds. Hearty plants produce green, aromatic leaves (the scent is downright fruity). Overall height is between 1 and 3 feet (0.3 and 0.9 m), spreading habit.

» **Kangaroo paw,** *Anigozanthos* species and cultivars. Growing from stout rhizomes, these dramatic plants deliver incredible flowers on long, leafless, branching stems — shades of red, usually, though orange and yellow versions are also available. Strappy green or gray-green leaves. Gets 1 to 3 feet (0.3 to 0.9 m) tall and wide.

» **Lupine,** *Lupinus.* Native. The lupines you want in low-water settings are native to the West and Southwest. Glorious, dense spires of blue-and-white flowers adorn silver bush lupine, *L. albiflorus*; gets as tall as 5 feet (1.5 m). The arroyo lupine, *L. succulentus,* has blue-and-purple spikes on 3-foot (0.9 m) plants. Other worthy species are sometimes found at a native-plant nurseries.

» **Mariposa lily,** *Calochortus* species. Native. These beautiful wildflowers go by wonderful common names: star tulip, globe lily, fairy lantern. They tend to be white or cream with contrasting markings in the blossom's interior of red, pink, yellow, and white. They grow from corms or bulbs and are between 1 and 4 feet (0.3 and 1.2 m) tall, depending on the species.

» **Mexican bush sage,** *Salvia leucantha.* A favorite, but justly so. Dependably generates scads of handsome, tall, purple-and-white flower spikes that pollinators adore. Plants get big, around 4 feet (1.2 m) high and 6 feet (1.8 m) wide.

» **Mexican tulip poppy,** *Hunnemannia fumariifolia.* Native. The small, bright yellow flowers do resemble little tulips. Foliage is finely textured and blue-green. Plants get about 1 to 2 feet (0.3 to 0.6) high and wide.

» **Milkweed,** *Asclepias* species and cultivars. Native. Yes, some milkweeds are well-suited to dry, hot gardens, if nurturing caterpillars of endangered butterflies or simply enjoying their beauty is your goal. They tend to have gray-green, narrow, thick leaves; flower colors vary from white and pink to red and purple.

REMEMBER

They reproduce by seed and by creeping roots (rhizomes), so pick a spot where they're free to spread.

>> **Monardella,** *Monardella* species. Native. Clusters of long tubular flowers adorn low-growing plants of gray-green or blue-green foliage. *M. macrantha* has fiery red to orange-red flowers, whereas *M. villosa* has purplish-pink ones. Both remain about 1 foot (0.3 m) tall and spread out around 2 or more feet (0.6 m) wide.

>> **Monkeyflower,** *Mimulus* or *Diplacus*. Expect a good show of orange, cream, yellow, or red blossoms, depending on the species or cultivar. Foliage is glossy, dark green, and resinous. About 1 to 3 feet (0.3 to 0.9 m) high and wide.

>> **Moroccan daisy,** *Rhodanthemum* cultivars. White daisies with contrasting dark centers on a neat mound of gray-green foliage. Typically 12 inches (30.5 cm) tall and 12 to 18 inches (30.5 to 45.7 cm) wide. 'Casablanca' is a classic.

>> **Mule's ears daisy,** *Wyethia amplexicaulis*. Native. Another tough little sunflower-daisy type bloomer, with large, 3-inch (7.6 cm) bright flowers in singles or multiples on a leafy plant (the floppy, lance-shaped leaves are the source of the common name). Reaches 2 to 3 feet (0.6 to 0.9 m).

>> **New Zealand flax,** *Phormium tenax*. Delivers plenty of attractive tubular red-orange flowers on branched stalks that are either fairly erect or arching. Foliage below is a contrasting bronze-green. These are big plants, in time reaching 10 feet (3 m) tall and 8 feet (2.4 m) wide. Because the flower show doesn't last that long, you may wish to select for foliage. Those of the aptly named 'Dusky Chief' are purple-gray. A smaller version is 'Tom Thumb', 2 to 3 feet (0.6 to 0.9 m) tall and wide, with red-edged olive-green leaves.

>> **Pacific coast iris,** *Iris* species. Native. Many to choose from — white, yellow, purple, reddish, and chocolatey brown, as well as combinations. They're a cross between two native species and prized for their beauty and sturdiness. Clumps need to be divided every few years. Generally no more than a foot (30.5 cm) high.

>> **Peruvian lily,** *Alstroemeria* hybrids. Clusters of colorful flowers in many shades top strong stalks above green foliage. Plants tend to grow 2 to 3 feet (0.6 to 0.9 m) tall and spread out to about 4 feet (1.2 m) after they're mature.

>> **Phacelia,** *Phacelia tanacetifolia*. Native. Clusters of blue-purple flowers, durable, divided green foliage. Reaches 3 feet (0.9 m) tall and wide over time. Very popular with pollinators.

>> **Pozo blue sage,** *Salvia* 'Pozo Blue'. Grow this hybrid for its beautiful lavender-blue flowers. Gray-green foliage, bushy habit, grows 3 to 5 feet (0.9 to 1.5 m) tall and wide.

» **Prairie clover,** *Dalea.* Native. A low-grower that can be used to fill in broad areas, on average a foot (0.3 m) tall and spreading to 4 feet (1.2 m). Lots of tiny yellow flowers, aromatic green foliage. Very tough.

» **Purple lavandin/lavender,** *Lavandula* species and cultivars. Cherished for its sweet, romantic fragrance and handsome foliage. Many choices. Watering can be tricky; although lavender needs irrigation to get established, overwatering leads to rot — well-drained soil is a must. Usually 2 to 4 feet (0.6 to 1.2 m) tall and wide.

» **Sea thrift,** *Armeria maritima.* This is a smaller plant, popular in rock gardens. Little ball-shaped flower clusters of bright pink or white top short stalks above grassy, dense foliage. Grows only 4 to 6 inches (10.1 to 15.2 cm) high and spreads to 18 inches (45.7 cm) wide.

» **Silver mound,** *Artemisia schmidtiana.* Aptly named, forms dependable, dense mounds of silver-gray foliage. Tends to need supplemental summer water or it gets ratty-looking. Normally about 10 inches by 10 inches (25.4 by 25.4 cm). 'Nana' is a dwarf version, about half the size.

» **Spurge,** *Euphorbia* cultivars. Easy to grow, with attractive, narrow, slender green or gray-green leaves; many choices with colorful and variegated foliage are available. Forms patches by self-sowing and underground rhizomes, so plant it where you don't mind it spreading. Flowers are technically bracts, usually lime-green.

» **Triplet lilies,** *Triteleia* species. Native. Darling little starry white flowers in clusters; need good spring moisture to bloom well. Loose, grassy foliage. Grows from small corms, spreads via offsets.

» **Verbena,** *Verbena* species and cultivars. Tall, branching stems show off ball-shaped or rounded clusters, usually in the purple to pink color range; self-sows. Foliage is a bit sparse. Plants get approximately 4 feet (1.2 m) tall and half as side. 'Lollipop' is a smaller, shorter plant.

» **Yarrows,** *Achillea* species and cultivars. Some are good for groundcovering, whereas others are mounding plants. They spread by seed and rhizomes and grow thickly after they're established. Leaves are soft-textured, finely divided, and lightly fragrant. Flowers are flat-topped and present well. Scads of species and cultivars are available. Three popular ones are

- 'Moonshine' is a classic, with yellow flowers; about 2 to 3 feet (0.6 to 0.9 m) high and wide.

- 'Island Pink' has rosy pink flowers. Gets a foot tall (0.3 m) and up to 3 feet (0.9 m) wide.

- 'King George' has chiffon-yellow flowers. Stays low, about 3 inches (7.6 cm) high, but spreads. Nice for rock gardens.

>> **Woolly sunflower,** *Eriophyllum lanatum.* Native. Loads of small, cheerful yellow flowers over mats of gray-green leaves. Reaches 2 feet (0.6 m) tall and spreads to 3 feet (0.9 m). Self-sows and fills broad areas.

Summer stars

Summer color is always a treat. Here are my top choices:

>> **African lily,** *Agapanthus* species and cultivars. Big, loosely ball-shaped flowers of blue, white, or purple on erect, leafless stalks. Strappy leaves. Grows from a bulbous rhizome. Can get as tall as a person, but for most landscapes, those in the 2 or 3 feet (0.6 or 0.9 m) range are best.

>> **'Ascot Rainbow' spurge,** *Euphorbia × martinii* 'Ascot Rainbow'. One of the showiest euphorbias. Variegated leaves of yellow and green gain red hues in cooler fall weather. Green flower bracts with tiny red flowers. Gets 18 to 24 inches (45.7 to 61 cm) high and wide.

>> **Bear's breeches,** *Acanthus mollis.* Undeniably spectacular with its erect, purple-and-white flower spikes and dark green foliage. ***Note:*** It spreads. Grows 3 to 4 feet (0.9 to 1.2 m) tall and a bit less wide.

>> **Blackfoot daisy,** *Melampodium leucanthum.* Native. These daisies are reminiscent of white zinnias and do well in summer heat. Plants grow 6 to 12 inches (15.2 to 30.5 cm) tall and 1 to 2 feet (0.3 to 0.6 m) wide.

>> **Blanket flower,** *Gaillardia* species and hybrids. Native. Brilliant, multihued flowers of garnet, crimson, rust, yellow, and orange. Butterflies adore them. Habit is mounding; foliage is green to gray-green. About 2 feet (0.6 m) high and wide.

>> **Blazing star,** *Liatris* species and cultivars. Native. Loose, grassy-leaved plants displaying nice, dense spires of purple, lavender, or white flowers that draw butterflies. Generally up to 2 feet (0.6 m) tall and a bit wider.

>> **Buckwheat,** *Eriogonum* species. Native. These shrubby perennials have small, gray or gray-green foliage and clusters of tiny flowers in rusty red, tan, or brown. Here are three notable ones (size varies):

- *E. fasciculatum* has pink to white flowers.

- Ella Nelson's buckwheat, *E. nudum,* has yellow ones.

- Those of *E. grande* var. *rubescens* are cherry red.

>> **Bur marigold,** *Bidens.* Native. Long-lasting yellow daisies (1 to 2 inches, 2.5 to 5 cm) over dark green, fine-textured foliage. Lots of cultivars. Plants get about 1 foot (0.3 m) high and to 2 feet (0.6 m) wide.

>> **Cape rush,** *Chondropetalum* or *Elegia* species. Unique and graceful grassy-looking plants. Stem ends have clusters of tiny dark flowers; the effect is stunning. Check out the following:

- 'El Campo' is a compact selection.

- *E. elephantina* will be up to 6 feet (1.5 m) high and wide.

>> **Catmint,** *Nepeta* species and cultivars. The abundant light purple flowers are a favorite of pollinators. Silvery to green foliage. Eventually gets about 3 feet (0.9 m) tall and 4 feet (1.2 m) wide.

>> **Chocolate flower,** *Berlandiera lyrata.* Native. Gets its name not from its flowers, which are yellow daisies with dark centers, but from its chocolate-scented, gray-green leaves. Thrives in summer heat. Grows 1 to 2 feet (0.3 to 0.6 m) high.

>> **Horehound,** *Marrubium.* The flowers are tiny and nothing to write home about, but the thick, attractive, lime-green foliage is fabulous. Gets 2 to 4 feet (0.6 to 1.2 m) tall and half as wide. 'All Hallows Green' is widely available.

>> **Hummingbird mint,** *Agastache* species and cultivars. Natives. Gray-green foliage is joined by tubular flowers in various appealing hues and bicolors. I recommend the tougher, drought-tolerant types, orange hummingbird mint, *A. aurantiaca,* licorice mint, *A. rupestris,* and Texas hummingbird mint, *A. cana.*

>> **Matilija poppy,** *Romneya coulteri.* Native. Its other common name is "fried-egg flower," and the big white poppies centered by yellow do fit! Blue-gray foliage. Be forewarned that this becomes a big plant, attaining 10 feet (3 m) tall and 4 feet (1.2 m) wide.

>> **Meerlo lavender,** *Lavandula × allardii* 'Meerlo'. Notable for its large lilac-purple flower spikes and its variegated leaves edged in white. Gets between 2 and 3 feet (0.6 and 0.9 m) tall.

>> **Oregano,** *Origanum vulgare.* These are casual-looking, heavy-blooming plants, generally with small pink or purple flowers that bees love. You can eat and cook with the leaves. Plants get around 2 feet (0.6 m) tall.

>> **Ruellia,** *Ruellia.* Native. The blue or purple flowers look like small petunias and draw hummingbirds and butterflies. Glossy, dark-green foliage. Plants get 5 feet (1.5 m) high and wide.

>> **Russian sage,** *Salvia yangii* or *Perovskia atriplicifolia.* This plant can get big and full enough to seem like a shrub, but it's a perennial. Once established, it's trouble-free. Lavender-blue to purple flower spikes and fragrant, silvery green leaves. Hummingbirds, bees, and butterflies love it. Normally in the range of 2 to 3 feet (0.6 to 0.9 m) high and wide.

- **Sea holly,** *Eryngium* species and cultivars. Branched stems are topped by thistle-like blue flowers with spiny bracts. Leaves are often bluish-green to match. A number of worthy species and cultivars available with color variations. Plants are about 2 feet (0.6 m) tall and wide.

- **Silver carpet,** *Dymondia margaretae.* A South African native that forms dense mats of grayish foliage, which is joined by small yellow daisies. Expands to about 3 feet (0.9 m) wide, but only gets 1 or 2 inches (2.5 to 5 cm) high.

- **South African geranium,** *Pelargonium sidoides.* Prized for its burgundy-red, slender-petaled flowers, carried on 6- to 10-inch (15.2 to 25.4 cm) stalks. Foliage is classic geranium but small. Plants get 1 foot (30.5 cm) tall and wide.

- **Sundrops,** *Oenothera fruticosa.* Native. An upright-grower with multiple branched stems, prized for the way its red flower buds open to sunny yellow saucer-shaped blooms with orange stems. Reaches 1 to 3 feet (0.3 to 0.9 m) with an equal spread.

- **Thyme,** *Thymus* species and cultivars. Low-growing or mat-forming, small fragrant leaves, tiny flowers beloved by bees. Add interest by growing a variegated-leaf one. Size varies.

- **Wright's buckwheat,** *Eriogonum wrightii.* Native. A bushy, matting plant with small, tough gray leaves and slender stalks of white to soft pink flowers. Grows 18 inches (45.7 cm) tall and a bit wider.

Fall (and perhaps into winter) stalwarts

Flower color in autumn is a treat. The following fill the bill:

- **California aster,** *Symphyotrichum chilense.* Native. The original species is loaded with small white daisies with yellow centers. Cultivars extend the color range to light and dark purple. Green foliage, casual habit. Attains 1 to 3 feet (0.3 to 0.9 m) tall and 2 to 3 feet (0.6 to 0.9 m) wide.

- **California fuchsia,** *Epilobium canum* or *Zauschneria californica.* Native. Brilliant, thrilling late-season color — fiery orange-red, all the more dramatic against the gray-green foliage. Of course, hummingbirds love it. Gets 1 to 2 feet (0.3 to 0.6 m) tall and 3 feet (0.9 m) wide.

- **Giant coreopsis,** *Leptosyne gigantea.* Yellow daisies for later in the gardening year. In milder climates, blooms right through winter. Bright green, dissected foliage. Grows 3 to 5 feet (0.9 to 1.5 m) high and wide.

- **Naked lady,** *Amaryllis belladonna.* These grow from bulbs and send up tall, 2- to 3-foot (0.6 to 0.9 m) leafless flower stalks topped with pink trumpet-shaped flowers. The plants have strap-shaped green leaves.

- » **Pink muhly grass,** *Muhlenbergia capillaris.* The common name comes from the late-season flower show, a haze of pink covering the grassy mound. Prior to that, the grass blades are soft green to blue-green. Overall size is about 2 to 4 feet (0.6 to 1.2 m) around.

- » **Spurge,** *Euphorbia* species and cultivars. Refer to the previous section. For color later in the year, seek out gopher spurge, *E. lathyris,* or myrtle spurge, *E. myrsinites.*

Appreciating some shade

You may be able to grow some of these perennials in sun or part–day sun, but I segregate them here in case you do have some dry shade in need of dressing up. These perennials do better when they get at least some relief from hot midday or afternoon sun and, in fact, require less water when not growing in the path of hours of direct, hot sunshine. After they're established — doing well in the same spot for a few years — they may not need much or any water. Check out these:

- » **Bear's breeches,** *Acanthus mollis.* Refer to the section, "Summer stars," earlier in this chapter.

- » **Bergenia,** *Bergenia* species and cultivars. These clump-forming plants have broad, leathery, purplish leaves and pink- to purple-red flowers on stalks — a unique look. They get 1 to 2 feet (0.3 to 0.6 m) high and wide at maturity.

- » **Bush penstemon,** *Penstemon fruticosus.* Native. A bushy plant, it grows broader (up to 2 feet, 0.6 m) than tall (up to 16 inches, 40.6 cm). Foliage is dark green until cooler fall weather, when it reddens up . . . just in time to be joined by lots of clusters of rosy-purple flowers.

- » **Cranesbill geranium,** *Geranium* species and cultivars. Handsome, long-lasting flowers of blue, pink, violet, purple, or white over handsome, dissected green foliage. Not all varieties do well in drier settings, however; seek out *G. macrorrhizum* or *G. endressii,* or see what your local nursery has in stock. Flowers are 1 to 2 inches across (2.5 to 5 cm); plants, over time, can get 2 or 3 feet (0.6 to 0.9 m) wide.

- » **Epimedium,** *Epimedium* species and cultivars. Mounds of attractive leaves that vary from almost heart-shaped to lance-shaped. They can be bronzy in spring and redden in fall's cooler temperatures. Spring brings sprays of pretty but small yellow or white flowers. About 1 foot (30.5 cm) tall and wide.

- » **Hardy cyclamen,** *Cyclamen purpurascens* and **ivy-leaved cyclamen,** *Cyclamen hederifolium.* Cousins to the popular, larger house or bedding plants, they have the same round or heart-shaped leaves (sometimes prettily patterned) and a flurry of cream to pink to lilac flowers with reflexed petals late in the gardening year. No more than 6 inches (15.2 cm) tall and wide.

» **Heuchera,** *Heuchera* species and cultivars. Refer to the "Spring-blooming favorites" section earlier in this chapter.

» **Hummingbird sage,** *Salvia spathacea.* Native. Check out the section, "Spring-blooming favorites," earlier in this chapter.

» **Lamb's-ears,** *Stachys byzantina.* Prized for its lance- or paddle-shaped, felt-textured silver leaves. The flowers are pink and not that showy. Plants get no more than 10 inches (25.4 cm) high and spread a lot, filling in open areas and flattering other plants. Easy to tear out sections if they get too enthusiastic.

» **Spurge,** *Euphorbia* species and cultivars. Height varies from 1 to 2 feet (0.3 to 0.6 m) See the description in the section, "Spring-blooming favorites," earlier in this chapter.

Avoiding Commitments with Annuals

As the previous section discusses, perennials are long-haul flowers. Annuals aren't. They act fast, going from seedling to mature flowering plant in a matter of a couple of months. Then they're done. They stop flowering, they begin to look lousy, and they flop on the ground and/or dry out. At which point, you're free to tear them out and toss them on the compost pile. Annuals are a short-term romance!

The exception is those that reseed, which can be a blessing (reliable color) or a curse (too many plants, to the point of becoming invasive or weedy) for the gardener. They keep generating new generations, thus they "act like perennials." Examples include African daisy, baby's breath, bachelor buttons, clarkia, collensia, phacelia, and rudbeckia. Whether this happens in your yard depends on the plant and your local climate — I would just say, be alert to the possibility and be ready to yank out unwanted new plants.

REMEMBER

Annuals do tend to be tough and durable, often almost amazingly so. Plant snobs sometimes disdain them as a short step up from plastic flowers, but that assessment isn't fair. In situations where it's hard to make a garden look nice or you don't have the time, money, or energy to invest in lots of perennials, shrubs, succulents, and more, annuals are a dependable source of beauty. Carefully chosen and deployed, they can look great. Ahead, I explain how to get going with annuals and ways to showcase them.

Here are some wonderful annual flowers, in many hues and forms. Check what's available locally if you need large quantities. Mix and match — have fun with your plantings. (I provide both common and scientific names, so you can be sure you are getting what you want.)

Jump-starting your annuals

Flowering takes a lot of energy for plants. Even though annuals are wired to bloom quickly and generously, they can't do it without a little help from you. Consistent water and perhaps even a little sheltering shade (a lawn chair will do — it's temporary!) is definitely needed, especially in their first days and weeks in your yard.

REMEMBER

As a rule, annuals tend to be shallow-rooted. The upper layers of soil where their roots live dry out faster. Weigh their water needs and your available water before taking the plunge.

If you decide to go ahead with annuals, in order to prevent their soil from drying out and to prevent the water from evaporating, you must mulch your annuals. An inch, or more, really helps! (Chapter 15 discusses various mulching materials.) If your watering visits happen to wash away the mulch, be sure to replenish it.

Showcasing your annuals you plant

You have options when displaying annuals. They don't have to go directly into the ground. You can raise them in containers: individual pots, urns, windowboxes, hanging baskets, and more. Refer to Chapter 17 for the full scoop.

Still, I admit it, annuals are a short-term solution. Plant annuals where you:

>> **Want quick color.** Annuals deliver bright and bountiful color. They're often blooming or about to explode into bloom when you buy them.

>> **Want temporary color.** You don't really want the annuals in a certain spot for long, but you know they'll pump out colorful flowers for you as long as they're in residence.

>> **Want to fill in between perennials or trees and shrubs.** Plant annuals, especially if those bigger plants are new to your home landscape and it will be a while (a season? two or three years?) before they reach their mature sizes.

>> **Haven't decided on your long-term plans.** No commitments when you plant annuals, just color for now.

>> **Want to take real estate away from weeds/unwanted plants.** As the saying goes, "nature abhors a vacuum," and you're aware you shouldn't leave gaps and open areas.

>> **Need a placeholder plant or patch.** Annuals work when a perennial or other plant has failed, or you're waiting for a new plant to arrive.

>> **Are willing and able to water them.** If your choices need water to survive and remain good-looking, you'll have to decide if you can.

Raising annuals from seed (rather than buying seedlings) is an option, assuming you have the time and inclination and especially if you need a lot of them. Some are super-easy from seed, notably nasturtiums, cosmos, bachelor buttons, morning glories, calendula, and sunflowers.

You may wonder, why are some flowers considered annuals in some places and perennials in others? The short, sweet answer is a plant's designation really comes down to whether it can survive your winters. For example, African daisies are able to last for years in milder climates, but if your area gets cold enough to freeze, they'll perish and thus be considered annuals.

Choosing sun-lovers

Plentiful sunshine is easy to fill with bloomers — so many of them thrive. Here are my top picks:

>> **African daisy,** *Osteospermum.* Yes, this is the one Californians call "freeway daisy" because it has been so popular in landscaping embankments. Their usually blue-purple centers contrast beautifully with petals (technically ray flowers, like other daisy petals) of orange, red, rose, pink, purple, white, yellow, you name it. Height varies from about 10 to 18 inches (25.4 to 45.7 cm).

>> **Bachelor button,** *Centaurea cyanus.* Often included in wildflower mixes, this jaunty true-blue flower blooms dependably. Butterflies like it. Grows between 1 and 3 feet (0.3 and 0.9 m) tall.

>> **Calendula,** *Calendula officinalis.* Plentiful and bright orange and yellow daisylike flowers, usually about 3 inches (7.6 cm) across abound on branched stems. Bushy plants, reaching 1 to 2 feet (0.3 to 0.6 m) tall, depending on the cultivar.

>> **California poppy,** *Eschscholzia californica.* Native. Technically a perennial, this favorite blooms and self-sows enthusiastically, so if it likes your yard, you'll have plenty. The original, wild one is luminous orange, but now you can also get these in red, white, pink, yellow, and even multihued versions. Blue-gray foliage; plants are rather floppy, reaching about 1 foot (30.5 cm) high and wide.

>> **Cosmos,** *Cosmos.* Easy and easy-going, these offer carefree, fun color in many hues. The plants themselves are rather long, slender, and wispy-looking; some can get as tall as a person!

>> **Creeping zinnia,** *Sanvitalia procumbens.* Small, all-yellow daisy flowers cover a low-growing plant, about 6 to 12 inches (15.2 to 30.5 cm) tall and spreading out to 18 inches (45.7 cm). Very heat-tolerant.

>> **French marigold,** *Tagetes patula.* Your source for tough, fiery colors on dependable, compact plants. Generally 6 to 12 inches (15.2 to 30.5 cm) high and half as wide.

>> **Globe amaranth,** *Gomphrena globosa.* Loose, open-branched little globe-shaped flowers. Purple is the classic, but they come in other colors nowadays, including red and white. Mature height is 24 to 30 inches (61 to 76.2 cm) and mature spread is 8 to 10 inches (20.3 to 25.4 cm). Great for dried bouquets.

>> **Lantana,** *Lantana.* If you can get past the acrid scent, these jaunty, pink-and-yellow flower clusters are valuable in a dry landscape, delivering lots of color and attracting hummingbirds and butterflies. Also available in other colors — the contrasting ones are more interesting than the solid colors. Typically grows 2 to 6 feet (0.6 to 1.8 m) high and wide.

>> **Morning glory,** *Ipomoea.* Fast-growing, climbing vine adorned with, in the case of the beloved heirloom 'Heavenly Blue', large, 4- to 5-inch (10.1 to 12.7 cm) blossoms. Heart-shaped leaves. Check out some of the other colors and flower sizes if blue isn't for you.

>> **Moss rose,** *Portulaca.* Valued for its low (around 4 to 6 inches, 10.1 to 15.2 cm), sprawling growth habit, the plant is quite tough, thanks to almost succulent foliage. Often sold in color mixes of red, yellow, orange, and white.

>> **Nasturtium,** *Nasturtium.* Easy to grow in poor, dry soil, these cheery plants are quite tough. Big, rounded leaves, available variegated. Flowers typically come in orange, red, and yellow, individually or in mixes. You can find bushy ones and trailing ones.

>> **Spider flower,** *Cleome.* Such substantial, bountiful, fast-growing plants, it's amazing that they're annuals. Bell-shaped clusters of unique flowers in white, pink, violet, and cherry rose. Lavish, dense dark-green leaves. Can get 4 to 5 feet (1.2 to 1.5 m) tall or more. Wonderful along a fence.

>> **Sunflower,** *Helianthus annuus.* This favorite and easy bloomer has received so much attention from plant breeders that you now have all sorts of choices: tall or short; single bloom to a stem or multiple flowers; huge flowers or smaller ones; pollen-free ones; and big centers and small ones. They tolerate drought once established.

>> **Vinca,** *Catharanthus roseus.* Prized for its abundant, bright, simple flowers; pink, white, red, purple, lavender and bicolors, often with contrasting center "eyes." Stay around 1 foot (30.5 cm) tall.

>> **Zinnia,** *Zinnia.* Splashy color guaranteed with so many different kinds and colors; some with plush blossoms, some multihued. Easy to grow, great for bouquets. You can grow taller ones, but there are many in the 12- to 18-inch (30.5 to 45.7 cm) height range that are quite manageable and appealing.

Selecting for less-sunny settings

Some annuals do fine and flower well in part–day or even full shade, if your yard has those conditions. Both flower and leaf colors will be better if they aren't being blasted by hot sun.

REMEMBER

Annual plants grown in less sun still need consistent water and, if mulched, will live on that moisture for longer than their full–sun counterparts simply because there will be less evaporation. Here are some great choices:

>> **Coleus,** *Coleus.* The cliched red-and-green leaved ones are still around, but you can find some wonderful alternatives, including tropical orange, maroon and lime-green, ruby and crimson, and so on. Plant size and width varies a lot.

>> **Flowering tobacco,** *Nicotiana.* These trumpet-shaped flowers have a sweet scent, which draws pollinating moths and hummingbirds. Colors vary from scarlet to lime-green to white to pink. Tall ones can go in the back of displays, dwarf ones in the front or in pots.

>> **Forget-me-nots,** *Myosotis scorpioides.* Wee, pretty blue flowers with yellow centers, about ¼ of an inch (0.6 cm) across. Can form dense mats over time. Tops off at about 2 feet (0.6 m) high.

>> **Lobelia,** *Lobelia.* Small but exuberant, these sentimental favorites come in blue, white, purple, red, white, pink, and bicolors. Some varieties are 6 inches (15.2 cm) high or less, others are bigger; be sure to check when buying.

>> **Spider flower,** *Cleome.* See the previous section.

>> **Sweet alyssum,** *Lobularia maritima.* You'll get a profusion of lightly scented little ball-shaped flowers on low-growing, mat-forming (to 4 to 8 inches or 10.1 to 20.3 cm high, usually) plants. White is used a lot, but there are other choices, including pink, purple, lavender, rose, and apricot-orange.

IN THIS CHAPTER

» Exploring low-growing types

» Getting to know the many kinds of sedums

» Looking at larger, clump-forming succulents

» Thinking about colors of leaves as well as flowers

» Considering different types of cacti

Chapter 7

Selecting Succulents

A dmittedly, succulents are almost synonymous with low-water landscaping. How could they not be? They've evolved and are well-adapted to living in habitats of sun and heat with minimal water. The trick is to include ones that are attractive, ones that you like, and ones whose appearance makes your yard more interesting and beautiful.

This chapter tours some of the many options. The plant lists here aren't exhaustive, but I hope you get the heartening impression that a big palette in terms of form, size, and vibrant colors of foliage and flowers is available. Resolve to be adventurous in your choices!

REMEMBER

I don't bother to list cold hardiness with every plant listed in the upcoming pages. That's because, as a rule, all of these plants are potentially safe to grow in USDA Zones 7 or 8 to 11 and 12, in areas where winter freezes never happen or are rare. Some selections may slow down or go dormant when temperatures cool, whereas others respond by changing, often deepening, their foliage color. (I discuss USDA Hardiness Zones in Chapter 6.)

If you have any concerns about a choice's ability to survive winter in your garden, ask when you buy it. If a plant is being sold locally or thrives in a neighbor's garden, you don't have to worry.

TIP

To get away from the cliché of a scrubby, sparse-looking landscape of succulents, aim for lush. Rather than dotting succulents here and there, create areas where they're massed together. Don't jam them together; doing so creates pruning and separating work down the line — just plant them adjacent to each other. (They aren't static and will spread out by running stems, making offsets, and just naturally growing bigger and wider over the years.) Put in plants in a variety of different foliage colors — including different shades of green — so the eye travels.

WARNING

Killing a succulent by overwatering is a lot easier than by underwatering. Though their thick or juicy foliage may cause you to believe these plants don't need much water, that's not always or necessarily so. Certainly, newly planted plants need help getting established in your yard with some regular water and mulching. Should your selections begin to look dried and distressed, however, watering is what they want. But, yes, as a rule, these plants never like being drenched; in fact, overwatering can be fatal.

Recognizing Trailing and Groundcovering Types

Succulents that expand or form colonies, to cover broad areas or drape over rocks or walls, are especially valuable in drought-prone landscapes. They make appealing, rambling carpets of foliage, often to the exclusion of weeds, or lay down a horizontal tableau that you can punctuate here and there with other, contrasting, bigger plants or garden ornaments or furnishings.

Trailing and carpeting succulent plants are good-looking, low-maintenance choices for dry gardens, including yards with poor, lean, or gravelly ground. They're a practical alternative to other water-hogging groundcovers including lawn grasses. Ahead are my recommendations.

Eyeing the wonderful world of sedums

Common names for plants are frequently revealing. Even though many nurseries, plant catalogs, and gardening books (including this one) tend to refer to the plants here as *Sedum*, which is the correct scientific name for this large genus, occasionally they're referred to as *stonecrops*. That name actually is a helpful visual. The plants thrive in rocky terrain, among stones and gravel, often spreading and trailing their unique succulent foliage like a crop? Perhaps, if you use your imagination and view them from above, yes, that works!

WHEN ALL ELSE FAILS, USE THE PLANT'S COMMON NAME

You may walk into a garden center or specialty nursery with sedums on your wish list and find plants that aren't what you expect. Traditionally included in the genus *Sedum* are upright-growing, large, clump-forming, or mounding perennial plants, sporting big flower clusters that resemble a head of broccoli. The most famous, widely planted one is called 'Autumn Joy'. Its lime-green flowers deepen to pink-red in autumn's cooler weather. How can these sorts of plants be lumped in with the often-diminutive stonecrops?

The answer is, they aren't any longer. Botanists have sensibly separated them off into their own genus now, *Hylotelephium*. However, the new name hasn't really caught on. Everyone's so accustomed to calling them sedums. Some places at least label them as "border sedums," which helps because many are well suited to perennial borders in terms of their size and colors.

Note: Not all the stonecrops are called Sedum anymore. *Amerosedum, Phedimus, Petrosedum,* and others have entered the scene as botanists continue to fine-tune. My advice? Try asking for the one you want by its common name.

Speaking of using your imagination when contemplating these unique plants, here's another visual. A few years ago an intriguing garden in a residential neighborhood in southeast Portland, Oregon, was given over almost entirely to a great variety of different sedums. One time when I paused to admire it, the gardener came outside and we had a conversation that I never forgot. "I like imagining that this is my colorful under-the-sea garden," she confided. (Belatedly I see that wasn't a completely original thought because there is a cultivar called 'Coral Reef', which I include in the following list.) Though many sedums are wonderfully drought-tolerant, I've never stopped seeing them in this romantic if watery way — even if it sounds a bit odd!

Their natural toughness isn't the only reason to appreciate these plants. As a rule, garden pests such as rabbits and deer don't trouble them, and they aren't toxic to animals or humans (some are actually safe to eat). Disease problems are rare. When they bloom, pollinators flock to their tiny but often profuse flowers. The plants spread out but generally aren't considered invasive.

Here are some good, low-growing, low-water stonecrop-type sedums. So many different colors of foliage and flower! You may get inspired to grant them plenty of space and mix and match:

>> **Angelina stonecrop,** *S. rupestre* 'Angelina'. Golden yellow to chartreuse foliage; turns golden-orange in fall. Summer flowers are bright yellow.

Fast-growing. Mature size is 4 to 6 inches (10.1 to 15.2 cm) tall and spreading 12 to 24 inches (30.5 to 61 cm).

» **Blue Spruce sedum,** *S. reflexum* 'Blue Spruce'. Blue-green, needlelike foliage does remind you of the tree it's named for. Summer flowers are yellow and long lasting. Mature size is 6 to 8 inches (15.2 to 20.3 cm) tall and spreading 12 to 24 inches (30.5 to 61 cm).

» **Cape Blanco stonecrop,** *S. spathulifolium* 'Cape Blanco'. Powder-blue foliage; yellow flowers in summer. Mature size is 4 to 6 inches (10.1 to 15.2 cm) tall and spreading 8 to 12 inches (20.3 to 30.5 cm).

» **Cascade stonecrop,** *S. divergens.* Small green leaves grow quickly, thickly and form mats — only plant it where you don't mind its exuberance (it can overwhelm other small plants). Summer flowers in clusters are yellow. Mature size is 4 to 6 inches (10.1 to 15.2 cm) tall and spreading 12 to 24 inches (30.5 to 61 cm). *S. divergens* var. *minus* is dark green and has a fuller habit.

» **Chinese sedum,** *S. tetractinum* 'Coral Reef'. Green and yellow foliage turns bronze-pink in autumn. Flowers are yellow. Trailing habit, terrific on slopes. Mature size is 3 to 4 inches (7.6 to 10.1 cm) tall and spreading 10 to 18 inches (25.4 to 45.7 cm).

» **Cliff stonecrop,** *S. cauticola.* Blue-gray leaves touched with rosy pink; pink flowers later in summer, becoming darker red as they age. Mat-forming. Mature size is 2 to 4 inches (5.1 to 10.1 cm) tall and spreading 10 to 12 inches (25.4 to 30.5 cm).

» **Coppertone stonecrop.** *S. nussbaumerianum.* Bright orange-yellow foliage, even bolder orange with more sun exposure. Small white flowers in spring. Mature size is 10 to 12 inches (25.4 to 30.5 cm) tall and spreading 24 to 30 inches (61 to 76.2 cm).

» **Dragon's blood stonecrop,** *Phedimus spurius.* Green leaves rimmed in red turn fully, dramatically red by fall — spectacular! Pink-red flowers mid-summer to fall. Mature size is 4 inches (10.1 cm) tall and spreading 18 inches (45.7 cm).

» **Gold moss stonecrop.** *S. acre.* Bright green foliage, accompanied by bright yellow flowers in summer. Mature size is 2 to 4 inches (5.1 to 10.1 cm) tall and spreading 12 to 24 inches (30.5 to 61 cm).

» **Golden sedum,** *S. adolphii.* Yellow-green foliage deepens to orange in bright settings. Flowers are white. Mature size is 10 inches (25.4 cm) tall and spreading 24 inches (61 cm).

» **Japanese stonecrop,** *S. sieboldii.* Blue-green leaves edged in pink; cooler fall weather kicks it up to a show of pink, yellow, red, and orange. Bright pink flowers in late summer and fall. Mature size is 6 to 10 inches (15.2 to 25.4 cm) tall and spreading 12 to 18 inches (30.5 to 45.7 cm).

- » **Jenny's stonecrop,** *Petrosedum rupestre.* Blue-gray to light green foliage with yellow flowers in summer. Mature size is 2 to 4 inches (5.1 to 10.1 cm) tall and spreading to 24 inches (61 cm).

- » **Lance-leaf stonecrop,** *S. lanceolatum.* Gray-green foliage, but with more sun develops purple coloration and may turn red in winter. More cold-hardy than most sedums, grows well at higher elevations. Mature size is 4 inches (10.1 cm) tall and spreading to 8 inches (20.1 cm) across.

- » **Murale sedum,** *S. album* 'Murale'. Green foliage that darkens to chocolate brown in fall. White flowers in midsummer. Mature size is 4 inches (10.1 cm) tall and spreading 12 to 18 inches (30.5 to 45.7 cm).

- » **Orange stonecrop,** *Phedimus kamtschaticus.* Rich green leaves; this common name seems to refer to the summertime flowers, which are yellow with lots of bright orange stamens. Mature size is 6 inches (15.2 cm) tall and spreading up to 18 inches (45.7 cm).

- » **Pacific stonecrop,** *S. divergens.* Tricolor foliage: red, dark green, and light green create a sparkly show in this spreading beauty. The stems diverge, hence the species name. Yellow flowers in summer. Mature size is 4 inches (10.1 cm) tall and spreading up to 3 or 4 feet (0.9 to 1.2 m).

- » **Pork-and-beans sedum,** *S. rubrotinctum.* Chubby foliage of bright green with red tips. Another common name is jellybean sedum. Yellow flowers in summer. Mature size is 12 inches (30.5 cm) tall and spreading up to 2 feet (0.6 m).

- » **Purple stonecrop,** *S. spathulifolium* 'Purpureum'. Wine-purple leaves with a gray waxy coating! Bright yellow flowers in spring. Mature size is 4 inches (10.1 cm) tall and spreading 12 to 18 inches (30.5 to 45.7 cm).

- » **Voodoo sedum,** *S. spurium* 'Voodoo'. Deep red to reddish-green foliage; summer flowers are rosy-pink. Mature size is 4 to 5 inches (10.1 to cm) tall and spreading 12 to 15 inches (30.5 to 38.1 cm).

- » **White sedum,** *S. album.* Green leaves turn reddish-brown in fall. Flowers are white to pink. Mature size is 4 inches (10.1 cm) tall and spreading 18 inches (45.7 cm).

TIP

You won't have to spend long viewing these sedums to be impressed with their color shows. A word to the wise: color does vary. Truly, it varies over the growing season — it's common for a sedum to start off in spring plain green and darken or become redder or more orange when fall's cooler weather arrives. Color also changes depending on exposure. More sun tends to inspire bolder color. And sometimes those little clusters of flowers set up a terrific contrast to the foliage. You'll come to appreciate all their beautiful, continually interesting phases.

Considering other succulent carpeters

These succulents aren't sedums, but they're used in similar ways in landscapes — to fill open, sunny spots. They, too, like well-drained ground and should never be overwatered:

» **Blue chalk fingers,** *Senecio mandraliscae* or *Curio repens.* Blue to blue-gray blades with a light waxy coating, growing upright — the common name is perfect. Expands quickly and thickly, making it a great base for a garden of mixed succulents. (Flowers are insignificant and may be cut off if you don't like them.) Mature size is 8 to 12 inches (20.3 to 30.5 cm), spreading up to 4 feet (1.2 m).

» **Campfire plant,** *Crassula capitella* 'Campfire'. Fiery hues of bright orange, rust, gold, and red, especially in cooler temperatures. At other times it will be green to chartreuse. Growth slows or halts in hot summers. Mature size is 6 to 8 inches (15.2 to 20.3 cm), spreading up to 2 to 4 feet (0.6 to 1.2 m).

» **Flapjack plant,** *Kalanchoe luciae.* Green and red with a unique look; round, flat disks crowd the stems to create a full, if jumbled, look. Yellow flowers in spring. Mature size is 8 to 12 inches (20.3 to 30.5 cm), spreading up to 8 inches (20.3 cm).

» **Ghost plant,** *Graptopetalum paraguayense.* Powder blue-gray, grayish-white, palest lavender-pink — this trailer is a beauty. Little rosettes form on slowly expanding stems, so it's great spilling out of a pot or softening the edge of garden steps. Summer brings tiny yellow flowers. Mature size is 4 to 5 inches (10.1 to 12.7 cm), spreading.

» **Hens and chicks,** *Echeveria.* This plant has all sorts of colors and sizes, and it's such fun to mix and match! This is a large group, beloved for its variety and easy-going nature. Many spread by forming offsets. Basically they're plump, handsome rosettes, resembling miniature agaves. When they flower, usually late spring to early summer, you get little nodding bells carried on arching stalks well above the foliage. Size varies, but individual plants are usually 4 to 8 inches (10.1 to 20.3 cm) tall and between 4 and 12 inches (10.1 to 30.5 cm) wide.

» **Houseleeks,** *Sempervivum.* Green and gray-green foliage; look closer, and you'll observe each succulent leaf has a pointed tip, sometimes in a contrasting color. Forming smaller rosettes than *Echeveria,* these become dense colonies over time. Flowers on short stalks in late spring or summer tend to be in the red-purple range; be advised that individual rosettes bloom once, then die . . . but are quickly replaced by their offsets. Mature size is no more than 4 inches tall and wide (10.1 cm).

» **Ice plant,** *Delosperma.* Pink to purple flowers cover thick mats of green foliage; some have white centers, which helps them stand out more. Several similar species and cultivars are available. Less invasive than *Carpobrotus*. Mature size is in the range of 3 to 6 inches (7.6 to 15.2 cm), spreading up to 1 to 2 feet (0.3 to 0.6 m).

» **Ice plant, hottentot fig,** *Carpobrotus edulis.* Yellow flowers, sometimes light pink with yellow centers, bigger than those of *Delosperma*. Blooms mainly in late winter and spring. The rest of the year, you get thick, often ragged mats of green foliage. The state of California would probably fall into the sea if this nonnative invasive plant (originally from South Africa) wasn't clinging to every beach embankment and cliffside. That said, you can use it to secure an eroding slope. Mature size is in the range of 4 to 8 inches (10.1 to 20.3 cm), spreading up to 10 feet (3 m).

WARNING

Ice plants — which two similar plants answer to (see the two preceding bullets) — are so widely used in dryland landscaping, that I felt duty-bound to include them. Sure, they'll cover broad areas. Sure, their flowers are bright. Sure, they help prevent erosion on embankments and pretty up other difficult spots. Sure, they're no trouble — bulletproof is a common description. But they're also overused and aggressive. Before you deliberately add them to your home landscape, consider some of the alternatives presented in this chapter.

TIP

How do you get these plants to do what you want them to, which is spread out and make a living carpet somewhere in your yard? You have to plant plenty of them, but not so closely that they grow up to crowd one another; heed the "mature size" information in the preceding list or as provided on the nursery tag. Mulch bare areas in between the baby plants (and yank out any weeds that try to encroach) until they're able to fill in, which they will, given time!

Planting Clump-Forming/Solo Types

A bounty of appealing larger succulents can beautify your landscape. The categories I create here are, admittedly, not official botanical groups — they're growth-habit descriptions. (Some of these plants can appear in either "rosettes" or "bushy form," depending on their setting, age, or how fast they grow — these lists are meant for guidance.) I group the plants generally in these two ways to help you better envision how to use them.

While you may punctuate a carpeting groundcover or position some along a garden path or in a border, understand that they tend to expand over the years. Many form offsets — that is, solitary plants don't always remain so!

Adding rosettes

A *rosette*, in the plant world, is a circular arrangement of leaves. Often they're ground-hugging plants or at low to the ground or emerge in a vase shape (*basal rosettes*). Other times, rosettes are presented on short stems or clumps of stems. Squint and imagine that an individual rosette is a plush blossom, only composed of leaves rather than petals. An example familiar to everyone is the dandelion rosette.

For gardening in low-water areas, rosette-forming succulents are practical choices because they're compact-growing and, for the most part, self-sufficient. Supplemental watering is needed when they're getting started and perhaps occasionally to sustain them through long drought periods.

REMEMBER

Rosette-forming succulents don't last forever. After as many as ten years getting established, they may send up a flower stalk or stalks, after which the mother plant usually dies back. If you don't like the look of the stalks or their small flowers, preferring to grow the plants for the beauty of their foliage, you can cut them off. When you allow flowering to proceed, you'll enjoy just one show. But all isn't lost; these plants inevitably leave behind offspring and the cycle begins anew.

In any event, these larger succulents are versatile, attractive, and potentially important garden candidates:

>> **Aeonium,** *Aeonium.* Planted for their often-variegated foliage, this is a large and versatile group of succulents. The leaves of the classic 'Kiwi' are green blushed with yellow and rimmed in red, for a tricolor show. 'Cyclops' presents its green-dark red rosettes on stout stems. The foliage of 'Zwartkop', also carried on stems, is deep purple to almost black. Stalks bearing tiny yellow flowers may develop. Plant heights and girth vary quite a lot.

>> **Afterglow echeveria,** *Echeveria* 'Afterglow'. An aptly named, plump rosette in hues of soft blue, pink, rose, and violet. Mature size will be 1 to 2 feet (0.3 to 0.6 m) high and wide.

>> **Agave,** *Agave* species and cultivars. These succulents have bigger rosettes meant for important garden roles, in a wide range of forms (from tight rosettes to ones with exuberantly splaying leaves) and hues. If you want your agaves to stand out, consider *variegated* ones — ones with green-and-white leaves, or yellow- or cream-bordered leaves. You can also find gorgeous blue, blue-gray, and blue-green selections. This genus also includes some distinctly formal-looking varieties, thanks to the fact that their toothed edges are a contrasting darker color, making each leaf look outlined. Sizes and shapes vary widely, so be sure to check first and allow enough space.

>> **Aloe,** *Aloe.* Landscaping aloes are a diverse and fascinating group. Foliage is generally various shades of green, sometimes tinged red. Many send forth

dramatic spires, sometimes several per plant or in candelabra formations; colors are hot, mainly in the red-orange range. Hummingbirds love aloe flowers. Plant size varies a great deal, from short ones you can use as edgings or display in pots to ones that are practically tree-size.

» **Amole,** *Beschorneria yuccoides.* Related to agaves but with a softer look, amoles have blades that are smooth-edged, never toothed or spiny. Established plants will send up a towering flower stalk, hot pink to red, with small lime-green flowers. After that, the plant fades away but leaves behind offspring to carry on. Mature plant size is substantial, up to 6 feet (1.8 m) high and wide.

» **Bear grass,** *Nolina.* Depending on the species or cultivar, the leaves vary from plain green to yellowish or gray-blue hues; they tend to be slender, sometimes even grassy-looking, and a bit stiff. Branched stalks deliver flowers of creamy to greenish-white. Mature rosette size is usually in the 3- to 5-foot (0.9- to 1.5 m) range.

» **Bright Star yucca,** *Yucca* cultivar. Although many yuccas grow with trunks, this one is more of a rosette-former. Its claim to fame is bright foliage — a mature one is quite a show in sunny yellow and lime green. (However in cooler conditions or prolonged periods of drought, they develop pink tints.) Tall stalks with white flowers. Mature size is 2 to 3 feet (0.6 to 0.9 m) high and wide.

» **Bulbine,** *Bulbine frutescens.* Individual plants aren't large or tall but form colonies. Blades are narrow and grasslike. Flower stalks are bright yellow. Mature size is about 1 to 2 feet (0.3 to 0.6 m) high and wide.

» **Chaparral yucca,** *Hesperoyucca whipplei.* Gorgeous gray-green foliage with rigid, narrow, and spine-tipped leaves. If it flowers, they're white to purple and carried on stalks as tall as 15 feet (4.6 m). Plant grows about 4 feet (1.2 m) high and up to 6 feet (1.8 m) wide.

» **Datil,** *Yucca baccata.* Very full, bristly rosettes of stiff, blue-green leaves. Flower stalks, up to 6 feet (1. 8 m), tall are creamy white with purple blush. Offsets are common. Mature plants are shorter than wide, about 3 feet (0.9 m) high and 5 feet (1.5 m) wide.

» **Green aloe,** *Furcraea foetida.* Long, strappy, slightly wavy green leaves carried on a stocky plant, sometimes on a short stem. If stalks develop, they can rise tall, up to 20 feet (6.1 m)! Flowers are greenish-white and don't smell wonderful. Gets 4 to 5 feet (1.2 to 1.5 m) tall and up to 8 feet (2.4 m) wide.

» **Hens and chicks,** *Echeveria.* See the description in the section, "Considering other succulent carpeters," earlier in this chapter.

» **Linear-leaved yucca,** *Yucca linearifolia.* A ball-shaped plant of slim green leaves. Gets 2 to 3 feet (0.6 to 0.9 m) high and wide. Flowering stalk will be only about 3 to 4 feet (0.9 to 1.2 m); flowers are white.

>> **Lipstick echeveria,** *Echeveria agavoides* 'Lipstick'. Singling out this hens-and-chicks because of its unique, attention-grabbing foliage, which is dark green rimmed in red. Flower stalks and flowers are red-pink. Forms offsets. Under 1 foot (0.3 m) high and wide.

>> **Macdougal's century plant,** *Furcraea macdougalii.* Blades grow upright and tall. Flowering stalk, if it develops, towers 15 to 20 feet (4.6 to 6.1 m) tall, with greenish-white blooms. Plant will get 6 feet (1.8 m) tall and wide.

>> **Macho mocha plant,** × *Mangave* 'Macho Mocha'. Odd-looking name is because it's a cross between *Agave* and the splashy-leaved *Manfreda* succulent genus. Unique foliage resulted: flesh, flexible, and mottled in wine-colored spots on a gray-green backdrop. Flowers, on a thick stalk, are white, plentiful, and irresistible to hummingbirds. Mature plants are 1 to 2 feet (0.3 to 0.6 m) tall and up to 6 feet (1.8 m) wide.

>> **Mojave yucca,** *Yucca schidigera.* Thick grower that, over time, forms one or more stems. Foliage is rigid with marginal fibers; color varies from blue-green to yellow-green. Plants get up to 4 feet (1.2 m) high and wide, and the stout flowering stalk will be thick with beautiful rose-tinged white bells.

>> **Puya,** *Puya.* Grow this one for the handsome foliage color, generally in the powder-blue to silver-blue range. Leaf blades are long and narrow and sharply spiny. Forms colonies over time. Flowers, when they happen, are trumpet-shaped, substantial, and blue-green. Mature size is around 2 to 4 feet (0.6 to 1.2 m) high and wide, depending on the species or variety.

>> **Soapweed yucca,** *Yucca glauca.* Gray-green foliage that's stiff and narrow. Flower stalks sporting greenish-white blossoms are in scale with the compact plants. Mature plants are around 3 to 4 feet (0.9 to 1.2 m) tall and wide.

>> **Sotol,** *Dasylirion.* Look for ones with gray-green foliage; they're beautiful (for example. *D. wheeleri* or *D. longissimum*). Blades are narrow and stiff. Flowering stalks bear white flowers, sometimes blushed with pink or brushed with light green. Mature plants top out at 5 to 6 feet (1.5 to 1.8 m) high and the same size or wider in spread.

Examining bushy forms

This section is admittedly rather vague or arbitrary — any succulent that you plant in quantity and/or spreads out on its own could be said to create a brushy profile in your landscape over time. But if your wish is to get that look sooner rather than later, these are good choices:

>> **Candellia,** *Euphorbia antisyphilitica.* The common name refers to the plant's resemblance to a gathering of little candles — although, to be honest, the stems are slender. Birthday candles, maybe? They're blue-green and waxy and

become dotted with tiny white-pink blooms. Mature size is 1 to 2 feet (0.3 to 0.6 m) tall, spreading to 3 feet (0.9 m) wide.

» **Crown of thorns,** *Euphorbia milii.* Sharp thorns abound — you've been warned — but in the right spot, this plant is sensational. Multibranching stems bear bright-green foliage; the long-blooming flower clusters adorning branch ends are scene stealers. Color is bright and generous: red, hot pink, orange-pink, softer orange. Plants get up to 4 feet (1.2 m) tall and 3 feet (0.9 m) wide.

» **Dudleya,** *Dudleya.* Gray-green foliage, red-tipped in some varieties, spreading by offset after offset. Summer brings reddish-branched stalks with yellow flowers clustered near the tops. The overall effect is colorful and pretty. The plants do need excellent drainage; soggy ground kills them. Grows around 10 to 12 inches (25.4 to 30.5 cm) tall and wide.

» **Flower dust plant,** *Kalanchoe pumila.* Lovely, purple-blushed powder-blue foliage cover a thick, mounding plant. Early spring flowers are lavender-pink. Plants stay in the 12- to 18-inch (30.5 to 45.7 cm) high and wide range.

» **Jade plant,** *Crassula.* Maybe this genus is overused, but when this plant is growing well, it's undeniably handsome. Small, rounded, thick glossy leaves, edged in red, cover rangy stems; their color will darken when plants get some shade or extra water. This succulent has clusters of starry-white, pink-tinged flowers. Size varies, but a denser, bushy look is easier to get when you plant a dwarf variety, of which there are a few; check your local nursery.

» **Lavender scallops,** *Kalanchoe fedtschenkoi.* The appeal of this species is the happy combination of flowers and foliage — fortunately, it blooms from spring into summer. Chubby, scalloped leaves are blue-green or may be blushed with lavender, whereas the tubular flowers appear in profuse clusters. They're pink on the outside and darker orange-red on the inside. Plants get 15 inches (38.1 cm) tall and spread out.

» **Pig's ear,** *Cotyledon orbiculata.* Rounded, red-rimmed green leaves gathered under slender stalks of clusters of bell-shaped, orange flowers (in summer). The contrast is pretty. Mature size is 2 to 3 feet (0.6 to 0.9 m) tall and wide.

» **Red yucca,** *Hesperaloe parviflora.* Narrow, stiff gray-green bladelike foliage, joined in summer by tall reddish stalks with tubular flowers, usually red or yellow, although you may find other hues at a well-stocked nursery. No matter the color, hummingbirds love them! Stunning when massed. Mature size is 3 feet (0.9 m) high and wide.

» **Slipper plant,** *Pedilanthus macrocarpus.* Weird and wonderful, a tangle of multiple lime-green stems! They'll be longer and wavy in partial shade and more upright with more sun. Leaves are few and usually insignificant; little flowers are a curiosity (bright pink, sometimes orange-pink bracts on stem tips in spring and/or fall—they don't look like slippers, actually). Individual plants grow up to 4 feet (1.2 m) tall and half as wide.

GOING FOR DRAMA — FLOWER SPIKES

Some succulents are justly valued for their foliage, and you may be inclined to ignore or trim off any flowers that appear. For others, though, the flowers can be fabulous and are to be prized and admired while they last.

Succulents will bloom, sometimes once a season, sometimes prolifically, sometimes once in their lifetime (the wild agave called *Agave americana,* is an example — though the event isn't precisely after 100 years of rosette growth — more like 20 or 30 years).

From a landscaping point of view, imagine how best to show off the flowering spikes when they do appear and position your plants accordingly. Flower color options range from white, cream, or yellow, to fiery shades of red and orange, to violet and purple; oftentimes the stems on which they're borne are a contrasting color. If a plant isn't blooming when you acquire it, don't forget to find out these important details. Check out the following lists (refer to the descriptions in this chapter for more about each succulent).

At maturity, flowering spikes are taller than a person. These succulents are good for creating drama and, perhaps, framing or even blocking views:

- Aloe
- Amole
- Green aloe
- Macdougal's century plant
- Yucca

Knee- to waist-high flower stems or spikes arise. These succulents can be good garden citizens, complementing or flattering the extent of your displays and other plants in their vicinity:

- Bear grass
- Bulbine
- Crown of thorns
- Dudleya
- Flower dust plant
- Jade plant

- Lavender scallops
- Lipstick echeveria
- Macho mocha plant
- Puya
- Sotol

Contemplating cacti

Your choice of a cacti isn't to be taken lightly — it's a major landscaping decision. You aren't going to be able to avoid spines, so select a spot out of the path of foot traffic. Color considerations include not only the body itself, but the spines and, if they appear, flowers and perhaps even fruit.

REMEMBER

There are no guarantees with flowers and fruit; some cacti don't form them or don't form them until many long years go by, whereas others are prolific. How much a cactus flowers can be a matter of how much sun the plant gets, its age, and/or pollination. Celebrate if it happens!

REMEMBER

Cacti shopping will be easier if you have a handle on some of the terminology, so here are the basics:

>> **Areole:** Circular clusters of spines. An *areole* is where flowers bud and new stems emerge.

>> **Glochid:** Applies to opuntia cacti. Tufts of short spines, found at the areoles.

>> **Glaucous:** A waxy layer on the surface of the plant, helps retain moisture.

>> **Rib:** Vertical structure on stems/trunks of columnar plants. (Can expand or contract depending on the amount of water the plant receives.)

>> **Spine:** Spines are actually modified leaves. Some people incorrectly call them prickers, barbs, or thorns.

Check out the nearby sidebar for more information about shopping for cacti.

The following lists are curated, not comprehensive. I organize plants by potential height, to make choosing easier.

Reaching for the stars — Taller cacti

Big/taller cacti (maturing to higher than 6 feet, or 1.8 m, tall), contribute significant architecture to your landscape (as landscape architects say). Here are my suggestions:

>> **Blue columnar cactus,** *Pilosocereus pachycladus.* A mature plant has a trunk and branches; color is light blue-green to turquoise. Spines are plentiful and translucent. Flowers, should they appear, are white with touches of green or red. May get 30 feet (9.1 m) tall.

>> **Blue flame cactus,** *Myrtillocactus geometrizans.* Branching like a candelabra, green to blue-green, with dark spines. Flowers will be starry and white. Attains 13 to 16 feet (4 to 4.9 m) tall.

>> **Candelabra cactus,** *Myrtillocactus cochal.* Large and sprawling. Dark green; flowers are pale green. Gets 10 feet (3 m) tall — and almost as wide.

>> **Candelabra spurge,** *Euphorbia ammak* var. *variegata.* Branching, of course. Color ranges from creamy yellow to pale blue. Dark brown spines. Grows 15 to 20 feet (4.6 to 6.1 m) tall.

>> **Mexican lime cactus,** *Ferocactus pilosus.* Barrel-shaped to columnar growth habit with especially prominent ribs. Green with red spines; flowers are fiery orange-red. May get 6 to 8 feet (1.8 to 2.4 m) tall.

>> **Mexican post cactus,** *Pachycereus marginatus.* Forms slender columns from 3 to 8 inches (7.6 to 20.3 cm) in diameter; composed of five to seven ribs. May start branching from the base when mature. Small pink to greenish flowers. Attains 12 to 16 feet (3.6 to 4.9 m).

>> **Old man cactus,** *Cephalocereus senilis.* Distinctive and instantly recognizable, thanks to its gray-white appearance. Also the stems, up to 18 inches (45.7 cm) in diameter tend not to be branched, so they stand as tall sentinels in a dry landscape. Reaches 20 feet (6.1 m) or more.

>> **Organ pipe cactus,** *Stenocereus thurberi.* The columnar, ribbed stems do resemble traditional organ pipes. Green to yellow-green. Flowers may be white, pink, or purple, depending on the variety. Clumps will become 20 to 30 feet (6.1 to 9.1 m) tall and wide.

>> **Prickly pear,** *Opuntia ficus* 'Indica'. Justly popular in low-water gardens, it always makes a handsome appearance with its big, broad pads, colorful, proportionately sizeable flowers (4 inches, 10.1 cm, and yellow in this particular cultivar) and red or yellow edible fruits. (See the nearby sidebar.) May get 10 to 15 feet (3 to 4.6 m) tall and half as wide.

>> **Silver torch cactus,** *Cleistocactus strausii.* Light silvery-green columns, forming clusters over time. Tubular flowers, red to burgundy, stick out from the sides of the columns. Mature height is 8 feet (2.4 m).

SHOPPING FOR CACTI

When you shop for cacti, your first impression may be: so many choices! But just as when shopping for any garden plant, you want to keep your head. Know before you go how big a space you want to fill and resolve to pick an appropriate candidate (too big, and you'll be pruning or cutting back; too small, and it will never look at home).

When looking at specific plants, keep the following in mind:

- **Check the soil.** Cacti are sold potted. Is the potting mix dry? You want it to be dry. If it's wet or drenched, the nursery has been overwatering it, which isn't good for the plant's health.

- **Look to see whether the cactus is leaning.** Plants develop toward a light source and if the nursery didn't turn the pot periodically or set it in sufficient sun, this bad habit starts young. You can correct it, depending on where you site the plant when you get it home, but it's easier to start with a plant that exhibits nice, sturdy, upward growth.

Tip: Bring a box or crate for transport. If your new plants tip over as you drive home, they can get bruised and their (dry) mix can spill.

>> **Star cactus,** *Astrophytum ornatum*. Columnar habit, with a twist; the green columns, with prominent yellowish spines, literally twist as they grow upward. Bright yellow flowers. Reaches 1 to 3 feet (0.3 to 0.9 m).

>> **Totem pole cactus,** *Lophocereus schottii.* No spines or ribs, but rather a distinctive, rough, knobby appearance to the stems. Grows 10 to 12 feet (3 to 3.6 m) tall and about half as wide.

Staying lower to the ground — shorter cacti

The following cacti include little/shorter ones (under 6 feet, or 1.8 m):

>> **Beavertail cactus,** *Opuntia basilaris.* Prickly pads of blue-green. Flowers will be bright pink. Mature size is up to 20 inches (50.8 cm) tall and rambling to 6 feet (1.8 m) wide.

>> **Black spine prickly pear,** *Opuntia violacea* var. *macrocentra.* Pads are purplish, providing a handsome backdrop for the spring flower show. Showy flowers, proportionally large for a plant of this size, are yellow with red centers. Plants get 2 to 3 feet (0.6 to 0.9 m) tall.

- » **Claret cup cactus,** *Echinocereus triglochidiatus.* Forms a gathering of stout stems, studded with bright orange flowers (the edible fruit that follows is also orange). Mature size is 3 feet (0.9 m) high and 6 feet (1.8 m) wide.

- » **Fishhook barrel cactus,** *Ferocactus wislizeni.* Green. Large and stout. The thick spines, as the name reveals, are hooked. Flowers are orange. Gets between 3 and 6 feet (0.9 and 1.8 m) tall.

- » **Golden ball cactus,** *Parodia leninghausii.* Even though its habit is globular, in later years growth becomes more columnar. Green studded with yellow spines to give it that golden look. Reaches about 3 feet (0.9 m) tall and wide.

- » **Golden barrel cactus,** *Echinocactus grusonii.* Round, almost ball-like, and ribbed. Looks great in clusters. No more than 4 feet (1.2 m) tall at maturity.

- » **Hedgehog cactus,** *Echinocereus viridiflorus.* Rounded to columnar ridged stems, around 4 inches (10.1 cm) that are studded with spines. The spines come in a range of colors and may have dark tips. Flowers also vary in color, from white to yellow to red. Forms clusters. Mature size is under 1 foot (0.3 cm).

- » **Mammillaria,** *Mammillaria polyedra.* A pretty little rounded cactus that forms colonies over time. Flowers are cherry red with yellow centers — pretty! Mature plant size is 1 foot (0.3 cm) tall and about half as wide.

- » **Peanut cactus,** *Chamaecereus silvestrii.* Cylindrical form and low-growing. Late spring brings bright scarlet flowers, which make a fine contrast to the dark green stems. Only gets about 1 foot (0.3 m) tall.

- » **Strawberry hedgehog cactus,** *Echinocereus engelmannii.* Gets its name from its profuse show of pink flowers. The plants form mounds or clusters of (mostly) upright stems. Very spiny, though! Grows 24 to 28 inches (61 to 71 cm) tall.

- » **Turk's cap cactus,** *Melocactus matanzanus.* Just a little rounded plant; if it flowers, the flower sits on top and is reddish. Mature size is under 4 inches (10.1 cm) high and wide.

PRICKLY PEARS — HAVE YOUR CACTUS AND EAT IT, TOO

Among the many worthy cacti, perhaps the most familiar is the prickly pear, *Opuntia.* Dozens of species exist, not just native to dry-climate North America but from all over the world's more arid climates. This chapter includes a few, and I encourage you to explore the genus: in other people's gardens, at parks and botanic gardens, and, of course, at well-stocked local nurseries. You have lots of options!

Their green to blue-green leaves, or pads, are technically stem segments. Typically big and shaped like paddles, the leaves are fleshy and, in fact, tasty. They're the source of *nopales,* chunks or slices whose spines have been plucked out and their outer covering peeled off before being eaten fresh and crisp, or cooked or pickled. Often nopales are included in stews and soups and added to tacos. The pulp is also turned into juice or thicker beverages (smoothies). Flavor is mild, reminiscent of a slightly sweet bell pepper. The flesh is low in sugars, calories, and carbs.

Prickly pears also produce pretty flowers, in yellow or pink, depending on the species. These are followed by the fruit, or pears (similar size and shape), also termed the *tuna.* The fruit may turn out to be green, yellow, pink, or red, depending on the species and degree of ripeness. Before eating, you must remove the small, rough, spine-filled bumps as well as the outer peel. The flavor is mild, a bit sweet, reminiscent of a ripe melon. Try these in juice, sorbet, or salad!

The spines of the prickly pear cacti are undeniably daunting — spiky and sharp. This is how the plants protect themselves from predation and hoard that moisture for their own survival. The sharp spines don't prevent the plant from being a good garden candidate, though; just site it behind other plants, or several plants along a property line or other area where you want to discourage people or critters from coming through.

Chapter **8**

In It for the Long Haul: Shrubs, Vines, and Trees

E very landscape benefits from shrubs, vines, and trees. These plants fill out and help define a landscape for years and years. Like any long-term invest-ment, you want to be thoughtful and careful in planning, selection, and care.

As these plants grow and mature, they bring a home into scale with its yard, while also acting as buffers between your property and the neighbors and/or between your yard and gardens and the streetscape. If you're fortunate to live in a spot where you have a view (for example, mountains or a cityscape in the near dis-tance), these substantial plants can help frame it.

In a setting where water is precious, they can also be extremely practical. Shrubs, trees, and yes, even vines can create welcome shade and shelter from the hot sun. Their presence raises the immediate humidity and can slow evaporation. Depend-ing on where you site them, they can also offer protection from sun and drying winds to the plants growing under them or close by. Not to mention, you'll appre-ciate the relief from the blazing sun when working or lounging outdoors.

Selecting appropriate plants when your landscape faces the constant challenges of limited water is extra important. Some suck water and nutrients from the soil to the detriment of other plants. Maples, willows, and sycamores, I'm afraid, are often guilty of this crime and so I don't tout them in this chapter. No banana trees. No shrubby hibiscus. Nope, nope.

This chapter looks at some options that work. As with the other chapters in Part 2, I don't aim to be comprehensive. If a plant I list captures your interest, go look for it. When you find it, have a frank chat with the nursery or garden center staff about its prospects in your particular landscape, particularly its water needs. If this conversation raises doubts about its ability to thrive or your ability or willingness to give it the irrigation it needs, pivot to alternatives.

TIP

Important in early days: When you bring home a new shrub, tree, or vine to add to your yard, keep in mind that no matter how drought-tolerant it is supposed to be, it won't be so immediately. Be prepared to supply your new introduction(s) with supplemental water their first days, weeks, and months so that they can settle in and their roots can quest deeply into the soil. That's true whether a new plant is small or you've invested in a more mature one. Later in its life, happily established, it may require little or no water. Refer to Chapter 10 for more details.

Identifying Shrubs for Dry Settings

Selecting shrubs is a big decision, not just because of their size or the expense and trouble of acquiring and planting them. You also don't want to have to repeat the choice. You want to get it right the first time so the plant settles in and holds its position well and attractively.

Think about what you want in terms not only of foliage but potentially of flowers and the fruit that may follow. Some questions to ask yourself:

» What is the mature size? Is a slow-growing shrub okay? Are you willing to wait for it to fill in? If it grows faster, will you trim it or prune off stems or branches to shape it and keep it in bounds?

» What type of leaf size do you want? Do you want green or gray-green year-round (an evergreen plant)? Would it be nice to have fall color? Will leaf litter make a mess?

» Can you find the color of flowers and fruits you like and a color that fits into that part of your yard/goes with other flowering plants in the vicinity? How long is the bush in bloom? Will fruit follow, and is that fruit edible for you and your family, or for birds/wildlife? Do falling flower petals or fruit make a mess?

The following sections identify shrubs and bushes that have shown to be good choices for arid and low-water landscapes, divided into useful landscaping categories for easier reference as you ponder your options. For clarity, I include the botanical name as well because common names vary from place to place or, sometimes, two different plants share the same name (for example, daisy bush).

Recognizing natives and nativars

Let me repeat myself: Plants native to the arid and mountain West and Southwest are smart and practical, proven landscaping choices. They're adapted to the climates, seasons, and soils, as well as to regional insects, birds, and animals. They're less prone to pest and disease problems.

Often a native plant was brought into cultivation when a horticulturist or botanist judged it had *garden potential* (a plant with promising qualities, such as plentiful and attractive flowers or a compact growth habit). Sometimes it's even a naturally occurring hybrid or variation. When grown "in captivity" so to speak, these plants may flourish because they're getting a little care from you and they don't have to contend with the competition or other challenges (bad weather, flash flooding, nibbling animals, fires, and so on) of their wild homes. Scan the following sections and marvel with me about how many and varied they are.

When you go shopping, you may spot a native-shrub variation with yellow instead of red flowers, or one that is touted as more compact-growing. You don't have to be a native-plant purist when you spot these alternative selections. They can be great.

TIP

Even though you may be open to planting native shrubs, you may be concerned that some are too bulky, or not pretty enough, for your yard. Don't rush to this judgment. Find and visit a nursery in your area that offers them or stroll through a regional botanical garden and have a closer look. You'll be pleasantly surprised. I guarantee it.

The following are all fine low-water garden candidates:

>> **Apache plume,** *Fallugia paradoxa.* Small leaves and whitish bark, but the main attraction is the flurry of single white flowers that set fluffy pink seedheads. Mature size is 4 feet (1.2 m) high and wide.

>> **Barberry,** *Berberis.* Small green leaves on thorny bushes; fall and winter color may be red to purple. Yellow or orange flowers, followed by red, blue, or dark purple berries. Some species are considered invasive, but native ones are good garden choices: *B. aquifolium, B. aquifolium* var. *repens,* and *B. nevinii.* Mature plant size is around 4 to 6 feet (1.2 to 1.8 m) high and wide.

>> **Bush anemone,** *Carpenteria californica.* Glossy green leaves are furry and gray-white underneath. White flowers centered in yellow are carried in profuse clusters. Around 8 feet (2.4 m) high and wide; 'Elizabeth' is a compact version with proportionally smaller flowers.

>> **Bush penstemon,** *Keckiella.* Informal and fun shrubby plant reminiscent of the popular perennials. Enjoy the attractive, tubular-shaped flowers in spring and the glossy green foliage the rest of the year. *K. antirrhinoides* has yellow flowers. Generally 3 to 5 feet (0.9 to 1.5 m) tall.

>> **California lilac,** *Ceanothus.* Naturally thick, rangy shrubs with smallish, dark green, crinkled leaves. Early in the gardening year and often for weeks, they burst forth with striking, almost ball-like flower clusters, usually blue but may be lilac, purple, and even white. Many species and cultivars, heights ranging from 6 to 20 feet (1.8 to 6.1 m). Here are two noteworthy ones:

- The blooms of *C. arboreus* 'Powder Blue' are gorgeous.

- Aptly named *C. thyrsifolius* var. *thyrsifolius* 'Snow Flurry' has fabulous white blooms.

Do shop around until you get the combination of size, habit, and flower color that you love best.

>> **Coffeeberry,** *Frangula californica.* Valued for its handsome, rugged foliage, dark green and pale green beneath. Flowers are nothing to write home about, though showy red fruits follow, darkening with age. 'Leatherleaf' is a superior choice. Mature size is 6 to 8 feet (1.8 to 2.4 m) tall and wide.

>> **Conebush,** *Leucadendron.* Slender, almost needlelike gray-green foliage and lots of informal daisylike blooms in shades of purple or pink with yellow centers. Gets its name from the woody, conelike seedheads that follow. From 3 to 10 feet (0.9 to 3 m) tall, depending on the species and cultivar. I recommend 'Winter Red', as cool weather darkens the foliage to wine-red; blooms are red and white.

>> **Fairy duster,** *Calliandra.* Small dark or gray-green leaves cloak smallish shrubs that grow 3 to 6 feet (0.9 to 1.8 m) high and wide. Flowers in spring, summer, or both, with showy, tufty flowers (no petals, all stamens).

>> **Fernbush,** *Chamaebatiaria millefolium.* Big, bountiful clusters of fragrant white flowers on a bush of olive-green foliage; handsome seedpods ripen bronze. Grows 6 to 8 feet (1.8 to 2.4 m) tall and wide.

>> **Flannelbush,** *Fremontodendron.* Spring and summer bring a big show of large, cup-shaped bright yellow flowers all over the bush. The common name refers to the heavy, felted evergreen foliage. Fast grower, up to 20 feet (6.1 m) tall and wide.

» **Flowering currant,** *Ribes* species and cultivars. Small, lobed foliage and small, pretty flower clusters in pink, white, or rose. No spines on the currants; the closely related gooseberry does have sharp spines. Heights from 3 or 4 feet (0.9 to 1.2 m) to 10 feet (3 m). Here are a couple options:

- *R. malvaceum* var. *viridifolia* 'Ortega Beauty' has garnet flowers.

- R. *sanguineum* var. *glutinosum* 'Inverness White' has white ones.

» **Juniper,** *Juniperus.* Don't pass this stalwart; with its range of species and cultivars, all are dependable, trouble-free growers. Prickly, green to blue-green foliage, needlelike when young and scalelike when mature. Heights and foliage colors vary.

» **Lemonade berry,** *Rhus integrifolia.* Lustrous, dark green leaves, lightly serrated. Early in spring, it bursts forth with tiny white to pink flowers. The acidic red, berrylike fruits that follow give the plant its name. Grows between 3 and 10 feet (0.9 and 3 m) tall.

» **Manzanita,** *Arctostaphylos.* These shrubs are prized for their interesting, somewhat twisty growth habit and colorful shredding, peeling bark. Foliage is thick and green to gray green, little urn-shaped flowers hanging in clusters are in the white-pink-rose range, and berry-like fruit follows. Usually between 6 and 10 feet (1.8 to 3 m) tall. *A. bakeri* 'Louis Edmunds' has pretty pink flowers against a dark gray-green backdrop.

» **Mexican marigold,** *Tagetes lemmonii.* Fragrant, slender leaves and, in fall and winter, it's covered with cheerful yellow daisy flowers. Can get up 8 feet (2.4 m) tall and half as wide. The cultivar 'Compacta' lives up to its name, staying around 2 feet (0.6 m) tall and somewhat wider.

» **Monkeyflower,** *Mimulus* (or *Diplacus*) *aurantiacus.* Lower-growing, thick with glossy green leaves and studded with orange or yellow tubular flowers. Grows up to 3 feet (0.9 m) tall and wide.

» **Mountain mahogany,** *Cercocarpus.* Multitrunked plants have small, tough evergreen leaves of green to gray-green. They grow slowly and can get 10 to 15 feet (3 to 4.6 m) tall and wide, depending on the species. White flowers are nifty; though small, they grab attention when they go to seed, developing little white plumes.

» **Pacific wax myrtle,** *Morella* (or *Myrica*) *californica.* Multitrunked and grown for its dense evergreen, glossy green, aromatic foliage. Between 10 and 20 feet (3 and 6.1 m) tall and half as wide.

» **Pitcher sage,** *Lepechinia.* These evergreen shrubs are tough with soft, felted gray-green foliage and tubular flowers at branch tips. They can be white, soft purple, pink, or even magenta, a pretty contrast to the leaves. Matures 3 to 8 feet (0.9 to 2.4 m) tall, depending on the species and cultivar, so do check.

>> **Silktassel,** *Garrya.* Gets its name from the long tresses of silvery-green catkins that adorn the bush in early spring. Dark green, leathery leaves. Here are a couple choices:

- G. *elliptica* grows to 15 feet (4.6 m) tall.

- G. *fremontii* only gets 6 to 8 feet (1.8 to 2.4 m).

>> **Styrax,** *Styrax redivivus.* Multistemmed deciduous shrub with round-shaped dark green leaves that turn nice hues of orange and gold in cooler fall weather. White, waxy-textured, clusters of scented flowers in spring and then followed by green fruits that mature tan. Silvery gray bark. Plants get 6 to 10 feet (1.8 to 3 m) tall and wide.

>> **Summer holly,** *Comarostaphylis diversifolia.* Slow grower, eventually reaching 20 feet (6.1 m) tall and about half as wide. Glossy dark green leaves are toothed. Interesting shredding bark. White, urn-shaped flowers in clusters in spring, followed by bright red holly berries.

>> **Texas ranger,** *Leucophyllum frutescens.* Silver-gray, felted foliage with tons of beautiful lilac-pink flowers. 'Green Cloud' has darker, purple flowers and green foliage; 'White Cloud' has white flowers and gray foliage. Matures to between 5 and 8 feet (1.5 to 2.4 m) tall.

>> **Toyon,** *Heteromeles arbutifolia.* A sturdy evergreen shrub most recognized for its profusion of long-lasting fall-into-winter red berries that are preceded by flat-topped clusters of white flowers. About 6 to 8 feet (1.8 to 2.4 m) high and 4 to 5 feet (1.2 to 1.5 m) wide.

>> **Tree poppy,** *Dendromecon.* Tough, fast-growing plants of evergreen, blue-gray leaves. Earns its common name when bright yellow flowers appear in late spring and summer; they're followed by dangling seedpods. 8 to 10 feet (2.4 to 3 m) tall and wide.

Considering nonnative options

Many good plants for gardens originated in other parts of the world with similar climates or soils. Nurseries, botanic gardens, parks, public gardens, and commercial landscaping often feature these plants — indeed, nowadays the plant palette (like so many other things) is decidedly global. Origins range from Australia and New Zealand, the Mediterranean region, South Africa, the Canary Islands, Mexico, and Central and South America. These fabulous and interesting plants widen your choices dramatically.

WARNING

Similar origins aren't the same and not a guarantee a plant will thrive far from its native haunts. My Australian brother-in-law was excited to plant his dear, familiar wattle in his Southern California garden — climate and soil, he figured, similar to his hometown of Sydney. It did fine for a few months, then the neighborhood gophers discovered it. They destroyed the root system and killed the plant in a matter of a few days. After a period of mourning, he tried a native ceanothus in that spot — no further gopher problems.

REMEMBER

A plant whose native or original setting is sandy, gravelly, or rocky soil tends to perform better in lean, well-drained soil. In fact, some plants will grow well in conditions that aren't like their native ones. Do your best to make a match, but don't overthink it. Garden-grown plants almost always have a better, plusher life than they would in the wild because someone — you — is attentive to their needs and care.

Here are some worthy, attractive nonnative shrubs to consider (I note which ones are evergreen):

>> **Baeckea,** *Baeckea.* Medium to yellow-green, fine-textured evergreen foliage that can turn copper-red in cooler weather. Flowers are usually small and white. *B. virgata,* "tall baeckea," gets 8 to 10 feet (2.4 to 3 m) tall and 6 to 8 feet (1.8 to 2.4 m) wide.

>> **Banksia,** *Banksia.* Exotic-looking but not hard to grow, provided its soil has good drainage. Flowers are in the yellow-orange-red range and held aloft in conelike or cylindrical spikes. Foliage is usually needlelike. Reaches 6 to 20 feet (1.8 to 6.1 m) tall, depending on the species.

>> **Bay laurel,** *Laurus nobilis.* A classic evergreen shrub or small tree, with multiple trunks, grown for its dark, fragrant leaves. Can get 25 to 30 feet (7.6 to 9.1 m) high and half as wide.

>> **Blue hibiscus,** *Alyogyne huegelii.* The arid-climate answer to hibiscus or Rose of Sharon, this upright evergreen shrub delivers big, blue to purple flowers over a long period. Dark green, rough-textured foliage. Gets 6 to 8 feet (1.8 to 2.4 m) tall and wide.

>> **Bottlebrush,** *Callistemon.* An exuberant show of rounded to cylindrical flowerheads bristling with colorful stamens. Often but not always red. Green to gray-green leaves and a thickety growth habit. Height varies with the species.

>> **Cassia,** *Cassia.* Members of the bean family, these woody shrubs form bright green to chartreuse, pendant pods that age brown to copper — an intriguing sight. Foliage is green to gray-green, depending on the species. The abundant flowers in spring are sunny yellow. Reaches about 6 feet (1.8 m) tall and wide.

>> **Chaste tree,** *Vitex.* Fast-growing deciduous plant with gray-green, fragrant leaves. Flowers carried in spikes are also scented and in the blue-to-purple range, depending on the species and cultivar. Expect 15 to 20 feet (4.6 to 6.1 m) in height.

>> **Daisy bush,** *Brachyglottis greyi.* The main impression of this plant isn't actually the bright yellow summer daisies, but rather the color of the mounding foliage — it's silvery-gray. A slow grower, it eventually reaches 3 to 5 feet (0.9 to 1.5 m) high and a bit wider.

>> **Daisy bush,** *Olearia × haastii.* Glossy, rich green leaves, with contrasting soft white underneath, cover a good-size plant that tops out at 6 feet (1.8 m) tall and wide. White flowers in clusters, fragrant.

>> **Grevillea,** *Grevillea.* A lot of variation in this genus; you can expect narrow leaves and bright, showy, often multihued flowers in clusters. Some are low-growing. 'Long John' has watermelon-pink flowers, needlelike green foliage, and gets 15 feet (4.6 m) tall and wide.

>> **Hopbush,** *Dodonaea viscosa.* You may want this evergreen bush for its fall-to-winter foliage color, which deepens to red-purple. The rest of the year, the long, narrow leaves are green to purple-green. Flowers are inconspicuous followed by durable winged seedpods. Matures to 15 feet (4.6 m) tall and 12 (3.6 m) wide.

>> **Lemon verbena,** *Aloysia citrodora.* A casual-looking, exuberant plant with an upright growth habit, attaining up to 8 feet (2.4 m) tall and half as wide. Full of lance-shaped, bright green, aromatic leaves; flower clusters are white or light purple.

>> **Mexican orange,** *Choisya ternata.* A dense-growing evergreen with glossy green foliage. The white flowers appear in summer in clusters and are sweetly fragrant. Grows 5 to 8 feet (1.5 to 2.4 m) high and wide.

>> **Myrtle,** *Myrtus communis.* A full, slow-growing bush with small leaves that start out red but turn dark green. Little white flowers with long yellow stamens cover the plant in summer and waft a sweet scent. 'Variegata' is a nice cultivar with white-edged green leaves. Plants get 6 to 10 feet (1.8 to 3 m) tall and wide.

>> **Pincushion,** *Leucospermum.* No mistaking these unique, exotic flowers that earn their common name with rounded blooms consisting of colorful tubes of curled petals in sunny yellow to orange to red, often in the same blossom. Leaves are downy and green to gray-green. Plants generally get 6 to 8 feet (1.8 and 2.4 m) tall and wide.

>> **Pomegranate,** *Punica granatum.* Mostly grown for its easy-going nature and lush looks, not necessarily for edible fruit. Green leaves, often with golden color in fall's cooler conditions. Brilliant red flowers. Fruit only appears on

established plants that are at least 5 years old. Typically 15 feet (4.6 m) tall and wide, though shorter cultivars are available.

» **Rockrose,** *Cistus.* So popular in California. Narrow green foliage on mounding plants. The main attraction is the bountiful, pretty flowers, with petals like crepe paper, reminiscent of small poppies. They come mainly in white, pink, and purple, often with contrasting red spots to the centers. Most are 4 to 5 feet (1.2 to 1.5 m) tall and wide.

» **Rosemary,** *Rosmarinus officinalis.* Thick-growing plants with that wonderful, sleepy resinous-pine scented foliage, and tiny blue, purple, pink, or white flowers. Lower-growing ones are great fillers and sprawlers; taller ones can become 5 feet (1.5 m) tall and wide.

» **Rosemary everlasting,** *Ozothamnus rosmarinifolius.* An evergreen shrub of small, dark green, needlelike foliage. In spring, bright pink buds open to tiny white flowers. Gets 4 to 6 feet (1.2 to 1.8 m) tall and wide.

» **Santolina,** *Santolina.* Thick, low, spreading growth, typically 1 to 2 feet (0.3 to 0.6 m) tall and spreading to the sides. Fragrant foliage is dissected; tiny yellow flowers in summer. Two top choices are

- *S. chamaecyparisissus* has gray leaves.
- *S. rosmarinifolia* has bright green leaves.

» **Shrub daisy,** *Euryops.* Delivers yellow daisies, tons of them, on green to gray-green mounding, shrubby evergreen plants. You'll need to prune the plants back hard every few winters to reboot; otherwise they become scraggly. Grows 3 to 5 feet (0.9 to 1.5 m) tall and wide.

» **Smoke tree,** *Cotinus.* The name refers to the airy, light red or pale orange-hued flowers, but the main attraction is the colorful, roundish leaves. Often wine-red, it can go the range from apricot to purple in a season. *Deciduous* (drops leaves in fall). 'Royal Purple' has the darkest purple foliage. Grows 8 to 15 feet (2.4 to 4.6 m) tall and wide.

» **Sunrose,** *Helianthemum nummularium.* Oh, what a flower show! Spring and summer bring loads of poppy-like blooms with contrasting yellow centers; orange, red, hot pink, and more, depending on the cultivar. Plant has evergreen, gray-green foliage and generally stays under 1 foot (0.3 cm) high but spreads to the sides.

» **Tea olive,** *Osmanthus.* Slow-growing evergreen, typically with heavy-textured, dark green leaves that may have toothed margins. Fragrant flowers are tiny, borne in small clusters all over the plant. Size ranges from 8 to 20 feet (2.4 to 6.1 m) tall and wide.

» **Wattle,** *Acacia* species and cultivars. Fast-growing and often thicket-forming, so some are considered invasive — spend time at the nursery making a selection that suits the site you have in mind! That said, their abundant, fragrant yellow flower show against a gray-green bush is undeniably appealing. Most easily reach 10 feet (3 m) tall.

>> **Waxflower,** *Chamelaucium*. Gets its common name from the waxy petals of the little white to pink, long-lasting flowers. The foliage is evergreen, needle-like, green to gray-green, and lightly scented. Two options include

- *C. ciliatum* gets 3 to 4 feet (0.9 to 1.2 m) tall and wide.

- *C. uncinatum* becomes 6 to 10 feet (1.8 to 3 m) tall and wide.

Adding low-water hedges to your yard

A hedge is a particular deployment of shrubby plants, with the goal of creating a dense row or line. Here are the reasons you may want a hedge:

>> It can act as a living fence along a property line.

>> It can define or separate different areas of your yard, creating different garden rooms.

>> It can act as a privacy screen, blocking out both sights and sounds of the street or neighbors.

>> It can be windbreak, buffering your yard from drying winds and protecting the plants within from wind damage such as toppling or snapped branches.

>> It can form a backdrop for other plants and flowers.

Hedges do take time to fill their role, particularly of course when you start with small plants. Watering is necessary, certainly in the initial stages (the plants' first year or so).

Stress or neglect means the hedge may not fill in and look good, so you must weigh those needs with a hopeful eye to the day, several years from now, when your hedge is much more self-sufficient.

TIP

To get a hedge off to a good start, begin with young and healthy plants, and get them in the ground in the spring or fall when rains may help out with the water needs. Space them closely (how close? Depends on the plant; ask at the nursery for guidelines) and mulch around the roots to conserve soil moisture and keep out competitive weeds. More advice, including planting instructions, is in Chapter 10.

The following shrubs have shown themselves to be capable of making nice, thick, handsome hedges in low-water landscapes. Refer to the lists in the previous sections for descriptions:

- >> **Baeckea,** *Baeckea.*

- >> **Bay laurel,** *Laurus nobilis.*

- >> **Bottlebrush,** *Callistemon.*

- >> **California lilac,** *Ceanothus.*

- >> **Coffeeberry,** *Frangula californica.*

- >> **Hopbush,** *Dodonaea viscosa.*

- >> **Laurel sumac,** *Malosma laurina.*

- >> **Lemonade berry,** *Rhus integrifolia.*

- >> **Manzanita,** *Arctostaphylos.*

- >> **Myrtle,** *Myrtus communis.*

- >> **Pacific wax myrtle,** *Morella californica.*

- >> **Silktassel,** *Garrya.*

- >> **Summer holly,** *Comarostaphylis diversifolia.*

- >> **Tea olive,** *Osmanthus.*

- >> **Toyon,** *Heteromeles arbutifolia.*

Identifying recommended roses

Despite the impression you may have of roses as high-maintenance, fussy shrubs, many actually perform quite well in low-water landscapes. They still need water and mulch to help hold moisture around their root systems, but as they grow and mature, they adapt to what they get — and you'll find that they are pretty tough. Pretty and tough!

Here are my top picks, but you should also peek in neighbors' yards and visit a local nursery — excellent places to find which roses thrive where you live:

- >> **Beach roses,** *Rosa rugosa.* Rough, textured, dark green leaves; very thorny bush. Spicily scented single-form flowers are usually pink, hot pink, magenta, or white, followed by edible fruits (*rose hips*). Plants can get large: 8 to 10 feet (2.4 to 3 m) high and wide isn't unusual.

- >> **China rose,** *Rosa chinensis* 'Mutablis'. Dark-hued foliage. Flowers are multi-hued, starting out soft yellow, changing to pink, and darkening to almost red. Mature plant size is 10 feet (3 m) high and 6 feet (1.8 m) wide.

- » **Flower Carpet roses,** *Rosa* cultivars. Shiny green leaves and clusters of single-form flowers in abundance — surprisingly tough and long-blooming. Available in many colors, from red to yellow to peach. Around 3 feet (0.9 m) tall and wide, hence the name.

- » **Knockout roses,** *Rosa* cultivars. A very popular series of rugged, heavy-blooming shrubby roses. Available in white and shades of red, pink, and yellow. Generally 3 to 4 feet (0.9 to 1.2 m) high and wide.

- » **Lady Banks rose,** *Rosa banksiae* 'Lutea'. Dark green foliage, thornless stems, and scads of fluffy little yellow flowers. Forms a bountiful shrub or can be trained as a climber. Can reach 15 to 20 feet (4.6 to 6.1 m) tall.

- » **The Yellow Rose of Texas** (also called 'Harison's Yellow'), *Rosa* × *harisonii*. Gray-green, ferny foliage, prickly canes. Deep yellow, fluffy little flowers. Can reach 8 feet (2.4 m) high and half as wide.

- » **Zephirine Drouhin old-fashioned/vintage rose,** *Rosa* 'Zephirine Drouhin', a Bourbon type, so it has richly fragrant flowers, bright pink. Medium green foliage, thornless stems, grows best trained as a climber. Can reach 10 feet (3 m) high and 6 feet (1.8 m) wide.

Hanging Low — Fine Vines

Vines are always welcome in a garden, but I'd argue that they're even more appreciated where summers are bright and hot. That's because they can create comfortable dappled shade for you as well as any plants I recommend in this section. Ways to use them include the following:

- » Climbing up and covering over a pergola or slatted shelter or over a seating area or patio.

- » Covering a fence or porch, both decorating it and adding privacy.

- » Clambering up a trellis, arch, or other upright support.

- » Enveloping or draping over a divider or lattice fence to hide or distract from view items like recycling and trash bins, a compost pile, or other items.

- » Concealing an old stump.

- » Adding interest and color to a tree. For example, a flowering vine twining in an old evergreen tree.

You can grow the following vines in low-water landscapes (once established), and they'll readily cover supports with lots of foliage and flowers:

- » **Blue plumbago,** *Plumbago auriculata.* Evergreen. Small glossy green leaves. Scads of five-petaled flowers in blue or violet. Can reach 20 feet (6.1 m) tall.

- » **Bougainvillea,** *Bougainvillea.* Evergreen or partially deciduous. Green leaves, thorny stems, and gorgeous, papery blooms (technically *bracts* around tiny true flowers) in white, yellow, red, orange, pink, red, magenta, purple — established plants can be astoundingly drought-tolerant. Able to reach 30 or more feet (9.1 m) high.

- » **Chinese jasmine,** *Jasminum polyanthum.* Evergreen. Bright to dark green leaves and loads of pink buds that open to richly perfumed white star-shaped flowers. A fast grower, it can reach 20 feet (6.1 m) high.

- » **Climbing roses,** *Rosa* cultivars. See the preceding section for more about this type.

- » **Cross vine,** *Bignonia capreolata.* Evergreen. Dark green, almost purple foliage and distinctive, red, orange, and yellow tubular flowers. A vigorous, fast grower, it can reach 30 feet (9.1 m) or more.

- » **Lilac vine,** *Hardenbergia violacea.* Evergreen. Lance-shaped, dark green leaves and spectacular flowers — they're purple and yellow and carried in clusters. Can get 30 to 50 feet (9.1 to 15.2 m) tall.

- » **Star jasmine,** *Trachelospermum jasminoides.* Evergreen. Dark green leaves and clusters of small, richly fragrant white flowers that age to cream. Height ranges from 10 to 20 feet (3 to 6.1 m) high.

- » **Trumpet creeper,** *Campsis radicans.* Deciduous. Green foliage, and orange, red, or yellow blooms. A strong grower! Needs support and training. Easily gets 20 to 30 feet (6.1 to 9.1 m) tall.

WARNING

You may notice the absence in this list of two familiar vines: ivy (*Hedera helix*) and firethorn (*Pyrancatha*). That's not an oversight! Although heavily used in mild-climate landscaping in years past, both have worn out their welcome. They're rampant and invasive. Ivy is a haven for slugs and snails. Firethorn berries make a mess. Don't consider them, even for a minute — and if your property has one already, tear it out and replace it with one of the preceding recommendations.

WHEN VINES WILT — WHAT TO DO

Plants in need of water will show their distress by wilting, but vines are a special case. Because if you delay your response, the plant will be hobbled, damaged, or die. Think about it — moisture has to travel quite a distance from the roots to the farthest extent of the longest trailing stem.

(continued)

(continued)

Here's how to practice vine triage:

1. **Check the limp vine over and remove dead, browned, dying leaves, and browned buds and flowers.**

   They're not going to come back to life.

2. **Trim back stems to viable green, juicy growth.**

3. **Water slowly at the root zone so it soaks in deeply.**

   Then, mulch or replenish mulch to prevent evaporation.

4. **Resolve to water not only more deeply but consistently, going forward.**

   A plant on a schedule will rally and recover, even start to put out new growth if conditions aren't too challenging.

Here are other possible causes of vine wilting:

- **Actual mechanical damage to the stems:** For example, someone or something mashed or snapped a stem.

- **Disease:** Clematis wilt is a debilitating fungal disease for those species.

- **Pests:** Sucking insects are after the moisture and sugars in plant parts. You'll have to investigate one of these causes if water alone doesn't revive a flagging vine.

Having a Need for Trees

Some people have the misconception that low-water gardens are all rocks and succulents, essentially a desert landscape in miniature. Not only is that not true, but it's not that desirable. Think for a moment of an oasis in the desert, and how the weary, thirsty traveler longs to get to that destination, not just for rehydrating but for rest under and among the shelter of trees.

Trees do a lot of essential and important things for people and for their surroundings:

>> They provide shade, which is cooling. When adjacent to a house or other building, this service is valuable and appreciated for comfort (also helps reduce cooling/air-conditioning bills) and the comfort and survival of other plants.

>> They provide shelter from wind and storms/rain.

SELECT TREES APPROPRIATE FOR LOW-WATER LANDSCAPES

I remember visiting my parents in Santa Barbara the year they spent the money to have a beautiful mature birch tree installed in their front yard (they didn't want to wait for a baby tree to grow tall). Its white bark and jaunty, pretty green leaves did indeed look great against their stucco house, but my heart sank at the sight because birches require lots of water for survival. Their tree didn't last three years and, good kid that I am, I was on hand to suggest appropriate replacements after they sadly took it down. The tamarisk they chose, a dryland native tree, grew about as tall as the birch but turned out to be much happier in that spot.

>> They define space, both overhead/vertically and to the extent of their branches, actually making their domain more intimate.

>> They anchor a place, acting as a landmark, a claim, and setting a tone or personality for their surroundings.

>> They nurture their environment. People notice birds and squirrels . . . but why are they in the tree? Food and shelter. Food? It could be literally provided by the tree (leaves, fruits, nuts). Or it could be the many insects that make a tree a home, seen and unseen under the bark. A healthy tree is teaming with and sustaining life.

So it makes sense to have or retain trees in a home landscape and perhaps especially so in hot, dry areas.

Listing the best trees for low-water landscapes

You can't go wrong with trees that are native and/or well-adapted to local and regional weather and soils. As they grow and mature aboveground, they're also growing and maturing belowground, out of sight.

And probably more than any other plants, trees have the ability to send their roots deeply into the earth, where they can find and use soil moisture to sustain them through hot summers and prolonged periods of drought.

Here are some of the toughest and most attractive:

>> **Acacia**, *Acacia*. Refer to the section, "Considering nonnative options," earlier in this chapter. They're considered big shrubs or small trees.

- » **California buckeye,** *Aesculus californica.* Multitrunked, gray bark, dark green leaves. Panicles of white to pale pink flowers; sweet fragrance. Plants get 20 to 40 feet (6.1 to 12.2 m) tall.

- » **Crape myrtle,** *Lagerstroemia* species and cultivars. Handsome bark, green leaves, fabulous flowers, and fall color — long, hot summers don't faze these trees. Mature size is in the 20 to 30 feet (6.1 to 9.1 m) range.

- » **Cypress,** *Hesperocyparis.* Handsome evergreen trees with gray-green, aromatic foliage. Choose from a number of attractive native species and many cultivars. Height varies from 20 to 50 feet (6.1 to 15.2 m).

- » **Desert willow,** *Chilopsis linearis.* Multitrunked small tree, with long, narrow gray-green leaves. Fragrant clusters of white, pink, or purple-hued trumpet-shaped flowers followed by dangling seedpods. Reaches 15 to 30 feet (4.6 to 9.1 m) high.

- » **Eucalyptus,** *Eucalyptus.* Many species and cultivars, offering all sorts of habits, heights, flower colors. Distinctive and different juvenile and mature foliage, peeling bark. Height varies a great deal, so be sure to ask before investing in something that might get massive.

- » **Incense cedar,** *Calocedrus decurrens.* Handsome, slow-growing evergreen with a narrow, upright form. Bark is red-hued when young and gray when older. Green foliage is in flattish sprays. Can reach 60 feet (18.2 m) or more.

- » **Madrone,** *Arbutus.* Easily recognized by its colorful peeling, shredding bark. Dark green leaves, clusters of light pink or white flowers, followed by orange or red fall berries. Often multitrunked. Many species and cultivars, ranging from 20 to 40 feet (6.1 to 12.2 m) high at maturity.

- » **Mediterranean cypress,** *Cupressus sempervirens.* Stately, elegant evergreen with dark green, aromatic foliage. Can get 40 to 60 feet (12.2 to 18.3 m) tall; some handsome shorter cultivars are available.

- » **Myrtle,** *Melaleuca* species. Gray trunks, narrow leaves, and clusters of unique little flowers; small and brushy. Color varies from red, to yellow, to white, depending on the species. Most grow to 10 feet (3 m) tall.

- » **Olive,** *Olea europaea.* Lance-shaped, gray-green leaves with silvery undersides. Small white flowers followed by fruit; if you don't want to deal with the crops, fruitless cultivars are available. Can reach 25 feet (7.6 m) or more but grows slowly.

- » **Palms.** Many options of species and cultivars are available; no need to go big if you don't want to. Instead, shop for shorter ones and fronds whose look you like. Some to consider include the following:

  - **Chilean wine palm,** *Jubaea chilensis.* Taller than wide, featherlike leaves of gray-green.

- **Hesper palm,** *Brahea*. Fan-shaped leaves off a stout trunk.

- **Mediterranean fan palm,** *Chamaerops humilis*. Typically stouter and shorter than other garden palms; sharp leaves radiate on stalks.

- **Windmill palm,** *Trachycarpus*. Long stalks bearing fan-shaped fronds.

» **Palo verde,** *Parkinsonia* × 'Desert Museum'. Attractive green bark, tiny, round, bright green foliage, and showers of fragrant, trumpet-shaped yellow blossoms. Unlike the wild species, this cultivar is thornless. Can reach 30 feet (9.1 m) high.

» **Pineapple guava,** *Acca sellowiana*. Dark green, oval leaves, silvery beneath. Fun little pink or white flowers with prominent red stamens; the fruit that follows is small and gray-green. Grows slowly to 10 to 20 feet (3 to 6.1 m) tall.

» **Pistache,** *Pistacia*. The foliage is recognizable: compound leaves divided into many leaflets; brilliant fall color. Flower clusters are greenish and small. Between 10 and 30 feet (3 and 9.1 m) tall.

» **Redbud,** *Cercis*. Small trees, sometimes multitrunked. Leaves are medium green and heart-shaped to rounded. Gets its name from the way it cloaks its branches in pink to magenta flowers in spring before the foliage appears. Two good natives are *C. canadensis* var. *texensis* and *C. occidentalis*. Mature height may be 10 to 15 feet (3 to 4.6 m) high.

» **Smoke tree,** *Cotinus*. Refer to the section, "Considering nonnative options," earlier in this chapter; they're considered big shrubs or small trees.

» **Tea tree,** *Leptospermum*. Green to gray-green needlelike foliage. Masses of small flowers in spring. Many pretty cultivars. Height and spread varies from 3 to 10 feet (0.9 to 3 m), so check that information before choosing.

Keeping existing trees healthy

Your property already has a tree or trees growing on it. You've identified what you have and confirmed that you like it, like its placement, and it appears to be in good health. Now the challenge becomes keeping it alive and well for the long term. Here's my best advice:

» **Observe.** Get to know each tree. Notice when it puts out new growth and how much. Notice when it flowers and try to discover who is visiting and pollinating. Notice what changes come in cooler weather and in hotter weather. Notice birds, insects, and other visitors. Does it drop leaves or needles and if so, when and how much? Does it appear healthy?

» **Tend.** Harvest the fruit or berries or, if you don't plan to use or eat them, leave for wildlife or clean up. Does it need dead or damaged limbs removed? You can do this at any time. Does it need pruning or trimming to improve its appearance?

WARNING

Always keep the lawn mower and string trimmer/weed whacker away from the base of trees, and never set or park anything heavy over a root zone (which causes unseen but debilitating damage).

>> **Nurture.** Watering is the number-one thing you can do for a tree in a dry climate or in dry periods. If one doesn't already exist, work to create a basin around the tree so water won't run off. Water deeply — a hose set at the base on a trickle is simple and effective.

Clean up leaf, flower, and/or fruit litter. Watch for signs of disease or distress such as decaying or splitting branches, yellowing/browning/burnt-edged leaves, and aborted fruit. Bring in a professional if you need help with diagnosis and treatment of anything that concerns you.

REPLACING A TREE

When a tree falters or outright dies, remove it on the grounds that it isn't going to make a miraculous recovery. (When in doubt, have a professional visit and assess.) Taking it out yourself is a matter of your strength and stamina, but it's also a matter of having the right tools — lopper, pruning saw, chainsaw.

Do the work in stages: Remove major branches, and then shorten the main trunk in manageable pieces until all that's left is a short stump. Dig out the stump and root ball if you can or repurpose the stump as a spot to display potted plants or garden décor. If the stump and root ball removal are beyond your capabilities, a tree company can do it with a chainsaw and stump grinder.

Seedlings or shoots might appear in ensuing years if some of a living root system or stump survives.

If you want to put a new tree in, after all this, my advice is not to use the same exact spot but rather to prepare a planting hole close by. Doing so is just easier. Shop, dig, and plant when the weather is conducive; in most mild-climate areas, fall is the best time to install a new tree because the stressful heat of summer is over and winter rains may help you water it.

Always dig a big hole for an incoming tree — twice the width and depth of the root ball is good, so the roots have room to expand. Current thinking is not to fill the planting hole with any special soil amendments, but instead to use native soil. It's tough love. A young tree should be compelled to and expected to thrive in native soil, for its best prospects for a long future in its new home.

> » **Figuring out where to raise food**
>
> » **Choosing successful types and varieties**
>
> » **Understanding when to get started**
>
> » **Discovering climate-appropriate veggies, herbs, and fruits**

Chapter **9**

Raising Edible Foods

Growing your own food, always popular, is more appealing than ever these days. It's a great way to repurpose parts of your yard — perhaps where a lawn must come out (good idea, see Chapter 11), where a rock garden or part of one has lost its appeal for you, or anywhere you have sufficient space. Being able to pop out the door and pick something fresh to add to a recipe is wonderful. And, of course, a wide range of interesting and delicious choices for crops are available that you may never find in a local market. Also, importantly, having control over a major, or even a small, portion of your food supply is empowering, fun, and gratifying.

But — and you knew this "but" was coming — people who live in areas where water is precious have particular challenges that people in wetter areas can't even imagine! Can you even do this?

Yes, you can raise certain vegetables, fruits, herbs, and even grains in low-water, hot, windy, dry, and/or drought-plagued areas, and they can be delicious. It's not just a matter of figuring out how and when to provide the water the growing plants require — Chapters 2 and 3 have many helpful, ingenious ideas and options for you in that regard. You also have to choose the plants and then plant and care for them wisely. That's what this chapter is all about.

Planning before You Plant

First things first: you have to figure out where to plant your edibles. Here's how to pick a good spot:

>> **Find a spot with plenty of sun.** That spot generally is about 6 to 8 hours in a day. Okay, that's common advice because most food crops need that much light in order to produce — but in hot and dry climates, you have to moderate this advice. Summers, in particular, can actually be too hot and too bright. Some shade, even partial shade from a tree, shadow from a building, or shade structure, especially in mid-day, can reduce stress for vegetable crops and fruits. If they're full-on blasted in the heat of the day, some plants will not only sunburn or sizzle, but they'll also slump because they require extra water.

>> **Attend to the soil.** Do some amending, that is, adding to and improving your existing soil. Unless you or the person who tended your landscape before you has spent years building organic matter in the soil, chances are the soil is sandy, gritty, and/or nutrient-poor. Lean and fast-draining soils also don't hold water well. To put it bluntly, these soil conditions aren't great for raising food. Refer to Chapter 4 for more details about improving your soil.

TIP

The short version is, add organic matter to the ground where you want to raise food. Consider using raised beds rather than fooling with your native soil (see the nearby sidebar).

>> **Make sure watering will be as easy as possible.** Don't site your food-growing area far from your water source (hose or rain barrel). Consider irrigation systems, from soaker hoses or more elaborate drip systems. I discuss a wide range of options, products, and ideas in Part 1.

>> **Start small.** Beginning small allows you to find out what plants work for you, lets you taste some success, and also helps you discover which watering and tending techniques suit your lifestyle. If all goes well, you can expand in the coming years.

REMEMBER

Many beginning food gardeners overestimate. How big is your household? Unless you plan to give away or sell your surplus or get into canning and preserving, scale back your ambitions. Put in fewer plants. A general rule is to plant about a half-dozen plants of any given type per person.

REMEMBER

Raising vegetables in pots, planter boxes, or hanging baskets is fun and easy — if you can provide the needed water, as containers dry out awfully quickly. Gardens planted in open ground consume more water than gardens planted in enclosed spaces, such as pots, planter boxes, and raised beds. In a hot, dry climate, making sure they have enough water may not be a practical idea, sorry to say. Consult Chapter 17 to see if this plan works for you.

THE PROS AND CONS OF RAISED BEDS

A *raised bed* is basically a bottomless box, often bounded by pressure-treated 2x6 lumber, though you could also repurpose discarded palettes, set up bales of straw, or use other materials, even stones or bricks. Digging pests like gophers and voles can be thwarted if you line the bottom with screen they can't breach.

Height, width, and depth are all up to you. Just remember you have to be comfortable with the size — anything wider than 5 feet (1.5 m) is hard for most people to work in. Consult *Gardening Basics For Dummies* by Steven A. Frowine and the National Gardening Association or *Vegetable Gardening For Dummies* by Charlie Nardozzi and the National Gardening Association for fuller information and/or watch some YouTube videos about constructing and maintaining raised beds.

Here are some pros using raised beds:

- **They allow you to use better soil.** If your native soil is lousy, hard to dig in due to compaction, rocks, or roots, and/or if it would be too much work to improve an in-ground spot sufficiently for raising food, then consider raised beds. You can fill a raised bed with good-quality enriched soil, compost, aged manure, or a combination of these. The soil within will warm up, retain moisture thanks to its organic-matter content, and basically pamper your crops.

- **They're more accessible.** That also means less bending over and sparing your back. Raised beds make yanking out any weeds, tending to the plants, and picking your harvests much easier.

- **They're tidier in your landscape.** If you put in several raised beds, space them far enough apart that you can get a wheelbarrow through. Mulch the paths (gravel, bark mulch, perhaps underlaid with plastic) so you don't have to contend with weeds.

- **They're suitable for intensive gardening.** A raised bed can be planted intensively for high production (larger harvests).

However, a con to using raised beds is in very warm climates, raised beds can heat up too much — and dry out too fast — making it difficult to keep up with necessary watering (no matter your method) and raise healthy crops. If you want to try, bigger is better.

Getting Started — Steps to Growing Your Own Food

With forethought and planning — the following is here to help you in that regard — you can plant appropriate food plants at the right time and in waterwise ways, in order to look forward to a tasty harvest.

Timing is everything

Addressing when to plant is an important decision. It depends on your particular regional climate. If your winters are mild with little rain, you can get started earlier than somewhere where temperatures drop to freezing. Here are some general and useful guidelines to follow:

>> **Start seeds indoors weeks or even a couple of months before the seedlings are due to go outside.** Consult the seed packets and/or seed-company catalog or website descriptions, looking for the information. Then count backward from the approximate date you want to transplant to the outdoors.

If you're new to raising food plants from seed, read the packets and descriptions carefully to see if you want to undertake the project — if you have the space indoors and are willing and able to nurture the little plants.

REMEMBER

Seed-raising isn't the time to be thrifty with water. Seeds need to germinate under normal conditions, and they must get enough moisture to start growing. Give them the water they need until they're established — that is, until the seedlings have developed several sets of leaves and are several inches high.

>> **If you buy small seedlings, you don't have to acquire them until spring or fall.** Shop early in the season for the best selection. Garden centers and box stores aren't the only sources; try a local farmstand or farmer's market. Check that the plants look healthy (not spindly, not sparse; no evident pests or diseases) and are well-rooted.

>> **Plant earlier in the spring and/or later in the fall.** Spring planting leverages warm weather and warmed-up soil so conducive to good growth. Fall planting leverages seasonal rainfall, sparing you from supplying all the water the young, burgeoning plants may need.

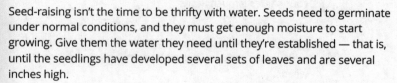

WARNING

If you garden in an area with punishingly long, hot, dry summers, follow the advice in this chapter but aim to raise food crops only in spring or fall — just skip the stress of summer altogether!

Choosing appropriate varieties

You need to consider what sorts of food crops to grow. I discuss specific types of plants in the section, "Going with Traditional Veggies," later in this chapter. But here are important guidelines for selecting ones that have a good chance in low-water settings:

>> **Look to smaller-leaved plants and varieties.** They're better able to cope with less water and drought than ones with big and broad leaves. That's because moisture evaporates more quickly on a bigger surface area. Notice how ornamental plants with smaller leaves, especially native perennials and shrubs, do better in dry and hot regions — it's the same principle. Thus hot peppers have an easier time of it than, say, lettuces.

>> **Seek out regionally adapted varieties.** You can find regionally adapted varieties not in the offerings of big national seed companies but rather in smaller, regional ones. Some garden centers and other outlets in your area may offer them; you'll know because they're labeled that way. Here are other good sources:

  - Nearby botanical garden shops and plant sales

  - Native-plant clubs and societies

  - Seed libraries

  Dig around online or ask savvy gardeners in your area to find them.

>> **Choose quick-growing, early-maturing varieties.** Look on the seed packet, plant tag, or description for the *days to maturity figure*. You want ones that produce sooner rather than later. If you're growing the crop in the spring, you'll want to harvest before the hottest days of summer arrive. If you're growing in the fall, you'll want to pick before the days get shorter and cooler, which slows growth.

TIP

  Optimize soil moisture. Raise plants that require more moisture to come to maturity in spring (or later in fall) — for example, Swiss chard. Allow plants that need less water to grow through the drier spells — for example, beans.

>> **Go small.** Dwarf and miniature varieties exist in most vegetable types. True, their fruits may be fewer and smaller in size, but consider them meal-size. These selections are shorter, more compact-growing, and have smaller leaves — all features that help them cope with less water and still produce.

Positioning plants

Garden layout isn't just a matter of making the patch or raised bed look nice. It also has practical benefits. Here are some ideas meant especially for low-water areas. You don't have to commit to any one method; you can try these layouts in different parts of your food garden or with different plants until you're satisfied that the plants are thriving and using water as efficiently as possible.

>> **Set the plants (or sow the seeds) in an offset or hexagonal layout, rather than in traditional straight rows.** This keeps the plants closer together, which allows their leaves to offer adjacent plants more shade. Two other benefits: it helps keep the soil a bit cooler and slows evaporation.

>> **Plant fewer plants and increase the spaces between individual plants.** If the recommended spacing (as noted on the seed packet, plant tag, or catalog website/description) is 3 feet (0.9 m), set them on 4- to 6-foot (1.2- to 1.8-m) centers. With less plants, there will be more water to go around, right?

>> **Group different types of plants together for their mutual benefit.** A classic example is the Native American *three sisters* method of growing beans, corn, and squash as companions. The beans climb up the cornstalks, and the squash leaves spread out over the ground, suppressing encroaching weeds and helping to keep the soil cooler. (The beans also help improve the soil by fixing nitrogen, that is, returning nitrogen to the soil.) Win-win-win!

Watering for productive harvests

Although water is obviously important throughout a plant's growing period, it's critical when the plant is forming and ripening fruit because that process demands extra water.

If they don't have enough water, the plants will set fewer and/or smaller fruit. You can imagine that some plants will get by on less irrigation for a spell, but as soon as fruits begin to form, the need for water ratchets up again. (If you're using drip irrigation, responding to this cycle is a matter of adjusting the system or using timers; refer to Chapter 5.)

Sufficient water also assures that a fruit ripens evenly and it looks nice and tastes good. Fruit flesh becomes marred and the interior dries out and can get distorted or even woody when there hasn't been enough water when it was most needed. Flavor, obviously, suffers.

WARNING

Water stress isn't pretty. A classic example is tomato fruits splitting, because they didn't get consistent water. Episodes of drenching (by you or a rainstorm) followed by drying out cause splitting.

So, without further ado, here are two ways to meet the water needs of ripening food crops:

» **Water consistently.** A watering routine, whatever it may be (it depends, of course, on what you're able to supply), is best. Don't subject your plants to an unpredictable or uneven schedule.

» **Water deeply.** Water delivered slowly and right at the root system is ideal, and if it soaks in deeply, plant roots are encouraged to grow more deeply. And the deeper they go, the better — because soil dries out quicker nearest the surface. That is, deeper ground holds moisture better. Basically, deep-rooted plants withstand dry spells and droughts much better than shallow-rooted ones.

Caring for your veggies

Here I address a few more things you can do to make life easier for your crops in a low-water environment:

» **Mulch.** Mulch has so many important benefits. It keeps the area around root systems cooler. It helps prevent the evaporation of soil moisture. It suppresses weeds. A thick layer (3 to 4 inches, 7.6 to 10.1 cm) can reduce water needs by as much as half.

BE INVOLVED FROM SEED TO FRUIT AND FLOWER

Over the trajectory of a food plant's life, you can act at certain points to assure its health and productivity. Consider the following:

- **Seedlings:** Thin and intervene when they're just an inch or two (2.5 to 5 cm) tall. Use a sharp pair of scissors and work carefully. Trim unwanted seedlings right at soil level, leaving the strongest ones in place. This chore also allows the remaining plants to get more water and nutrients; these valuable resources aren't wasted on plants that won't succeed.

- **Flowering plants:** Many vegetables need to be pollinated by insects (often but not always bees) to set fruit. Coax pollinators into the area by having other plants close by that they favor, such as flowering perennials and sunflowers. Coordinate the bloom time, though. For example, if you're raising fall vegetables, have some fall-blooming perennials available, such as catmint, New England aster, goldenrod, and zinnias.

- **Fruiting plants:** Keep them well- and consistently hydrated during the critical development period.

TIP

Use dried, chopped leaves; bagged bark mulch; dried grass clippings (if you haven't used high-nitrogen fertilizer or weedkillers on your lawn, that is); straw (which, unlike hay, contains no weed seeds). For more information about mulch, consult Chapter 15.

>> **Don't fertilize.** Fertilizer relies on water to become available to plant roots, and if water is sparse, it will only burn plant roots — to the detriment of aboveground growth. Also, fertilizing promotes fast growth, and slow-and-steady growth tends to consume less water over time.

>> **Evict weeds.** Weeds suck water and soil nutrients from desirable plants. That's especially true when conditions are dry — weeds are wily survival experts. Don't let them horn in. Yank them out early and often.

Going with Traditional Veggies

You can grow plenty of vegetable crops in a low-water setting. Understanding a bit more about their habits and needs can help you decide if you want to give them a try. The following break them into two sections based on their preferred growing season, with a few tips here and there.

Trying cooler/shoulder-season favorites

Certain food crops do best in spring or fall and should be grown then.

>> **Asparagus:** This is actually a perennial plant and therefore a long-term investment — it can be three years from planting time to your first good harvest. Give it its own spot, prepare the planting area well, and mulch to hold in soil moisture and keep out weeds. The roots will go deep, helping the plants survive dry spells.

>> **Beans:** All sorts of beans are possibilities, but pole beans (which take longer to bear than bush beans) are well-suited to a longer growing season. Some do very well in low-water areas/hotter climates: black-eyed peas, cowpeas, lima beans (butter beans), tepary beans, and yard-long beans. Your best bet is to find out which kinds are regionally adapted to where you are.

>> **Collard greens:** They can take heat, but they do best planted in the fall for a late-season harvest.

GETTING TO THE ROOT OF THE MATTER

Root vegetables are considered cool-season crops and thus are tricky in hotter, low-water areas. However, if you have poor, sandy soil, carrots and parsnips are at their sweetest with very little supplemental water. Some afternoon shade on hot days is welcome. Turnips are also drought-tolerant and do well in lean soil as long as the site is well-drained. It's a balancing act; turnips get bitter and woody if soil is dry, but rot if the ground is too wet.

>> **Spinach:** The plants don't mind warm weather but benefit from some shade; you can also raise spinach well in the fall months. *Bolting* in hot times (going to seed; leaves will turn bitter) is a threat; my advice is to seek out a variety billed as slow to bolt.

>> **Swiss chard:** This delicious leafy green is much slower to bolt than spinach. It grows well in fall for late-fall to winter harvesting.

Identifying hot-weather stalwarts

Certain food crops grow and ripen their fruit best in hot, sunny weather. Here are the classics:

>> **Bell and other sweet peppers:** Although they love warm temperatures, they may also — depending on the type and the variety — want more water than you may be able to supply. If the weather is too hot, they may jettison their flowers before ever forming fruit. Wait it out. Sometimes they kick in once the temperatures cool off a bit.

>> **Cherry and grape tomatoes:** Because the fruits are smaller, you may have better luck getting good-looking, sweet-tasting fruit. They tolerate heat and humidity better than the larger-fruited types.

>> **Corn:** You may think that corn is shallow-rooted because often you can see shorter roots spreading out from a stalk, but the feeder roots go deep into the earth. That said, the plants still need food and water to do well. Curled leaf edges are a sign of drought distress. Sweeten the crop's chances by mulching, keeping greedy weeds out of their bed, and removing little nonproductive stalks.

>> **Eggplant:** A true hot-weather lover! It does well in raised beds. The soil does need to be kept steadily irrigated, though.

>> **Hot peppers:** They originated in Central and South America and have been cultivated in Mexico and the American Southwest for centuries, so they're

adapted to hot and low-water regions. I challenge you to move beyond 'Jalapeño'. Many others in many shapes, sizes, and colors are available, so have some fun!

>> **Tomatoes, slicing and paste:** They can be tricky. Too-hot weather negatively impacts pollination and fruit doesn't form (low humidity causes pollen to dry out; pollinators aren't active or effective if temperatures are too high — higher than 90 degrees F/32 degrees C, for too long). The work-around is protecting the plants; grow them in morning, not afternoon sun, and/or shield them with shade cloth.

>> **Okra:** This native of Africa doesn't bolt, turn yellow, or die in summer heat; instead, it grows lushly and produces its edible pods over a long period. Enjoy!

>> **Popcorn:** Popcorn is a type of corn; make sure you get seeds for a variety that specifically states that it's for popping. Some ears are long and others short; my favorite is the aptly named, red-kernelled 'Strawberry Popcorn'.

>> **Squash:** A big group, but most all prosper in heat and long growing seasons. Moschata and Cushaw types do great.

TIP

Tomatoes, peppers, and eggplant flowers all benefit from some gentle shaking early in the morning to facilitate pollination before the day gets too hot. Although this sounds like a minor intervention, it helps keep the flowers from being jetti-soned during the hottest weather.

TIP

Fruits that naturally have a high water content are indeed a challenge to grow. Cantaloupe melons have shown themselves to be more tolerant of drought than watermelons, but you may still have to forgo them, sorry to say. You may want to consider the cantaloupe called 'Hale's Best' that performs better, thanks to its ability to send its roots deeper into the ground than other melons. I can also recommend two tougher watermelon varieties; their names are a clue to their potential. Look for 'Desert King' or 'Hopi Red'.

STEER AWAY FROM THESE CROPS

Unfortunately, some crops just don't perform well in hot, dry areas. Most fall into the "cool-season crops" category. Hot weather causes them to become tough and strong- or bitter-flavored. You'll probably have do without the following or, if a recipe calls for them, buy them in a market:

- Kale
- Lentils
- Lettuce

- Mesclun/mixed salad greens
- Mustard greens
- Peas, regular and sugar-snap types

Trying Offbeat Choices

As in other areas in daily life, the old cliché "when life gives you lemons, make lemonade" applies to food gardening. Instead of lamenting what you can't grow well in your climate, open your mind — and your yard — to new opportunities. The following sections list a few plants that may be fun to try.

Considering unusual, little-known veggies

Seeking a culinary adventure? Willing to try something different? Here are a few food plants that grow and produce well in hot, dry growing conditions — worth considering!

>> **Armenian cucumber** or **metki:** Technically, these plants are melons and the flavor isn't all that sweet, but neither is it bitter; it's reminiscent of watermelon rind. This is a vining plant — give it a sturdy trellis.

>> **Asian eggplant:** They look like the plump, dark-skinned eggplants you're used to, except they're slender. Flavor is mild and sweet.

>> **Malabar spinach:** This is a vining plant and needs support. Slightly succulent leaves stay mild-flavored even in hot weather and are tasty cooked or raw. Comes in plain green and red varieties.

>> **New Zealand spinach:** They're much bigger plants than regular spinach — plant them on 3-foot (0.9 m) centers, at least. They don't bolt, either.

Raising grains

In recent years, there's been a resurgence of interest in grain crops, loosely defined as members of the grass family. Some varieties, nearly lost, have been brought back into cultivation, and more are sure to follow as consumers seek gluten-free alternatives and agribiz seeks plants that are naturally tough. I reflect that part of their current popularity may turn out to be practical, as the planet continues its warming trend and people look to nutritious, protein-rich crops that tolerate heat and drought.

REMEMBER

Growing some of these plants in your low-water landscape, either for their novel looks or for food (cereals/mush, baking, brewing, feeding birds) is both possible and intriguing. Do some investigating with regional seed companies to find out what they offer and get growing advice.

To get started, here are a few basic ones to consider (corn is a grain; check out the section, "Identifying hot-weather stalwarts," earlier in this chapter):

>> **Grain amaranth:** Gluten-free. It's not technically a grain, though grown and harvested like one. It prospers in hot, dry conditions. (Some amaranth species are grown for their leaves or as ornamentals; clarify with your seed source.)

>> **Millet:** Gluten-free. Higher temperatures actually inspire plants to grow taller and faster. It doesn't mind infertile soil. Perfectly edible for humans; many bird species love it, too.

>> **Sorghum:** Gluten-free. Native to Africa and very tough, but be forewarned, the plants can attain 15 feet (4.6 m) in height. The seedheads are decorative. A sweet syrup can be made by pressing the stems and then boiling down the juice.

FURTHER AFIELD WITH UNUSUAL GRAINS

In recent years, interest in growing backyard grains has burgeoned and with it, a call for more choices. Some are heritage or ancient grains that deserve to be brought back into wider cultivation, for their flavor, health benefits, and often, ease of growth. Others are exotic simply because they hail from some far-off land. Delve in! Your homemade bread, pasta, and even wheat-berry salads will benefit hugely, plus, in your own small way, you'll be helping to preserve crop diversity.

Here are good heat- and drought tolerant ones to seek out:

- **Durum (semolina):** High gluten content. In Latin, *durum* means hard; semolina is coarsely ground durum wheat. Widely used for pasta and some breads, also for couscous and bulgar.

- **Eikhorn:** Low gluten. This is the oldest grain in the history of agriculture! Flavor is nuttier and toastier than regular whole wheat. The plant has tighter husks and smaller berries than modern wheat, which makes it a tougher plant.

- **Emmer:** Low gluten. A plus for this grain is that the seedheads remain intact (they don't shatter easily), which simplifies harvesting. The seedheads of some varieties ('Black Emmer' and 'Utrecht Blue') are gorgeous, adding appeal to your garden.

- **Tibetan purple barley:** Very low gluten. Contains more fiber than most other grains, heads are violet and shiny. Earthy, hearty flavor.

Growing Your Own Herbs

Raising edible herb plants in dry and low-water settings is easy, but they must first become established. That is, their root systems must get growing in the spot you choose for them, whether in-ground or in a container of some sort. Keep a watchful eye on young herb plants and water them lightly but regularly and don't overwater.

TIP

Are you growing your herbs in pots or other containers? Instead of dumping water on them from above with a watering can or spray from the hose, set the pot in a tray or pie tin of water and let the soil mix suck up moisture on an as-needed basis.

After a good root system forms, many herbs will carry on or even thrive on neglect. In some places some herbs are actually considered weeds because they grow so easily with so little care.

TIP

When growing an herb for its leaves, for best *flavor*, harvest before it forms flowers. After these plants bloom, they redirect their energy into the flowers and the production of the seeds that follow. Leaf production slows or stops and — most unfortunately — often the flavor becomes less intense.

When an herb plant starts to produce flowers, its leafy harvest often changes flavor. You can prolong a leafy herb's harvest period by snipping off the flower buds as soon as they appear (see Figure 9-1).

FIGURE 9-1:
Snip off the flowers and enjoy a longer harvest.

(c) John Wiley & Sons, Inc.

Here are some good bets, based on water needs.

Needing more or more-regular water

These herbs are more water-needy:

- >> Basil
- >> Borage
- >> Chives

- >> Dill
- >> Garlic chives
- >> Parsley

Needing less water/getting by with less

These herbs are less water-needy:

- >> Caraway
- >> Coriander
- >> Epazote
- >> Fennel
- >> Lavender
- >> Lemon verbena

- >> Oregano/marjoram
- >> Rosemary
- >> Sage
- >> Summer savory
- >> Thyme
- >> Winter savory

Planting Fruits

Before you think "growing fruit is too intensive" or "growing fruit takes too much water," pause and think: where are many commercial fruit crops raised? In central California's hot sunny days. Lemon and avocado orchards dot the American West. New Mexico is a major producer of peaches, pears, and apples. Cherries are Utah's state fruit.

Are the big orchards consuming too much water, or are these operations on to something? The answer is mixed. Long, sunny growing seasons and ample land certainly help, but some were planted when the current water-shortage crisis wasn't yet imagined. That said, an ordinary homeowner in an area with plentiful sunshine and a long growing season can certainly contemplate adding some fruits to their yard. These sections take a closer look.

Recognizing fruit-bearing trees

Depending on where you live, you can grow fruit trees already proven to prosper in your area. Also consider fruits of other arid regions. In many cases, they'll need water and coddling to get established but in ensuing years will be fairly self-sufficient, including drought-tolerant (depending on what you choose, your climate, and conditions in your yard).

Your first step, after you warm to this idea, is to visit a local or regional nursery. Walk around and see what kinds of fruit trees they offer.

Then flag down a staffer and ask questions:

>> How big, and wide, does this tree get?

>> Do I need to plant more than one for pollination purposes?

>> How long until it begins bearing?

>> Do I need to protect it from any insect or animal pests?

>> Does it need spraying to prevent disease or insect problems or is it possible to raise an organic tree?

>> Does it have special pruning requirements?

>> What should I do to encourage a harvest of delicious fruit?

>> How long does it live?

>> What are its water needs? (How do you recommend I meet them?)

TECHNICAL STUFF

Some fruit trees are *self-fertile*, which means a tree doesn't need another tree — the same or similar — nearby to cross-pollinate with in order to produce fruit for you to harvest. Bees often accomplish pollination, so in the case of a self-fertile tree, the bees can move pollen around from flower to flower on the same tree and fruit will develop.

Self-fertile trees are clearly what you want if you only wish to plant (or only have space for) one fruit tree. Examples include apricots, citrus trees, sour cherries, peaches, pears, and plums. However, I must point out two things:

>> Self-fertile varieties have been developed in other types of fruit trees. Definitely get this important matter clarified wherever you shop for your fruit tree. For example, the 'Stella' sweet cherry is self-pollinating. You have to ask!

>> Dwarf versions (see Figure 9-2) of fruit trees — suitable for smaller yards and sometimes even growing in a large container — are frequently self-fertile. The nursery industry clearly saw and filled a need for backyard gardeners.

FIGURE 9-2:
Most fruit trees
come in dwarf
versions.

If you want to add a fruit tree, consider the following:

>> Apricot

>> Asian pear

>> Avocado

>> Asian (Oriental) persimmon

>> Cherry

>> Fig

>> Guava

>> Jujube

>> Kumquat

>> Loquat

>> Mango

>> Olive

>> Pear

>> Pineapple guava

>> Pomegranate

On the other hand, these trees are often too water-needy:

>> Apple

>> Citrus (lemon, Meyer lemon, lime, orange, grapefruit)

>> Nectarine

>> Peach

>> Plum

Contemplating fruit-bearing shrubs

Shrubs, as I explain in Chapter 8, can be major contributors to a home landscape, thanks to their bulk and, in time, their low-maintenance dependability. Those that produce edible fruit can be a curiosity for garden visitors but also allow you to harvest something delicious. Here are my top suggestions:

>> Goji berry

>> Kei apple

>> Natal plum

>> Prickly pear cactus (turn to Chapter 7)

>> Strawberry guava

Trying fruit-bearing vines

A vine that flowers and bears fruit can do double duty in a small yard, that is, you can get shade, beauty, and food. Only grow a fruiting vine, though, if you intend to harvest the fruit. Letting fruit fall to the ground unharvested not only makes a mess (and may stain your patio, deck, or walkways), but it also attracts bees and other insects as it rots. Consider these fruit-bearing vines:

>> Grapes

>> Kiwifruit

>> Passionfruit

>> Scarlet runner bean

STRAWBERRY FIELDS FOREVER?

Perhaps you've seen the sprawling strawberry fields of Central California, that seem to stretch endlessly to the horizon and indeed, provide a bountiful harvest for supermarket shelves nationwide. As you may guess, they're special varieties bred to grow well in that particular climate and soil and to resist common diseases and pests. However, to be honest, they can be lacking in sweetness, and part or all of their interiors may be white and not flavorful. Like so many other crops, a homegrown harvest is always fresher and tastier.

(continued)

(continued)

Strawberries have different types, including the following:

- **June-bearing strawberries:** The most widely available, they're larger one-time harvest, bigger berries. They may be a practical choice where summers become very hot.

- **Ever-bearing strawberries:** They have two rounds of harvesting, early and late summer, smaller berries.

- **Day-neutral strawberries:** They can go all summer but slow down or stop producing when exposed to high temperatures.

With ample sunshine, good air circulation, and some open space, you can raise wonderful strawberries in low-water gardens. Here are some useful tips:

- **Select your variety with care.** You don't need big, huge fruits; smaller strawberries often have wonderful flavor. Where certain pests or diseases are a concern, a local nursery can guide you to resistant varieties.

- **Make sure the ground is well-drained.** Strawberry plants rot if they have *wet feet,* that is, if their root zones are saturated. Raised beds can be a good option.

- **Mulch!** Mulch, as I mention throughout this book, helps hold in soil moisture and keep weeds at bay — good for your growing strawberry plants. Black plastic, with holes cut to insert the plants, works well. You can also use straw. Straw around the plants and between rows is a great choice also because the developing fruit will stay drier and be clearly visible to you (could that be how they got their name?).

- **Ramp up water when fruits begin to form and water the plants consistently so the fruits develop without stress.** Take a leaf from the agricultural fields and use drip irrigation or soaker hoses (see Chapter 5).

You have one other option, so-called *alpine strawberries* (also known as *fraises des bois,* strawberries of the woods). They're tiny-fruited and a different species from the traditional types. The plants are compact enough to grow in a pot or hanging basket, and they'll produce all summer.

You won't get a big harvest in any sense of the word — the plants aren't large or spreading and the fruit is usually pea-size, though elongated, but the flavor is dazzling, almost as sweet as a ripe pineapple! Keep some plants around and pick for sprinkling on your morning cereal, yogurt, or ice cream.

Chapter **10**

Planting and Caring for Low-Water Plants

This book deals with low-water landscaping situations. You can return to and review the chapters about water and watering at any time, as needed. This chapter covers the rest of the story. It doesn't focus on watering techniques and methods, except where I can offer a specific tip for a certain type of situation. Instead, it's time to talk about how to buy and then get your plant choices into the ground . . . and the myriad other ways, besides watering, that you can use to help them thrive.

Considering the Many Sources for Landscape Plants

Do you like to prepare special meals for guests from time to time? When such an event is scheduled, do you then go out to get the best and freshest ingredients? (Refer to Chapter 9 for lists of items you can grow right out your back door.) Because, of course, then the results are as good as they can be. Good ingredients, good food. Well, the same principle applies to acquiring plants: Quality plants are the ingredients of a successful landscape.

Here I begin by touring your buying options. You can shop local, or you can try the plant catalog/website route. I include tips for both approaches, plus a few other ideas for additional sources. You don't have to pick just one — shop wherever you can get the best ingredients.

Shopping at local nurseries

Where you live and garden has bearing on what plant-buying outlets are available to you. But perhaps you don't know all your options. You may be able to get plants at places that aren't currently on your radar. Ask other gardeners. Look online. Go exploring!

Nurseries and garden centers are businesses. They want to make money. They don't want unhappy customers. Therefore you can assume that they'll stock appropriate plants of good quality.

REMEMBER

Big nurseries aren't necessarily better than small ones. Big nurseries have more plants, more space, more staff, and perhaps more categories of plants. But sometimes the smaller ones can be a better shopping experience because hardworking, dedicated owners operate them. Small nurseries are also sometimes *specialty nurseries* — for instance, a place devoted to nothing but succulents probably has a better selection than the big place trying to do it all. One that touts only native plants is your one-stop shopping if that's your landscaping goal.

The following takes a closer look at how to be a savvy shop-local shopper. I include helpful guidelines for finding a good source, judging the health and quality of the plants, and how to get your purchases home safely.

Finding good nurseries

Here are some tips for finding good nurseries in your area:

>> **Someone recommended the place.** But not just anyone, and not just a good review on social media or online. Other gardeners and other people you know whose landscape looks good (trusted friends, neighbors, and acquaintances) have given it a thumbs-up.

>> **Their parking lot is full.** Lots of customers is a good sign because it means other gardeners like shopping there.

>> **The place is organized.** Full-sun plants are in one area, shade plants in another, trees over there, vines over here, succulents in their own section, and so on. Really large and super-organized nurseries even group plants by size or

color (of foliage or flowers), which makes browsing fun, idea-inspiring, and helpful. This organization is for your convenience.

» **The grounds are tidy.** Clean isn't quite the right word because gardening and landscaping obviously involves dirt and mulch. But carelessness with discarded empty pots, jumbled merchandise, and ungroomed plants doesn't reflect well. Neat, accessible presentation of plants indicates that the staff cares about the appearance and looks after the health of what they sell.

» **Tags or labels are on everything.** Sections have large, readable signs. Directional signs help you find what you're looking for. And of course a smart garden supplier knows this information empowers you so what staff they may have on hand aren't overwhelmed.

» **The staff is clearly trained and helpful.** Flagging down a nursery worker when you're having trouble finding something or have a question about planting or care should be easy. When you do, they know their stuff. Best of all is when someone greets you upon arrival with, "Welcome, can I help you find something today?" Awesome! Loyalty-building!

Recognizing what you get

Local nurseries almost always offer plants growing in pots or flats of various sizes. The larger the pot, usually the larger and more mature the plant; the bigger ones are more expensive. If the plants you want come in different sizes, it's your call, depending on the space you plan to fill and your budget.

Trees may be offered with their root systems balled-and-burlapped. The nursery staff can explain what you need to do when you get the tree home, but basically, you should cut and peel that stuff off so the roots can grow freely in their new home in your yard.

The potting mix in a nursery pot often isn't like the soil where you'll be planting. It's a potting mix, conducive to raising and nurturing seedlings. Typically it contains organic matter studded with little pebbles of water-soluble fertilizer, perlite, and/or pumice (refer to the nearby sidebar for more information about soil mixes).

TIP

Be flexible. Getting your heart set on a certain plant (perhaps something you've seen in another garden, read about in this or another book, or spotted on Instagram) is natural. But sometimes when you go shopping, you can't find the exact same thing. That's okay — there's plenty of everything. For example, there's more than one blue-flowered penstemon in the world! Sometimes pivoting to an alternative, an almost-the-same plant, becomes a wonderful discovery.

INSPECTING WHAT'S INSIDE SOIL MIXES

The following are common items in soil mixes, used for many nursery-raised plants, including perennials and succulents. You can also buy bags of soil mix, and these ingredients should be listed; they're important for getting drought-tolerant plants going and keeping them healthy:

- *Perlite* is white, lightweight, and looks like super-tiny Styrofoam balls.
- *Pumice* looks similar but is more granular, and its color is grayish or brownish.

Rest assured, both are safe, inorganic, and pH neutral (neither acidic nor alkaline). Note that they won't decompose over time.

These materials are present because they help keep the mix aerated, preventing compaction. Plant roots need oxygen. They can also strike the perfect balance between helping water move through (so roots don't get soggy, which is fatal to low-water plants) and retaining just enough moisture to keep roots healthily hydrated.

If you're bringing home plants to grow in pots, perhaps even moving them into larger pots, purchase a bag of soil mix that has either of these additives ("Special Succulent Soil Mix" on the bag, for instance).

Assessing quality before buying

You're standing in the nursery, holding a potted plant, poised to add it to your shopping basket or cart and buy it. Before you commit, check it over. If you find problems, put it back, maybe select another. Inspect the plant closely, looking at the following (refer to Figure 10-1):

>> **Leaves:** Look for good color, hydration, and overall health. Notice if they're whole (a few nibbles isn't a deal-breaker, but chewed-up foliage is never a sign of good health). Inspect on and under/on the backsides of the foliage for signs of tiny insect pests, webs, or sooty residue. If you notice any, don't buy.

>> **Stems:** Check that they aren't damaged. Make sure they're strong and sturdy. Bent or limp stems aren't good. Sometimes the foliage is fine, but the flowering stems aren't — such plants are probably still worth buying; they can always make new flowering stems after you get them home.

>> **Roots:** Carefully turn the pot on its side or upside down (your fingers splayed over the soil mix so it doesn't spill or the plant doesn't fall out). If lots of white roots are coming out of the drainage holes, it's probably pot-bound, which isn't good because the roots are too compacted. If you can gently tip the root

When you use gravel, stones, and/or bricks to create a permeable walkway or patio, water soaks in rather than running off.

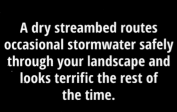

A dry streambed routes occasional stormwater safely through your landscape and looks terrific the rest of the time.

Native, multi-stemmed madrone trees prosper in a low-water landscape; they grow slowly, making them suitable for smaller yards (see Chapter 8).

To deliver maximum water with minimum waste to a freshly planted tree or shrub, create a basin around its root system (refer to Chapter 3).

Light-colored mulch such as straw reflects rather than absorbs heat (see Chapter 15).

zz up your yard by choosing vivid-colored succulents like yucca (see the many recommendations in Chapter 7).

Providing contrast makes your plants stand out (see Chapter 14).

hen choosing succulents, select different but compatible hues and place bigger plants to the back or middle (refer to Chapter 10).

Aim for contrasting colors when you plant drought-tolerant bloomers; find lists in Chapter

ative wildflowers, such as yellow black-eyed Susan and bright blue *Salvia guaranitica,* deliver lots of color (see Chapter 6).

Choose bloomers that attrac butterflies like the hyssop nativar 'Blue Fortune' (refer to Chapters 6 and 12).

A thick planting
African daisies
plentiful mulch
weeds and cor
soil moisture (
Chapter 15).

s are easy-
nt-tolerant
pectacular
hapter 12).

Install a rain barrel to access garden water as you need it. Be sure the spigot is down-low for optimum water pressure (see Chapter 2).

Drip-irrigation emitters (refer to Chapter 5) are wonderfully efficient — they release

If you paint your walls and trim in vivid hues, your dry garden gets a wonderful color boost (see Chapter 6).

A small in-ground garden pool actually doesn't consume a lot of water after its initial filling; just top off when some evaporates. See Chapter 18.

Visit a nursery that specializes in succulents and prepare to be amazed by the many colors and forms! Plant lists are in Chapter 7.

Small succulents in pots deliver a lot of beauty for very little fussing. Chapter 17 discusses container gardening.

system slightly out of the pot and look at the roots, do so. They should be white and healthy-looking. Are they growing well in the potting mix or do they fall right out? Ones that let go of their mix and fall into your waiting hand aren't sufficiently rooted. Carefully replace everything and put such plants back on the shelf.

>> **Buds and flowers:** If you're buying a plant for its flowers, pause and be rational. You can easily be seduced by a plant in full bloom, but the truth is, those flowers may fall off on the ride home or in the plant's first days in your garden. In fact, a blooming plant might be at its peak and the color show you see today will be over and done with for the year, meaning you'll have to wait to see it again next year. It's almost always better to buy a plant in bud instead. (If you're wondering what the color will be, check the tag.)

Leaves—look for good color, hydration, overall health

Stems—check that they are not damaged

Roots—these should be white and crisp; plant should not be potbound

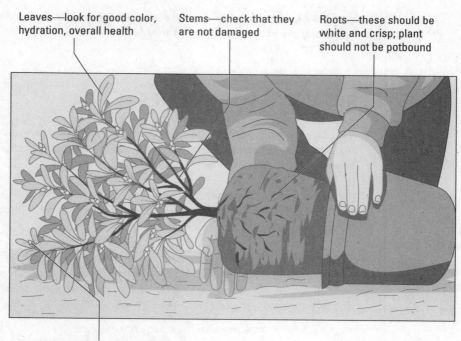

Buds—it's always wiser to buy a plant in bud rather than full bloom

FIGURE 10-1:
Before deciding to buy a plant, closely inspect it.

(c) John Wiley & Sons, Inc.

REMEMBER

Coming from a pampered life in a greenhouse, hoop house, or nursery row to life in a garden is a big change for a plant. If the move isn't easy, plants essentially enact triage. They don't just wilt, though that's a warning sign. They actually drop flowers and buds. If the stress continues — they're not getting enough sun or water, or their new soil isn't right for them — they'll start jettisoning leaves. Wilting, drying out of all plant parts, and collapse can follow.

Getting your purchases home safely

A hot day and a hot vehicle isn't a joyride for just-purchased plants. If you've noticed that they're a bit heat-stressed, ask someone at the nursery to give them a little water before you depart. Here are a couple other tips to make the trip home a little less stressful for the plants:

>> Bring a box, boxes, laundry basket, or milk crates, and secure the plants in them before driving off. Make sure they can't tip over, falling out, damaging, or snapping off foliage or stems, not to mention probably spilling their soil mix all over the back seat.

>> Drive safely (don't whip around corners) and go right home. The longer the plants are in the car, the longer they're stressed.

BIG BOX STORE BLUES

The garden center of a big box store is tempting. It's usually a sprawling area stuffed with plants and gardening supplies. Despite the apparently large selection, I don't recommend shopping there for plants.

The primary reason: They're middlemen. They didn't grow the plants. The plants were purchased in bulk from wholesale sources, big production greenhouses, or growing fields, which leads to a host of other issues:

- Box store garden centers often don't have knowledgeable staffers. They tend to hire caretakers, not horticulturists. That makes expeditions to such places frustrating. Finding someone who can answer your questions, direct you, or suggest alternative selections can be difficult.

- The selection isn't as good as it appears. You may find lots of plants, but often not a lot of variety. These outlets don't buy in small quantities, so if you're looking for plants that aren't widely popular, you probably won't find them.

- The appearance of the plants may be deceptive. Sure, they're lush and full of flowers, but that's because both the originating supplier and the box-store caretakers fertilize heavily (usually delivered via the watering system). In short, the plants are essentially jacked up on plant steroids to grab customers' attention.

- The quality isn't great. They often don't have enough staff to take care of all those plants, so you find dried-out plants for sale — a sorry sight. (Sometimes these plants are discounted and can be rescued with pruning and watering — that is, the root systems may still have life in them.)

- Because they didn't grow the plants, they can't vouch for correct labeling or plant health and they may decline responsibility for damaged, pest-infested, or diseased plants. That is, don't assume you can return disappointing plants for replacement or refund — ask about their policies at time of purchase.

If you do purchase plants at a box store, review the section, "Assessing quality before buying," earlier in this chapter.

Considering mail-order shopping

You may shop by sitting at your computer or scrolling through your hand-held device and clicking on what you want. Shopping this way certainly is the modern way and arguably saves time and resources because you don't have to travel to a shopping destination and you can shop any time of day or night. And it's a fine method for acquiring books, smaller household goods, clothing, and much, much more. But, live plants?

Yes. Here's why:

» You have a broader and more interesting selection than local nurseries that cater to popular items. That's because they don't have to stock mega-quantities.

» Almost always, they grew the plants themselves, which means no middleman. They offer intimate knowledge of — and responsibility for — the products.

CATALOG OR WEBSITE: WHICH IS BETTER?

You can shop for mail-order plants either via catalog or website. At times the two venues are essentially identical. A paper catalog that comes in the mail may be a teaser, with much more merchandise promised — and delivered — on the website. However, sometimes the nursery only offers a catalog because the nursery may be old school or maintaining a website is too much trouble. Hence, in the interests of thoroughness, check both catalogs and online.

(continued)

(continued)

Personally, I love to sit down with a colorful paper catalog, turning the pages in a leisurely way. I like to flag wish-list items with a marker or turn down corners of pages I want to revisit. Garden-catalog browsing is one of life's great pleasures, especially on a dreary winter evening when the days are short with little color outdoors. Better still with a glass of wine or a cuppa herbal tea — your mileage may vary!

If you're content scrolling on your phone or computer, I have an extra piece of advice: Bookmark, annotate, or make lists/notes. It's so frustrating when you can't remember where you saw a plant.

When ordering, always order online because it's fast and easy! In fact, I'm surprised mail-order catalogs still include bound-in order forms and sometimes even mailing envelopes. Maybe they're too busy raising and shipping plants to realize that their customers have modernized.

TIP

Value-added service from mail-order suppliers is increasingly a thing. Nowadays many of them have hotlines or live-chat options on their websites where you can ask a horticulturist. You can sign up for e-newsletters full of useful tips and advice, and all are free. They want to build a relationship with you. I recommend you look for and use these services.

TIMING IS EVERYTHING

Mail-order nurseries, with the help of increasingly sophisticated computerized modeling, are experts at sending your plants to you at the right time for planting. They tend to operate under the assumption that you prefer to receive a box of plants around Thursday or Friday for weekend planting; if that's not the case, just let them know. They monitor weather — not just normal outdoor temperatures but extreme heat waves and storm radar — aiming to ship to you when it is safe to plant.

All this handily takes the guesswork off your hands. All you have to do is plant when or soon after your purchases arrive!

TIP

When should you order? My advice is to plan ahead. Order as soon as you see the plants you want available for sale. Some mail-order nurseries are smaller businesses and may run out of the exact plants you want; others appreciate early orders so they can grow-to-order. In other words, you don't necessarily have to buy plants exactly when you want to plant them. Ordering weeks or months early may actually be better; practice patience, the wait is worth it. *Note:* Usually the nursery won't charge you until they ship.

PACKING AND SHIPPING ARE EXCELLENT

Almost all mail-order nurseries have packing and shipping of live plants down to a science. The quality is invariably good, and so is the customer service. They not only want you to be happy, but they also want the goods (plants) to succeed. They are the source. They grew the plants, and then their own trained staff packed and shipped them. They know their stuff!

TIP

When you're unpacking a shipment of plants, do so as soon as possible. When you open the package, you'll find an information sheet inside explaining recommended practices. Gently take out the plants, rehydrate the roots, and trim off any damage. If you can't plant them within a couple of days of their arrival, hold them in a protected spot, such as a shaded porch.

CUSTOMER SERVICE AND RETURNS ARE A PRIORITY

Experienced mail-order nurseries don't want to field calls or angry emails complaining about damaged or dead plants. They lose customers and money that way. Thus they prioritize providing hassle-free customer service. Typical policies include the following:

» Unlike online selling of household items, sending back unacceptable or damaged merchandise isn't a good option in the case of live plants. You can take a photo of the box of dead plants or their pathetic appearance and send it. Some mail-order nurseries may ask for photographic evidence before agreeing to refund or replace.

» The usual practice, though, is to believe you when you complain and offer a replacement plant or credit. Always check their guarantee and policies before buying, so there are no misunderstandings.

Knowing what to expect of mail-order plants

Mail-order plants often look different from plants purchased from local outlets. Read the fine print on the website or in the catalog so you aren't surprised. Shipped plants tend to look different from locally purchased ones in the following ways:

» **They look smaller.** The plants could be as mature as the same plant purchased locally, but for ease of shipping (and to reduce the weight of the box), they've been given a haircut — their topgrowth may have been trimmed down to stubble, which is okay. You're really buying a root system anyway. Get the plants in the ground, or container, and take good care of them and they'll recover quickly, soon putting on new growth.

» **They might be bareroot.** *Bareroot* plants aren't shipped potted. Instead, complete with the haircut just mentioned, their roots are carefully and professionally swathed in damp paper and/or wrapped in plastic to keep them hydrated and secure for their journey in a box to your door.

Bareroot plants are also dormant or just barely emerging from a period of dormancy. A big plus of these rather unimpressive-looking purchases is that they can be sent to you earlier in the growing season, and you can plant them earlier than pot-grown plants because they're dormant and won't be knocked back by cooler soil.

Special care details come with bareroot plants. The nursery tells you what to do if you can't plant quickly, such as, "store them in your refrigerator." Planting directions are clear: Handle with care, plant earlier than pot-grown plants, and look after them while they get established.

Acquiring plants at other places

Nurseries, local or mail-order, are the main options but not the only ones. Here are a few other places to seek out good plants:

» **Garden clubs:** Ask at a local nursery or check their community bulletin board if they have one. Attend a meeting, make new friends, and get good advice. You'll be clued as to when they hold a plant sale or fundraiser, which features plants provided by their members.

» **Native plant clubs and plant societies:** Try finding one the same ways, but also look online. Your town or city may not have one, but you can usually find one nearby if you're willing to travel a bit. Sometimes they're a national organization with regional branches.

If their website or social media has a "contact us" option, send them a query about how to join, about when they hold their meetings or scheduled events, or about where to get a certain plant. These folks are invariably enthusiastic, knowledgeable, and generous.

» **Botanic gardens/arboretums:** Not only are their display gardens wonderful to visit for inspiration and plant ideas, but they often have educational speaker programs and plant sales. The plant sales will have plants propagated from their own collections, which is a great way to get your hands on proven and/or special items.

» **Local neighbors/other good gardeners:** You don't have to tackle your garden and landscape alone when you can be making new friends and getting seasoned advice. Reach out to those who have yards and plants that you admire.

WILD-PLANT ETHICS

You may have admired native plants and pretty wildflowers on outings and hikes in your town or region. You can see that they do well, and you realize you want some in your yard. Not so fast.

Resist the temptation to dig up wild plants and bring them home for the following reasons:

- Many natural settings are already beleaguered thanks to all sorts of human activities, from construction and suburban sprawl to depleted aquifers. Removing a plant from its native habitat is a shame in that regard — you're taking it away from an environment where it plays a role for soil, wildlife (birds, insects, and more), and other associated plants.

- Poaching can be illegal. Poaching is when you help yourself to a plant on public or private land. Don't poach.

- Digging up wild plants and moving them into a garden isn't a recipe for success. It's stressful on a plant to be transplanted, especially if it's blooming, which takes a lot of resources and energy. You're also taking it away from its native soil, which may be teeming with visible and minute organisms and fungi that contribute to the plants' health and well-being. Quite frankly, it's a project destined for failure.

Deciding When to Plant

To give newly acquired plants a good start in your home landscape, be sensitive to what they need as well as what stresses them. Here I explain optimum timing and related concerns.

Planting in spring for quick transformation

In areas where spring starts early in the calendar year and very hot summer weather is a few months distant, spring planting is great. Plants are ready to get growing and are full of energy. At this time of year, their growth cycle is wired for upward and outward growth of foliage and stems, followed by flowers and perhaps fruit. In spring, they're also primed for eager and outward growth of their root system. Beauty and color should soon follow.

The following sections discuss the conditions you want for success.

Making sure the soil is warm

Focusing on warm air, pleasant weather is natural when trying to decide if spring has arrived, but for plants, warmed-up *soil* is paramount. Soil that was cold, frozen, semi-frozen, muddy, or just cool over the winter months isn't welcoming to roots. Literally they'll have a lot of trouble drawing up water from the earth, plus growing roots need a little air (not air pockets — just aerated ground) and hard or saturated ground is detrimental.

A general rule is to hold off planting most flowers, shrubs, trees, and vines until the ground is *workable* (not hard, not mucky) and soil temperature is at least 50 to 60 degrees F (10 to 15 degrees C). Temperatures in excess of 75 degrees F (24 degrees C), however, are too warm. Soil warms up gradually in spring. If you're attentive to the soil, you and your planting projects will have a window of opportunity of at least several good weeks or months, depending on where you live.

You may wonder how to determine soil temperature. Here are a few ways:

>> Use a thermometer stuck in the ground. Garden centers and mail-order suppliers sell soil thermometers. Just follow the directions about how to use and how to read.

>> Go low-tech and scoop up a handful of soil in the planting area and squeeze. If water drips out, it's too soggy and too early for planting. If the clod breaks into larger pieces, that's about right. If it crumbles into dust, it's too dry and too poor in organic matter — you'll want to do some soil improvement (the next section discusses good planting soil) first, depending on what you're planting.

>> Lie down on the garden area. No, I'm not kidding. The garden expert Roger B. Swain once suggested this, explaining, essentially, "If it's comfortable for you, it's comfortable for plants."

Making sure the soil is good

Even though plants vary in the type of soil they need, very often the soil in water-poor areas needs some help so newcomers can prosper. Native soil can be gritty, poor in nutrients, and high in salts. Or it may have high clay content and drain poorly. Soil remediation isn't hard or complicated — the addition of organic matter is always a good thing. (Turn to Chapter 4 for the information to improve your soil.)

Organic matter helps sandy, gritty, fast-draining soil hold moisture and improves its structure. It helps aerate slick, heavy clay soil. Materials you can add (bagged, homemade, or both) include mulch, potting mix, dehydrated livestock manure, chopped-up dried leaves, and compost.

Seeking a good day

Planting day should be easy on you as well as easy on the plants. Ideally the day is overcast and cool and, with great good luck, maybe drizzly. Work steadily and quickly, so roots aren't exposed to open air for any longer than the few moments when you pop them out of their pot and place them in the ground (or pot).

Planning ahead with fall planting

Adding plants to your landscape in the other shoulder season, the cooler days of fall, also works in many areas. In addition to sparing newbies the stress of the long, hot days of summer, here are other advantages to fall planting:

>> **Nursery offerings are often larger.** These plants may have been offered in the spring and didn't sell, so the nursery had to keep them alive over the summer and then offer them now — last chance for this year. The nursery, not you, had to water them in the hottest part of the year. If they survived, they also put on some growth and are bigger, more mature plants now.

Sometimes those fall plants are on sale. The nursery just wants to sell them before winter comes.

>> **Root growth is prioritized.** Fall-planted flowers and shrubs, as well as many trees, are wired not to put energy into new leaves or blooms in fall. Instead, their root systems take advantage of autumn's cooler soil and maybe some fall rains to get growing.

Because most of the activity and progress is taking place where you can't see it, underground, it may look like nothing is happening. But when spring comes around again, fall-planted plants have a significant head start over the spring ones. They'll grow faster and be more robust than their spring-planted counterparts. You'll be congratulating yourself!

Staying away from summer planting

The wrong time to plant is in the hottest part of summer. In fact, don't plant on any blazing-hot day.

Even experienced gardeners are tempted to break certain planting rules from time to time when they find a desired plant on sale (there's a reason the nursery is unloading it cheap — they know it's going to be hard to sell! Either that, or they know it's going to be hard to keep it alive and they'll soon have to discard it). Or sometimes a well-meaning friend gives you a plant. Politely turn them down if you think it's bad timing.

Hot days and high summer are bad for planting because transplants need a chance to adapt to their new home. In particular, they need to commence root growth, which not only anchors them in place but also supplies necessary hydration and nutrients to the aboveground parts. This critical process requires water — plentiful, consistent, probably frequent. In dry climates in hot summer weather, water is a luxury and a need you may not be able to meet for incoming plants.

Avoiding planting pitfalls

No matter when you add new plants to your landscape, you need to be mindful of certain practices so you don't harm them or limit their prospects:

>> **Don't overprepare the planting hole or bed.** Don't put new plants in a hole or bed that is 100 percent organic amendments. Doing so turns out to be counterproductive. Eventually their roots will hit an underground wall (where the enriched ground meets the native soil), literally, and at that point plant growth will stop or struggle.

REMEMBER

Instead, garden soil for incoming new plants should be a matter of tough love. Some gardeners use all-native soil. I prefer a mixture, so the incoming plants can enjoy a little boost, but still adapt to the site. Experiment with the proportions that work in your yard and with your plant selections, but half-and-half (half native soil, half amendments) is where I like to start.

>> **Be careful of plants with taproots.** Some incoming plants may be the sort that forms a *taproot* (the primary descending root) — and many desert natives do this, so they can survive drought. Plant a young rather than a big, mature plant, so the taproot isn't too developed as yet. Pick a spot where it will stay (this involves knowing its projected mature size and allowing sufficient space) because it *won't* want to be moved. (To know if the plant is a taproot-former, read up on it before purchasing and/or find out from wherever you acquire it.)

Focusing on Planting Techniques

If you have some plants ready to be planted, it's time to get them in the ground. Here I explain the basic, tried-and-true, one-plant-at-a-time method. I also look at some general water-wise planting strategies. Hang onto your hat — read this whole section before digging in.

Digging and setting in place

This section walks you through the step–by–step process of putting a plant in the ground.

TIP

A day or more before you start planting, irrigate the area where you'll be working, giving the water a little time to soak in. This way, the soil will be damp and much easier to work in.

Follow these steps:

1. **Gather tools and supplies.**

   A shovel and/or trowel is best. Perhaps use a dandelion fork, which can do more than help you pry out any deep-rooted plants in the way, and maybe a butter knife. Use heavy-duty trash bags, a bucket, or a wheelbarrow full of soil amendments, if you're adding them to the soil. Because you'll be on your hands and knees, something soft to kneel on is nice — a tarp, an old cushion, or even a garden stool kneeler.

2. **Prepare the spot.**

   I assume you've found out if the plant can grow in full sun or if it needs part-day shade, and you have an area in your yard in mind. Identify whether any weeds, lawn grass, or other plants are already present. If yes, evict them, root systems and all. If there are adjacent plants that may overhang or crowd the incoming plant, trim them back.

3. **Prepare the plant.**

   Water it until water runs out the drainage holes in the bottom of its nursery pot — so it's well-hydrated for its big move. Carry it to the planting area, leaving it in its pot and off to the side, so you don't knock it over or sit on it.

4. **Dig the hole (see Figure 10-2).**

   The general rule is a bit deeper and twice as wide as the root system going in. Eyeball the nearby plant or even check by temporarily putting it, pot and all, into the hole to verify the hole is deep enough.

TIP

   Take a moment to rough up the sides and bottom of the hole by raking with your fingers or the dandelion weeder. You want to make the adjacent soil a bit easier for the roots to enter when they're ready.

5. **Unpot the plant.**

   If it's hard to dislodge, squeeze and squish the pot to loosen it. If it's still stubborn, try running the butter knife around the inside of the pot. After it pops out, inspect it and tidy it up — pinch or cut off any rotted or wiry roots and loosen the rootball with your fingers.

FIGURE 10-2:
You can set incoming plants in place one by one after you dig the holes.

WARNING

Never get a potted plant out of its pot by pulling or yanking on the leaves or stem, which will damage or break it! Always handle it by the roots.

6. **Put the plant into the hole and backfill.**

   Because you dug a hole a bit deeper than the root system, scrape some soil in at first and then carefully hold the plant while putting soil back into the hole. Gently tamp the soil down as you work — you don't want any air pockets or compaction. Work all the way around until the plant is well-surrounded by soil and sitting in the ground neither below the soil level nor above it. Don't bury the plant's *crown* (the place where the root system meets the main stem). Proceed carefully and methodically.

REMEMBER

   You can fill a planting hole with a mix of the native soil you've removed and some amendments or 100 percent native soil. Review the section, "Avoiding planting pitfalls," earlier in this chapter for information and discussion about this important matter.

TIP

   Option: You can toss a handful of *worm castings* into a planting hole, a nice idea if you judge that your native soil is pretty lousy (dry, low in organic matter). They contain tiny microbes that provide nutrients and help increase moisture retention for the roots. Buy this product in bags at a hardware, home-supply, or garden store.

7. **Create a basin for watering at the outer edge of the rootball.**

   This way, when you water it, the water runs down into the root system below instead of running off. Create the berm out of the soil or soil/amendments mix you already have on hand and firm it into place.

8. **Apply a layer of mulch.**

   Doing so helps hold in moisture and hopefully also keeps encroaching weeds at bay.

9. **Water the plant by filling the basin once, letting it sink in and repeating.**

   This gets rid of air pockets and hydrates the root system some more.

Clustering your plantings

Chances are, you're putting in more than one plant at a time. When you do that, *clustering* (see Figure 10-3) is a good idea, which is when you install several plants at the same time, on the same day, in the same way, all close to each other. (You can add plants to a grouping later, but the downside is that they may not all be the same age or at the same stage of development, potentially complicating your care regimen. And returning to a planting area can be awkward as you try to work around the ones that are already established.)

TIP

Bearing in mind the future height and width of the flowers, herbs, succulents, or shrubs you're installing, place bigger and taller ones first and to the back of a bed or display and lower-growers and groundcovers in front, scooting yourself backward as you work. When they're all still young and new, they may all be of similar size, but down the line, the wisdom of such placement will be apparent because the taller-growing ones won't block or overwhelm smaller-size plants.

You may wonder whether you need to dig a planting hole for each plant or dig one big hole, bed, or trench, and put in several or many at once. The answer depends not only on how much time and energy you want to put in, but also on what you're planting. Keeping in mind their mature size, space new plants accordingly — that is, give each one elbow room. If digging out a big area is more convenient for you, go right ahead.

If the plants aren't bumping up against one another or intermingling today, eventually they will be. That's desirable because groups of plants not only look more natural and attractive, but they also block out weeds by shading intervening spaces, providing mutual protection. Close association also raises the immediate humidity and conserves soil moisture. In a word, clustering your plants is water-wise.

FIGURE 10-3: Grouping the same or similar plants simplifies care and can enhance their chances of thriving.

Source: www.swfwmd.state.fl.us/sites/

Grouping by water needs

In dry climates or areas that experience periods of drought, this principle — putting plants of similar water requirements together — is essential. Not only does it save time when watering, it saves water itself. Some forethought (when planning and shopping) really helps such schemes succeed:

>> **For a whole new bed or planting area:** Plan when shopping by researching plants with an eye to water-needs compatibility. For example, create an area devoted to succulents only or a culinary herbs corner.

>> **For an ongoing project:** Be practical and disciplined, not impulsive, when you're shopping for new plants to add to your landscape. Know what the conditions are in the spot(s) you're increasing or replacing plants in and how much space you have to work with, and then choose only suitable newcomers.

Find more details and ideas in Chapter 19.

Fertilizing Your Plants

Deploying fertilizer in home landscapes is ingrained in our culture and indeed, the gardening world, but I'm here to caution you. Low-water plants may not need to be fed. Here I examine this issue in greater detail.

Answering the question: To feed or not to feed?

Plants native to arid climates and their horticultural offspring and variations grow just fine in low-nutrient settings. They're accustomed to it.

Some research shows unneeded or overzealous fertilizing actually harms or at least suppresses the activity of soil microbes. Those soil microbes are helping to keep your plant roots and the soil they inhabit healthy and balanced.

Although some people fertilize to boost growth, inspiring dry-climate plant choices to grow faster can be counterproductive. Plentiful, lush growth is hard to sustain in low-water landscapes, plus it tends to be more appealing to pests.

Furthermore, fertilizer builds up in soil that isn't damp and runs off in soil that is kept damp — neither result is beneficial to the plants or good for the environment.

In short: you may skip fertilizer. You'll save money and time!

Understanding fertilizer and its use

You may feel you must provide at least some fertilizer to some of your plants, either because you really want and are willing and able to support some plants with lush growth, or you feel the plants are struggling and need a snack. (If you have an area of lawn, fertilizing turf grasses is a topic unto itself; check Chapter 3.) This brief section is for you.

Balanced fertilizers (see the nearby sidebar) so popular in other parts of the country aren't a good choice for low-water landscapes. They especially have too much phosphorus. The risk is that regular fertilizer will burn your plants' roots.

If you fertilize, only use formulations low in or lacking phosphorus, which may take some looking. The one exception: It's safe to use a balanced fertilizer on certain pot-grown plants (see Chapter 17).

Here is a very quick overview of fertilizer fundamentals. Fertilizers offer the following:

>> **Nitrogen (N):** For leaf and stem growth

>> **Phosphorus (P):** For root growth, but also for production of flowers, fruit, and seeds

>> **Potassium (K):** For general vigor and disease-resistance

Thus a 10-10-10 fertilizer, widely used in wetter climates, is called balanced because it contains all three macronutrients in proportion. If you must fertilize, I recommend something like 8-0-24 for a low-water landscape.

Knowing the best time to fertilize

Water-soluble garden fertilizers, by definition, are most effective when delivered along with water. Therefore you dose plants when watering. My advice is to be more gradual and conservative — deliver half the dose twice as often. It's easier on the plants.

As for the time of year, don't fertilize in fall or winter when growth is at its slowest or plants are dormant. Spring, when growth is ramping up, is best.

COMPARING ORGANIC AND INORGANIC FERTILIZERS

There are myths and misconceptions surrounding the two main kinds of plant fertilizers. Here I take a closer look at the facts of the matter; you can decide which kind you want to use after you're empowered with this information:

● **Organic fertilizers:** They're derived from natural sources such as rocks and minerals as well as living things such as plants and animals (including fish!). The passage of time — weathering and the action of soil microorganisms — helps them continue their natural decomposition process in your landscape. Thus their benefits as well as their inevitable breakdown are gradual.

- **Inorganic fertilizers:** Also called conventional or synthetic, these fertilizers are manmade and have been treated to act faster by being more soluble. They may be synthesized from petroleum products (and/or petroleum products are used to make them) or derived from minerals that have been treated with chemicals to make them more soluble.

Which to use? Your choice, taking into account your landscape's needs and your budget. Interesting to note: As far as plants are concerned, the nutrients are the same in either type.

Tending to Your Plants

Because plants are living things and because low-water regions can be challenging for many plants, even native plants, you must take good care of them. To be honest, maintaining your plants takes more time and effort at first. After your landscape is filled and has been growing for a couple of years — assuming your plant choices were practical — the work is less every year. Your enjoyment only grows! These sections discuss the critical mileposts in a plant's life in your landscape.

Taking care of them during the early days

Garden newcomers, no matter what type of plant they are, simply aren't water-wise right away. They need your help to get their feet under them, that is, to establish their root systems, which will sustain them in the years to come.

Watering is never more important than during the early days. Even though exact needs and water-delivery methods vary, you must water consistently and regularly until a plant is established. Don't get to the point where a plant wilts or droops or starts dropping buds or leaves. Don't let a plant go through extremes (cycles of drying and drenching). Don't skimp on water!

Mulching new plants really helps by holding in soil moisture and keeping weeds away. Replenish the mulch when it blows away, wears away, washes away, or breaks down. Chapter 15 discusses mulch in more detail.

How long will it be before your plants become lower-maintenance? Perennial flowers may take one or two years; shrubs and trees, two or three. Cacti and succulents tend to put on a growth spurt in their early days and then settle in and grow more slowly.

Training plants where you want them to grow

I once had an interesting conversation with a wonderfully talented indoor designer. We were standing in a home she had just painted and furnished for a client and I was admiring her work. The compatible colors, the handsome furniture, the varied décor — it was all so beautiful and interesting. So many different ingredients went into the composition and yet, it all worked together to make a space that was both comfortable and appealing. I was so impressed. But because I'm a plant person, I remarked, "No houseplants? No bouquets?"

She laughed. "Not a chance! Plants don't behave. You think you have a certain color of leaf or flower, and it turns out to be different. You think you have a certain profile or height, and the plant has other ideas! I could never work with plants!"

Plants definitely don't behave! When designing a landscape or outdoor space, and working with living things, matching your vision to reality is tricky because trying to get what you believe you want in terms of color combinations or the contrast between plant forms and their surroundings isn't easy.

My advice is, relax. Let plants do their thing. Unlike interior designers, outdoor designers can embrace variability and surprise. All that said, here are some useful management tips:

>> **Choose wisely from the start.** Find out how big or wide living elements are expected to get and seek matches between plants and spots.

>> **Consider light, both sources and amount.** The same plant grown in full sun or only morning sun will look different. Stems, flowering branches, and vines will lean toward the light. You can rotate potted plants on a patio or deck a quarter-turn every few days so they develop a balanced look, but you can't do that with in-ground ones. Cutting back or removing an adjacent plant can help let in needed light.

>> **Intervene to guide plants where you want them to grow.** You can train a climbing rose, flowering jasmine, or bougainvillea to cover a porch railing or gazebo by intervening and fastening exuberant stems to the support (use soft cloth so stems aren't abraded). Training stems when they're younger, greener, and flexible is easier; woody, older stems are stubborn and set in their ways!

>> **Trim and prune as needed.** Don't start cutting any time the spirit strikes, though. Make cuts — edit your plants — when they're growing well, generally in springtime, so they can recover. Colder weather can damage fall and winter cutting, and a simple cut can lead to a branch dieback. (More on pruning in the next section.)

Doing a lot of plant editing, which is time-consuming and annoying, is a sign that the plant isn't a good match for its spot.

Keeping your garden tidy

Patrolling your landscape from time to time isn't just fun, it's important. You'll notice things — plants that need your attention, weeds that should be pulled, problems that might be developing, and so on. You'll get ideas for tweaks and changes, so be attentive.

Here are some basic maintenance tasks that apply to low-water landscapes:

>> **Pruning:** Grab loppers, clippers, and perhaps a pruning saw and take out dead growth wherever you spot it. You can do this any time of the year because it does no harm; after all the branches or spent stalks are never going to come back to life. Remove rubbing or crossing branches in your shrubs and trees.

If a plant is starting to block a path or encroach an area where it shouldn't, you may cut it back. However, do this in spring when growth is strongest and the plant will recover best.

>> **Deadheading:** *Deadheading* means removing spent flowers. Some plants drop them on their own, but others don't or are slow to. The yard always looks better after a deadheading session. Plus, removing a faded flower cues the plant to make more flowers (rather than going to seed).

>> **Grooming:** Plants have seasonal cycles and keeping them neat may seem like fussy work, but taking out spent or unwanted growth clears the way for renewal/fresh new growth later.

>> **Dealing with dormant plants:** Many dryland plants slow down or appear to almost die back in the heat of summer; others do so in winter in response to cooler weather and shorter days. Either way, I advise clipping them back and getting rid of dead and bedraggled growth.

>> **Cleaning up debris:** Leaves and flower petals fall all the time if you're paying attention. They only need to be swept up and discarded if they're cluttering a rock garden or garden path, or if you have reason to think they're harboring pests.

Some trees litter like crazy, which can create a fairly daunting mess, not to mention their fallen leaves, flowers, or fruit can make a mess of, hide, or smother plants growing under them. If a broom won't do the job, try a shop vac (not a leaf blower, which just moves debris around). When done, you can dump the contents in your compost pile.

Dividing plants

There are good reasons to divide plants, principally perennials. Here's when to intervene and what to do:

>> **They're getting too big.** When a plant has been in place for a couple of seasons and is doing well, it outgrows the space you allotted. It may be crowding or running over other plants in its vicinity. Do the following:

1. **Wade in with a trowel or shovel.**

2. **Dig up the rootball.**

3. **Divide the plant into sections (each section should have a balance of topgrowth and roots).**

You don't have to save every last bit — some of this material can go to the compost pile. Then replant the pieces. Work quickly so the roots don't suffer stress while being exposed; get the pieces (the *divisions*) replanted quickly. If you don't have space for them, put them in pots and give them away.

>> **They're no longer blooming as well as they used to.** Oftentimes as they grow, plants develop a hole or dead area in the middle (irises are a good example). They also stop blooming as well. Dig up everything (follow the instructions in the preceding bullet), discard the unproductive center, and replant the remaining pieces.

>> **They're generating offsets.** Many succulents don't bloom often or early in their lives, but when they finally do, they're done. The mother plant dies, but when you dig it up, you find several little offsets. Discard the old root system and replant these babies in new homes, in the same area or even in pots. If you don't intervene, they'll manage, but they'll form a tight, crowded clump because they grow right where they are.

Transplanting and relocating

When you decide to move a plant from where it is to a new spot is another type of landscape editing. You may elect to do this for a variety of reasons:

>> Because it's getting too big for its spot

>> Because it doesn't appear to be thriving in its spot

>> Because you think it would look better in its new location

Dryland plants don't love to be moved around, though. The process is stressful because you're disturbing them and their root systems. Pulling them out of the ground where they enjoy shelter and some moisture and exposing them to drying light and air can be hard on them.

WARNING

Don't move larger plants with established taproots. Chances are you won't be able to get the whole thing. It will break off and the plant can't repair this damage, so it will struggle and likely die.

For best transplanting results, heed the following instructions and advice:

>> **Undertake the project at a good time for the plant.** Don't do this when the weather is hot or a plant is in full bloom, times that are bound to cause the plant extra stress and reduce its chances of survival.

>> **Have a plan.** Know what's being taken out and exactly where you're moving it.

>> **Prep the new home ahead of time.** Water it until the ground is damp. Remove weeds, rocks, and debris, and dig the hole.

>> **Do the work at a low-stress time.** Cool evening or early morning, never the heat of the day, is the best time. Ideally the day is overcast and cool.

>> **Prep the plant.** Cut off flowering stems. Shorten foliage or branches by no more than a third. These actions allow the plant to suffer less and direct energy into root development in its new location.

>> **Work fast.** The less time the roots spend out of the ground, the better.

TIP

Drape a damp rag over a plant when it's out of the ground, especially over the exposed roots, to minimize water loss. Or temporarily place the roots in a bowl or bucket of water.

>> **Provide aftercare.** Water the plant in its new spot and mulch. Check on it and give more water in the coming days and weeks, until it's established.

Understanding and Managing Plant Needs

Being an attentive steward of the plants in your home landscape can be a great source of satisfaction and joy, but it has its challenging moments, too. Here's some guidance on the most common and typical plant–care issues.

Identifying signs of stress

A horticulture teacher once shared this excellent advice: "Listen to your plants; they're talking to you." Well, I agree they're able to communicate their needs or woes, if you only know how to discern that information. Here I share some common signs of common problems and suggest a few remedies.

Realize that plants, like people, are susceptible to cascading woes when weakened. One thing leads to another, for example, a thirsty plant can't easily fend off an insect pest. Step in and help when a plant is stressed; the following are common scenarios that should get your attention:

>> **Plants that are getting too much sun:** Scalding and sunburn is also a concern with plants. Leaves bleach out, turn brown, die, and fall off. Bark on branches or trunks split. Twigs drop leaves and die back.

TIP

Remove the damaged plant parts; they aren't going to recover or come back to life. Provide shade in some way, at minimum, in the hottest part of the day, noon till midafternoon — perhaps a big umbrella, pop-up canopy, awning, or a shade cloth or burlap draped over the plant. You may want to build a shade shelter, slatted so some light still reaches the plants but not as much. If the plant is next to a wall or fence that is reflecting bright light, perhaps you can repaint it a lighter color or white.

>> **Plants that are getting too little sun:** Not as common a problem in hot and dry landscapes, but it happens to lower-growing plants under trees. Warning signs include yellow or pale growth and stems or branches becoming *leggy* (elongated, stretched out, often with fewer leaves along their length) as they reach toward the light they crave.

TIP

If this happens, move the plants to a sunnier location. Prune or thin out the encroaching, shading plants.

>> **Plants suffering from pests or diseases:** This includes slow growth, especially when you're otherwise taking good care of the plant or the weather is good. Damage can come on suddenly and includes aborted flowers, buds, or fruit, distorted foliage, foliage that is wilted or marred by nibbling, color changes, and browning. Close inspection shows tiny pests congregating on leaf undersides or branch nodes, sooty mold or webs, and so on.

TIP

Don't delay; spring into action before whatever the problem is becomes worse and kills the plant or spreads to other plants in your yard. Begin with diagnosis. Better than a broad search online, consider taking a sample of a damaged plant part to a good local nursery, garden center, or botanic garden and asking for help and advice.

>> **Plants that have been overwatered:** Foliage loses its bright green color, turning dull, bluish or brown, or leaves go limp. Investigating the roots, you see signs of rot. Wet, warm soil does lead to rot and molds that attack the dryland plant's root system and can kill it.

TIP

Stop watering! Pull mulch and leaf litter away from the base of the plant.

>> **Plants that are thirsty:** Classic symptoms include dry, dead leaf tips, dry soil at the base, limp leaves, dropped leaves, and slow growth.

TIP

Water slowly and deeply, and then maintain a layer of mulch.

Watering to rescue a plant

Maybe you went away and the watering system failed or the neighbor didn't do a great job of looking after your plants. Maybe there's been a period of prolonged drought. Whatever the reason, before you decide that a plant is a goner, try these ideas:

>> **Pitiful potted plants:** Immediately move them to a shady or sheltered spot. Set their containers in a tray of water rather than dumping water from above; the growing medium will soak up the moisture gradually and as needed. Give the plants a couple of days, topping off the tray water now and then.

>> **Limp, drooping plants:** Water slowly at the base right by the roots during the morning or evening when evaporation is less of a factor. Mulch the root systems so the soil retains some of the needed hydration. Keep this up for several days, watching for signs of recovery.

>> **Suffering shrubs and trees:** Deep watering is the answer here; shallow drinks won't help. If you don't have one, create a basin under each afflicted plant (the outer edge of the basin can be at the outer edge of the foliage growth) and set a hose there on trickle for an hour or more. Then check to see how deeply it has soaked in by digging down (see Chapter 2). Stop-start watering may be appropriate (refer to Chapter 3).

TIP

An ingenious cylinder-shaped gadget called the "Root Quencher" recently appeared on the market and checks how deep water soaks in around trees. It has a telescoping design with three chambers, so it can probe to different soil depths. It can be hooked up to an automatic watering system, too!

Preventing problems

An ounce of prevention *is* worth a pound of cure. Of course you can't always anticipate or understand everything that's going on with the plants in your yard, but you can take sensible steps to keep them in good health. Here are the basics:

>> **Select the right plant and right place.** Do your homework and make a good match. (The plant lists in Part 2 provide important if brief information about

each plant's preferences; clarify again what conditions a plant needs at time of purchase.)

>> **Be nurturing.** See to the necessary watering, mulching, and grooming or pruning. (Refer to the earlier sections in this chapter, "Tending to Your Plants" and "Understanding and Managing Plant Needs," for more detailed discussion.)

>> **Pay attention.** Visit your plants often and observe them. Try sitting down to look at them from their level!

3

Leaving Your Lawn Behind

Come to terms with taking out an established lawn.

Uncover the simple, effective steps to remove your lawn.

Consider alternative ways to get rid of an unwanted lawn.

Look at the many drought-tolerant, groundcovering alternatives.

Find out what's involved in installing a meadow planting.

Discover the amazing improvements in artificial turf.

Examine the creative ways you can use rocks and gravel in your low-water landscape.

Chapter 11

Taking Out a Lawn

I f you turned to this chapter, you realize that your lawn's days are numbered!

The very idea of removing a lawn used to be shocking and is still, to some people, upsetting. But more and more people are coming around to understanding that lawns have had their day in the sun, so to speak, and now become problematic in today's world — particularly, of course, in areas where water is precious. A broad swathe of lush green turf is too costly and too time-consuming to maintain anymore, not to mention the harm the resources it consumes do to groundwater, soil, and various creatures. But limited water is the primary objection; water is more urgently needed for other things. In many places, high-maintenance lawns have become not only a luxury, but unconscionable. It's time to move on.

In some areas (Las Vegas has been in the news a lot in this regard), nowadays lawns are outright banned. They must be taken out; violators are fined.

Here I recommend digging out your lawn because it's fast and effective. I describe other options and explain what's involved; understand that these take longer and may require vigilance in case any resilient bits are missed and try to resurge. In any event, keep your eyes on the prize: Removing your lawn is the first or a major step to converting to water-wise gardening.

There are two basic kinds of traditional lawn grasses:

>> Ones with fine roots (easier to remove or kill)

>> Ones with fat, fleshy roots (called *stolons*). The stoloniferous ones are more tenacious and harder to get rid of. Classic examples are Bermuda grass, St. Augustine grass, and zoysia grass.

Which kind do you have? Dig up a piece, you'll find out quickly.

Eliminating Your Lawn: Yes or No?

As you stand on the precipice of this major landscaping decision, the following sections discuss some pros and cons to removing your yard.

Getting rid of your lawn, the pros

Removing your lawn has many benefits, and surveying them can help motivate you. Here are the advantages of doing so:

>> **Less water consumption:** No argument here!

>> **Improved carbon footprint:** Not only will your water consumption drop, but also the amount of fuel/electricity used for mowing, trimming, and weed-whacking will decrease. Fertilizer and weedkiller use will also go down or cease (producing those products also consumes fossil fuels).

LAWN ORDER: LAWN RULES AND LAWS

Before you remove your lawn, check your municipality's rules and regulations. You may not have a choice, and lawn removal is now mandated. Find out if there is a deadline (and if you miss it, what the consequences/fines are).

If you live in a development or planned community with a homeowners association, you may discover that a lawn — even if artificial — is required. (Consult Chapter 13.) Some residents have gotten around that requirement by reducing the size of their lawn while installing/increasing their water-wise landscaping beds. They keep everything neat and attractive so their neighbors can see and their association can agree that it's still a handsome yard.

>> **More free time:** Mowing and edging are time-consuming, constant chores, certainly when the grass is growing. Watering, depending on your method, can also be time-consuming.

>> **Money saved:** Your water bill will go down, and other expenses in this list will also go down or no longer be a budget item.

>> **Better appearance:** A lawn that can't be maintained at a lush, green level actually begins to look lousy and detracts from your landscape's overall attractiveness.

>> **Better resale value:** Homebuyers these days don't want to be on the hook for the expense, trouble, and other downsides involved in keeping up a lawn in a low-water environment.

>> **Happy, nonjudgmental neighbors:** In some neighborhoods, peer pressure isn't pretty. Maybe you've been reluctant to get rid of your lawn and tried to keep it going, for whatever reason . . . and others have made comments. In the interests of neighborhood harmony and just because you may get some practical advice or even help, consider being proactive by letting others around you know that your lawn is coming out soon.

>> **Adaptable yard:** Your yard can be used for a wide variety of options if you remove the grass. Relandscaped, you can turn it into something practical and useful, including perhaps devoting space to raising food for you and your household (flip to Chapter 9).

REMEMBER

Eliminating a *monoculture*, an area of one dominant plant, is also ecologically responsible. Most lawns are made up of (usually nonnative) grasses that not only don't contribute to the local ecosystem but in fact deprive native creatures (birds, insects/pollinators, soil organisms, and more) of food and shelter. People mow down lawn grass before it can get tall or flower and go to seed — thus lawns offer neither food nor shelter.

Removing your lawn, the cons

Taking out an area of lawn has some downsides, and you'll miss some things. I mention some new directions here:

>> **You, your household, and your pets lose open space.** You ought to be able to fill this need in other places, from parks to hiking trails.

>> **Landscape framing is gone.** A lawn provides balance in landscape between vertical and horizontal elements. But take heart, you can replace it with horizontal or mainly flat items, such as a patio, or fill in the area with a groundcover or succulent garden.

SAD TO SAY GOODBYE TO YOUR LAWN

Maybe you really like your lawn area and even if you understand why it must go, taking it out breaks your heart. You've enjoyed sitting or even lying down on it, or your dog likes to snooze there after the sun moves around the side of the house and he can enjoy a little shade on the soft surface.

Maybe, to use landscape-designer language, you've appreciated its horizontal-surface relief in your landscape or contrast with adjacent vertical plantings like shrubs and flowers.

Maybe you enjoy the sight of green, finding it peaceful and soothing.

Maybe you like mowing, or at least enjoy the smell of fresh-mown grass.

Maybe you grew up this way or moved to your dry-climate home from a wetter part of the country, and changing your assumptions and habits is difficult.

I'm not going to deny or sneer at those long-held thoughts and beliefs. But the times, the climate, and the available water, they are a-changing. Maybe it will help to take a clear-eyed look at what's at stake, that is, actual water use, maintenance products, and potential alternative uses.

Consider:

- **Water use:** Irrigating a lawn with *potable* (drinkable) water was never necessary, just convenient. Turf grasses and, indeed, many other landscape plants don't need to be irrigated with municipally treated water to survive. If you're still trying to keep some area of lawn going, you can at least take the burden off your water bill (or well). Among your other options are collected rainwater, gray water, and reclaimed/nonpotable water; refer to Chapter 2 for more details.

- **Fertilizer and weedkiller consumption:** Although the use of fertilizers and/or weedkillers (including the popular weed-and-feed products) on your lawn may have been minimal compared to the nearest golf course, habitual use of them is manifestly bad for the environment. Often much or all of it drains off, entering the groundwater or area waterways (ponds, streams, and reservoirs, if any nearby). Algal blooms, dead fish, and harm to tiny creatures in the ground and aquatic environments result. Time to let go of this risk, this damage, and this expense.

- **Alternatives that aren't a radical reworking of the yard:** You can still have a horizontal/flat area in your landscape if you wish. Maybe it will become a stone terrace or patio, or you can install a low-care groundcover. Maybe your dog can still get those nice outdoor naps. Consult Chapter 12.

- » **Lawns capture storm runoff.** Water runs off most concrete, pavement, and paving stones, whereas lawn grass soaks it up. You can implement alternatives in Chapter 15.

- » **A lawn's role as a buffer (or firebreak) is now gone.** Hardscape such as a patio, terrace, or deck — as well as other plants — can fill this role.

- » **The benefits of cooling the air, photosynthesizing to generate oxygen, and even perhaps trapping particulates and dust from the air are now lost.** To replace these losses, landscape the area with living plants (and not hardscape like a patio). See Chapter 12 for suggestions.

- » **A lawn's flatness lets in light to garden areas, whereas a replacement may not do as good a job.** If this factor turns out to be important in your home landscape, whatever fills the space vacated by the lawn must also be low-growing. Check out the plant-selection chapters in Part 2.

- » **Mowed lawn areas manage or prevent *natural succession*.** This term refers to the encroachment of taller plants, including spreading flowers, bushes, berry bushes, tree seedlings, and invasive plants. You can still keep unwanted or invading plants at bay by cutting, pruning, weed-whacking, or mowing.

- » **Lawns make great play space.** Where are you going to play catch or kick a soccer ball? At a park or nearby athletic fields.

Phasing in the Big Change

You can reduce the size of your lawn or reduce it in stages assuming tackling the project is your choice and not a mandate. This approach is less exhausting and less expensive, and it helps you, your yardwork routines, the look of your property, and your neighborhood adjust. For instance, take out a third of your lawn this year, relandscape or repurpose the area, and then do another third the following year, and so forth.

Here are a couple of things you can do, as you move toward transitioning from a water-consuming, manicured lawn to something new.

Reducing lawn care

As you consider lawn removal, you can experiment with fussing over it less to see if you can live with the consequences, that is, if it still looks okay (doesn't die or look patchy or unkempt). This strategy saves work and money.

Mow less frequently

Let the grass grow a little higher, say 3 to 4 inches (7.6 to 10.1 cm) tall before mowing; higher than that, and the mower may not be able to cope, even on its highest setting.

REMEMBER

The grass plants will be better able to photosynthesize and thus keep their color when you reduce how often you mow; they'll be able to grow deeper roots that will sustain them better through dry spells. Creatures, including beneficial ones such as earthworms and beetles that prey on garden insect pests will be better able to survive and participate in the *food web* (the interdependent ecosystem of plants and animals) that exists. Even better, baby/emerging weeds may be shaded out.

Phase out your lawn's dependence on additives

Reduce the amount and/or frequency of application of additives and then stop all lawn treatments and garden chemicals — no more pre-emergent herbicides (weedkillers), no more high-nitrogen fertilizer, no more weed-and-feed products used by you or a lawn service.

Weed-and-feed products are widely available, familiar to most homeowners and gardeners. *Weed-and-feed* refers to lawncare products that have both herbicides (weed killers) and fertilizer. They're designed to fertilize your lawn while also killing weeds in your grass, like dandelions and clovers.

REMEMBER

By decreasing and then stopping the use of chemicals, you'll spend less money (and reduce demand for these products) and less time working on the lawn. The harm these products do to the soil, water, and creatures will cease.

Reducing or halting watering

You may wish to wean your lawn of heavy water consumption. Even when you proceed gradually, holding back on irrigating is the beginning of the end.

Different lawn grasses behave differently; even ones adapted to hotter climates slow their growth in summer. When you cut back on irrigation, the results are perfectly predictable. Growth slows down (which means less mowing!). Then your lawn may lose its green sheen and turn brown.

TIP

A way to keep a lawn — possibly appropriate for your situation — is to replace a water-dependent traditional grass lawn with a drought-tolerant native species or blend (see Chapter 12).

Dead-lawn alert! If you slow and stop watering in late spring heading into summer, your lawn will turn brown and look dead. "What have I done?" you may ask yourself. If you lose your nerve because it looks so bad and resume watering, chances are good it will spring back to life (with a huge jump in your water consumption and water bill, however). If you can wait it out and fall rains come, amazingly, most lawns green up again. That is, your lawn didn't actually die — it just went dormant for a while.

But let me be blunt. If you want to kill your lawn or a section of it, totally withholding water will eventually do it.

Digging Up Your Lawn

Here is the best way to eradicate an unwanted lawn. Before I get to the steps, let me cover some important preliminaries.

The good news is, compared to many other landscape plants, lawn grasses are shallow-rooted. You may have plenty of space to clear, but at least you won't be digging deeply. Most all turf grasses' roots only extend into the earth 4 to 6 inches (10.1 to 15.2 cm). By the way, this is another reason they aren't appropriate for low-water landscaping. The toughest plants develop deeper roots than that!

Never, ever reach for a rototiller, which is absolutely the wrong tool for this job! Its tines chop up the lawn grass and roots, and new grass generates from root fragments. Quite the opposite of what you want to happen!

Knowing the right time

Tackling this project in summer is a bad idea, not just because you and the helpers will suffer in the heat, but also because the grass is likely to be dry and hard to dig up. Spring is perfect — when the ground has some moisture but isn't soggy. Fall might work, too, provided the soil isn't too hard and dry.

Doing it right — handy tools to help

As with any project, the right tools make the work go so much more efficiently. Faster. Easier on your back! Here are my recommendations:

>> **Wheelbarrow and/or tarp:** For collecting turf and/or rocks and debris.

>> **Bucket:** For collecting rocks you dig up. You can find a use for them elsewhere in your yard later.

RENTING HEAVY EQUIPMENT

When removing your lawn, you may want to consider renting heavy equipment to make the job easier, although you don't need to do so. These following items do make the work easier and faster than hand-digging, to be sure, though of course they add to the expense of the project:

- **Sod lifter:** Also referred to as a *sod cutter,* this wheeled piece of equipment (manually operated or motorized) slices through soil horizontally to cut grass at the roots. This creates strips of grass. Big sod lifters are the size of a riding mower, whereas smaller ones are more on the order of a hand-held tiller. You could rent this device or hire a local contractor or landscaping firm who does this sort of work and comes with good reviews and insurance.

  However, this option is only cost effective if you're removing an extensive lawn. If you decide to go ahead and to operate it yourself, familiarize yourself with its operation and heed all safety tips. Note that maneuvering one takes upper-body strength!

- **Earth-moving machine:** This is another helpful piece of equipment to consider if the project is large and daunting. It makes short work of clearing out cut sod.

>> **Trowel:** For (some) hands-and-knees digging.

>> **Half-moon edger (see Figure 11-1a):** This is the best tool for the first portion of this project! The blade cuts easily into the lawn grass, and stomping on the flat top pushes into the turf efficiently.

>> **Garden spade:** Flat-bladed is best because it not only helps lift turf pieces but it can also be used for cutting.

>> **Garden fork (see Figure 11-1b):** The sort of tool that people use for pitching leaf piles or hay. It does a great job at prying up cut turf.

>> **Rake and/or shop broom:** For running over the ground after it's exposed and smoothing the surface.

>> **Sturdy gloves:** For preventing blisters.

>> **Sturdy boots:** Stomping on a shovel or edger is much easier and more effective, not to mention less stressful on your feet.

REMEMBER

Sharp tools are important! If the edges of some tools are dull, the work will be slower and more frustrating. Save yourself unnecessary exertion; make sure everything has a sharp edge before you dig in. If you don't know how to sharpen gardening tools properly, don't have files, or don't want to, take your tools to a local sharpening service. It's never a big expense, and it's worth it!

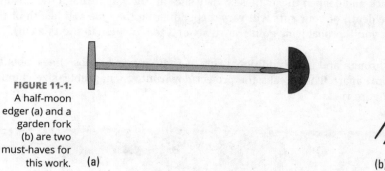

FIGURE 11-1:
A half-moon
edger (a) and a
garden fork
(b) are two
must-haves for
this work.

(a)

(b)

Doing the work, step by step

Many hands make light work. If the project size is daunting, you're not the fittest person, or you just want it to go more quickly, get help.

TIP

Tell and/or show your helpers the project area, so they know the scope; pick people who can work hard and stay on task; promise cold beer or lemonade.

On the workday, start early, and take a break in the hottest part of the day. Provide sunscreen to everyone. Explain and/or demonstrate the process before starting. Assign tasks so the work goes like an assembly-line: for example, one cutter, one peeler-and-shaker, one haul-awayer. The following sections break down the process step by step.

Step 1: Prepare your yard

Slightly damp ground is easiest to work in. Either work the day after a good rain (if any!) or water the lawn the night before.

TIP

If you're only taking out a portion of a larger lawn, mark the boundaries before you start. Use one of those bright orange electrical cords or sprinkle a line of flour along the ground. (Avoid using spray paint due to its toxic fumes and ingredients.)

Step 2: Slice into sections

Using the shovel or half-moon edger, mark lines about a foot (0.3 m) apart — all the way across the entire lawn. Horizontal or vertical, it doesn't matter, but try to make them parallel.

Double back and deepen those lines so they slice all the way through the turf and roots. The depth of your cuts will vary, depending on the type and health of the grass, but you'll probably be going down about 4 to 6 inches (10.1 to 15.2 cm).

Go back through and make additional cuts at right angles to those lines, about a foot (0.3 m) apart. This breaks the project down into manageable-size chunks. Consult Figure 11-2a.

 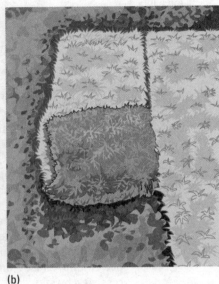

FIGURE 11-2: Cut the turf to divide it into manageable sections (a), and peel back the squares of lawn, roots, grass, and all (b).

(a)   (b)

(c) John Wiley & Sons, Inc.

WARNING

Chunks bigger than approximately 1 foot (0.3 m) square are harder to handle and can be surprisingly heavy.

You and your crew can work a row, or two rows at a time, if you prefer.

TIP

If you happen to be working adjacent to a sidewalk or driveway, when you get near it you may discover that it not only extends several inches into the ground but it's also tapered outward a few inches, thus encroaching on the area you're working in. If your digging tool encounters such an underground barrier, either angle your cuts to avoid it or get down on your hands and knees and use a trowel to pry out the turf along that border.

WARNING

Step 3: Peel and tilt

Using the garden fork, pry up the squares one by one. Peel them back (see Figure 11-2b) — they're like pieces of carpet — to confirm you dug deeply enough and are getting the majority of grass roots.

STEP 4: CLEAN OFF THE SOIL

Save the soil — the garden needs it. There's no point in discarding it, plus the squares would be heavy and unwieldy to discard.

Tilt each square and try to remove (and leave behind) as much soil as you can. To help remove the dirt, rake with your fingers and/or scrape with a trowel (refer to Figure 11-3a). After you get most of the soil, give it a few good shakes to remove the rest, which also makes each section lighter.

FIGURE 11-3:
Brush or scrape off as much soil as you can (a), and then cover the area (b).

(a)   (b)

(c) John Wiley & Sons, Inc.

TIP

Save the earthworms you encounter. They're garden friends, beneficial to soil, enriching it with their *castings* (waste) and aerating it. Temporarily put them in a bucket with a few handfuls of dirt to keep them cool and moist. Return them to the area at project's end, put them in your compost pile, or take them to another planting bed elsewhere on your property.

Step 5: Collect the pieces

Gather up all the grass squares. Don't toss the pieces on another part of the lawn, onto a garden bed, or into the driveway or sidewalk nearby. Doing so doubles your clean-up work. Instead discard finished squares on a tarp or in a wheelbarrow and dispose of them (see the nearby sidebar).

Step 6: Take care of finishing touches

When the area is cleared of lawn, rake the soil to get air in and break up remaining soil clumps. You may unearth a few more rocks; if so, toss them in a bucket. Then rake over the entire area neatly, leveling it if you can (just because doing so makes the area look nice and will help make whatever comes next look better).

Because you don't want weeds to invade, cover the cleared area (see Figure 11-3b) until you're ready to replant it, install the new patio or deck, or whatever your new low-water plans for the spot may be.

DISPOSING OF THE WASTE

When removing your lawn, the old grass comes up in sections. Just in the interests of sparing your local municipal-waste facility or landfill, the last thing you should do is bag it up and send it away in the trash. Here are other good options:

- **Use it on site, temporarily.** Flip it over so the grass is down and the roots are up and leave it on the cleared area for a week or two. This dries out the roots, allowing you to shake off a little more dirt. It also prevents weeds from moving into the cleared area until you're ready to replant or pave or whatever your new plan is for the spot.

- **Compost it.** Pile all the pieces in a stack or stacks in some out-of-the-way part of the yard and let everything break down over time, which can take months or even a year if conditions are quite dry.

- **Add it to your compost pile.** Don't add it all at once (so create a stack alongside), which would overwhelm the pile. Also toss the pieces in grass-side down to discourage opportunistic re-rooting within the pile.

- **Use it as a buffer or weed barrier in some other part of your landscape.** Place it grass-side down so it can't try to re-root. Line the edges of a flowerbed or vegetable patch to discourage weeds from encroaching. Even though it will break down after a while, in the meantime, it does a good job of keeping weeds at bay.

- **Relocate the lawn.** Maybe there's a scenario where you take all the pieces and put them in a new area elsewhere on your property. Or give or sell them to someone who wants to install a lawn area. Either way, two important things to bear in mind:

  - Prepare the new spot in advance so it can receive the pieces as soon as possible.

  - Don't let anything dry out! Dampen the prepared ground, lay down and fit into place the sod pieces, and then water again. Keep the area watered until the pieces establish in their new home, which could be several weeks.

Good covers include tarps, flattened cardboard boxes, rug remnants, or black plastic. Anchor the cover in place with rocks or boards. Alternatively, mulch if the material won't dry up and blow away.

Killing Your Lawn

Here are other, less labor-intensive but slower ways to get rid of your lawn. None of them require digging. I include remarks on their effectiveness (and, where applicable, risks), plus some tips.

WARNING

Unlike digging up the entire thing, these methods rely on not only killing the top-growth but also the roots below — but not by definition removing and disposing of them (though you can undertake that extra work). Possibly you'll miss some spots — often the edges — and the surviving remnants will sprout. Patrol the project for survivors and yank them out. Be patient and persistent.

Sheet mulching — smothering the lawn

This method is easy to do with a smaller lawn, and you certainly can do it with a larger one, too. The grass dies in over a period of eight or more weeks. Some people use black plastic, but the following approach works much better.

Sheet mulching actually preserves the soil structure. It transforms the area afterward with ornamental and/or edible landscaping. In other words, your evicted lawn actually sets the stage for its worthy replacements.

TIP

Do this in the fall so winter rains help keep the project damp, saving you the expense and trouble of watering. Follow these steps:

1. **Mow low.**

   Cut the grass as short as you can. Run the mower and then take a second pass with the weed-whacker. Save the clippings (see the next step).

2. **Cover the grass.**

   Use a layered approach (think lasagna mulching).

   1. Put down flattened pieces of cardboard, newspaper, or brown craft paper, which will block light and prevent growth.

   2. Overlap seams by 4 to 6 inches (10.1 to 15.2 cm).

   3. Follow with a thick layer of organic materials (6 inches, 15.2 cm): compost, bark mulch, dry grass clippings, or ideally a combination.

3. Soak the area.

If you don't get any rain, continue to keep it damp for a few months. As soon as the materials (yes, even the paper) break down, the old lawn should be dead and you have improved ground to plant in.

Solarizing — Cooking it to death

This method is called *solarizing* because it uses the light and heat of the sun to kill your lawn. Stick to the following steps:

1. Check your upcoming weather forecast and swing into action when you see a period of hot, sunny days coming up.

2. Mow low.

Cut the grass as short as you can. Maybe run the mower and then take a second pass with the weed-whacker (string trimmer).

3. Water the entire lawn, checking that moisture has soaked into the ground at least an inch or two (2.5 to 5 cm).

For ways to check, see Chapter 4.

4. Immediately cover the entire area with heavy clear plastic.

If you don't have one big-enough piece, go ahead and use several but do some overlapping to assure complete coverage.

The best clear plastic for this job is UV-stabilized and 2- to 4-mil thick.

5. Weigh down the plastic on the boundaries as well as here and there across the middle so it can't be disturbed or blown off.

You can use bricks, blocks, rocks, boards, potted plants, whatever you have that's heavy enough for the job.

The sun's heat will sweat or cook the lawn grass, killing it in about six to eight weeks. *Note:* This method also kills or drives out beneficial soil inhabitants such as microbes, earthworms, and little arthropods, but they do rebound quickly.

Encouraging it to die a natural death

Neglect and lack of water eventually kills any plant — as I'm sure you know. The lazy and slow way to kill your lawn, of course, is to stop caring for it altogether and wait. Don't water it. Don't care for it. Depending on what it's composed of and whether your area has any natural rainfall that keeps it going, the dying process can take a year or two.

Nudge its demise along by mowing the grass low (scalping it) often. This leverages another plant-care fact: without topgrowth or enough topgrowth to sustain them, roots will eventually perish.

Poisoning it

This method can be fast and effective. Weedkillers such as Round-up (glyphosate), Ortho Grass B Gone, Bonide Kleenup and others, where still legal, work. These products commonly are concentrated and must be delivered with water.

REMEMBER

When applying the poison, read and heed all label directions regarding timing, dosage, and safety. Using these materials can be risky to your health and the health of other creatures, including people, pets, and wildlife.

Protect your desirable plants from spray drift or you'll inadvertently kill them, too. Temporarily drape old blankets or upend cardboard boxes over them. Spray on a calm, windless day. Protect yourself by wearing heavy boots, long pants, a long-sleeved shirt, a hat, gloves, and even a mask and/or goggles. Then do laundry and take a hot, soapy shower after, just to be safe.

You may need to repeat applications to completely kill all the grass.

WARNING

Think hard before doing this method. Your lawn may have already done damage to your home landscape's soil, area groundwater, and the many creatures that inhabit the local ecosystem. Blasting it with an herbicide is adding insult to injury.

IN THIS CHAPTER

» **Pondering a new look**

» **Looking at the many drought-tolerant grasses**

» **Considering ornamental grasses**

» **Reviewing other low-growing plants**

» **Deciding on and installing a meadow area**

Chapter **12**

Replacing Grass with Low-Water Solutions

O ut with the old, in with the new! After your lawn is gone, or even while you're still contemplating or working on the removal project, you're ready to start looking at replacement options.

Whatever slots into the newly available space, it must consume less water. This chapter explores various options and approaches. I hope to inspire you to see this process all the way through and give your improved landscape a nice new *practical* look.

For some people, replacing a traditional lawn is more than just installing something appropriate to the realities of climate, weather, and soil. It's a paradigm shift. Chances are good that a lawn substitute, whatever it is, will look different than what you're accustomed to or have grown up believing in or liking!

And there's no downside to leaving your lawn, and all the maintenance, water, and other resources it consumed, behind. Allow a wilder, more natural, more colorful look. Embrace the seasonal and year-to-year changes and grow with it.

GETTING A BETTER GRASP OF GRASS JARGON

Here are some widely used terms that you'll run into wherever lawns are discussed and grasses and grass alternatives are sold.

- **Bunchgrass:** Also referred to as *clump-forming grass,* this term refers to a grass that grows as a distinct clump. Unlike sod-forming grasses, it doesn't have running roots. It gets bigger and bulkier over time but it won't spread out via offsets (like succulents) or roots (like sod).

- **Cool-season grass:** A species of grass that tolerates seasonally cold soil and cold winters.

- **Forbs:** Flowering herbaceous plants that are neither grasses nor sedges, but often grow among them — as in a meadow, field, or pasture. All produce flowers, but this particular term is used to distinguish those with conspicuous flowers.

- **Grass blends:** A mix (of different grasses or of several related ones) is more resilient when it comes to climate and weather variations. A mix is also smart when conditions vary in your yard (areas of sun and shade, for example). For instance, a bag may be labeled Turf Builder Grass Seed Sun and Shade Mix.

- **Lawn:** An area devoted to grass that is consistently mowed to remain short.

- **Lawn grass:** Also referred to as *sod-forming grass,* this grass uses running roots to spread out over time.

- **Ornamental grass:** A grass that's grown and valued for its attractiveness as a perennial plant (color as well as texture). As such, it may have interesting blades and attractive flowering spikes and reach a substantial size. These form clumps, which limits their spread and makes them useful in an ornamental garden.

- **Plugs:** A *plug,* also referred to as a *sprig,* is a small, individual grass plant. Plugs are grown and sold in quantity. Each one is generally about 4 inches (10.1 cm) long and 1 inch (2.5 cm) wide. A plug pack holds six; a plug tray holds three or four dozen little plants.

- **Rhizomes:** As pertaining to grasses, they're modified, thickened stems, below the grass's topgrowth. They travel underground, breaking the surface to send up new plants. Grasses expand their territory by rhizome growth.

- **Sedge:** A grasslike plant in the genus *Carex,* not properly a grass at all. Remember the saying: "Sedges have edges," whereas true grasses have node-segmented stems and blades.

- **Sod:** Pieces of turf, sold and installed in pieces or rolls.

- **Stolon:** Running roots, a bit like rhizomes, but aboveground, growing along the surface.

- **Turf, turfgrass:** Grass and its soil-holding roots, together, viewed/used as a whole.

- **Warm-season grass**: A species of grass that thrives in warmer regions and goes dormant in cooler weather (winter).

Examining Drought-Resistant Grasses

Being aware that you have choices other than traditional, water-sucking lawn grasses (including the ones so popular in wetter areas) is game-changing. A wide array of other grasses and grasslike plants are far better-suited to hot and dry regions.

TIP

You may be able to view alternative, more-appropriate grasses in parks, campuses, and even golf greens in your general vicinity. Many municipalities, schools, larger organizations and businesses (including country clubs) have already made the transition to drought-resistant landscaping. They're not just full of virtue, of course — these entities aim to save money and reduce maintenance.

This section looks at some of these alternatives. Here I examine their characteristics and why they're advantageous and then I mention some good ones for you to consider.

Recognizing advantages of these grasses

The alternative grasses I'm recommending have a lot going for them, specifically:

>> **They can get by with less water.** The main trait of drought-tolerant grasses is that they're adapted to low-water conditions. Their roots may quest deeper into the earth to sustain the plants and/or their root systems are better at holding moisture and enduring dry spells. It's no surprise, then, that some are native plants — I note which ones in the next section.

>> **They're lower maintenance.** Because they're adapted to less water, drought-tolerant grasses are less work. They respond well to efficient watering systems and practices (such as in-ground systems and deep, less-frequent watering). Refer to Chapters 3 and 5 for more about those systems. Often slower-growing, they don't have to be mowed as often.

>> **They're widely available.** Although it wasn't always true, it is now. Any well-stocked garden center, nursery, or native-plant outlet should stock drought-tolerant grasses — bags of seed, small plants/plugs, or sod.

>> **They complement dry and low-water landscaping plants.** Not just in their low-water needs, but also in their appearance. Their shades of green aren't as luminous or loud as the greens of Northern or East Coast lawns; their softer hues and their textures blend in better with other drought-tolerant plants.

Identifying top drought-resistant grasses

The following is a rundown of common grasses used for lawns that tolerate varying degrees of drought. Consider this section a launchpad for your selection process; for those that sound good to you, do more research before committing. Find out if a grass can be grown well in your region and your particular yard's conditions. Ask at local nurseries and ag-supply stores; query other gardeners; inquire at your nearest Cooperative Extension Service office. You then can make an informed match.

Grasses sold for use in lawns fall into these two main categories:

>> Cool-season grasses

>> Warm-season grasses

Don't automatically assume, just because you aim to conserve water, that a warm-season one is by definition drought-tolerant. These sections examine the two types.

WARNING

Don't mix the two types. The results are bound to have a patchy, uneven look.

Cool-season grasses

Cool-season grasses grow best when temperatures are between 60 and 75 degrees F (15 and 24 degrees C), and can withstand cold winters. These grasses can start fresh growth with fall rains, flower in spring, and go dormant in the heat of summer unless you're able to give them occasional water, which will extend or reactivate their growth.

Here are some top choices:

>> **Fine or "hard" fescues.** *Festuca* varieties. Fine texture. Fast germination and establishment; does well in less-than-ideal growing conditions, tolerates shade. Newer varieties offer insect-pest resistance. Often you'll see sheep

fescue, *F. ovina*, which is inexpensive. Better — more durable — especially for lawn areas in the arid West, is "Durar hard fescue," *F. brevipila* (older names include *F. duriuscula* and *F. ovina duriuscula*; as with other plants these days, botanical research is leading to updates/changes in scientific names).

>> **Kentucky bluegrass,** *Poa pratensis*. Fine texture, rich green color when fertilized. Spreading habit. Many disease-resistant varieties are available.

>> **Turf-type tall fescue,** *Festuca arudinacea* (or, more-current name, *Schedonorus arundinaceus*). Fast, upright, clumping growth. Nice green blades. Can form especially deep roots, helping it to weather prolonged dry spells.

>> **Western wheatgrass,** *Pascopyrum smithii*. Native, but can be aggressive if it gets extra moisture. Silvery blue-green leaves.

TIP

Western wheatgrass is worth considering if you want to cut back on or stop mowing because it only grows 1 to 3 feet (0.3 to 0.9 cm) tall.

Warm-season grasses

Warm–season grasses are in active growth when temperatures are above 80 degrees F (27 degrees C). Thus they look best starting in spring, flower in mid– to late summer, and tend to go dormant for winter. They like some heat during their growing season and can tolerate some winter cold.

Check out these types:

>> **Bahia grass,** *Paspalum notatum*. Naturally low-growing. Not as attractive as some other warm-season grasses because of its coarse texture. Can grow in some shade. Excellent heat- and drought-resistance.

>> **Bermuda grass,** *Cynodon dactylon*. May be coarse-textured or fine-textured, depending on the variety. Spreads quickly and is able to crowd out weeds. Needs frequent, close mowing to look good.

TIP

Common varieties of Bermuda grass can be grown from seed, but more recent (improved) hybrids are only available as plugs or sod. They aren't as weedy because they don't set seed.

>> **Blue grama,** *Bouteloua gracilis*. Native to the Great Plains. Fine-textured with flat, gray-green blades.

>> **Buffalo grass,** *Bouteloua dactyloides*. Native to the Great Plains. Fine-textured. Curled, gray-green blades. Requires little mowing. Can survive on as little as an inch (2.5 cm) of water per month.

TIP

Blue grama and buffalo grass, both natives, are often sold mixed together as a drought-tolerant blend.

NOT GRASS — BUT CLOSE ENOUGH?

Here are some plants that aren't grasses, but they have a grassy appearance or can create a lawn-ish look, tolerate dry spells, and thus perhaps fill a similar role:

- **California gray rush,** *Juncus patens*. Fine-textured, leafless evergreen stems of gray-green to gray-blue. Typically gets 18 to 24 inches (45.7 to 61 cm) high and wide.

- **Creeping thyme,** *Thymus spp.* The trick is installing it (do soil preparation and plant loads of little plugs), but after it's established, it forms a fragrant, low-care carpet that tolerates foot traffic. Lots of lavender-hued flowers change its look for part of the growing season.

- **Dichondra,** *Dichondra spp.* A morning glory relative, actually. Thick with little roundish leaves, it spreads via creeping stems that root at the nodes. It only gets 1 to 3 inches (2.5 to 7.6 cm) high. It was once very popular as a lawn replacement in hot, dry Southern California, but it fell from grace because it's hard to keep it looking nice (it must have full sun and excellent drainage) and, in some settings, it becomes invasive.

- **Dutch white clover,** *Trifolium repens*. It doesn't need mowing and, as a member of the bean (legume) family, it can improve your soil by fixing nitrogen. Butterflies and bees like it.

- **Foothill sedge,** *Carex tumulicola*. Native to California. A clump-former that gets only 12 to 24 inches (30.5 to 61 cm) high and wide, it can cover ground in your yard around garden beds, near walkways, or even in shady spots.

Many other plants, including low-growing succulents, can serve — consult Chapter 7.

>> **St. Augustine,** *Stenotaphrum secundatum*. Coarse-textured but tough. Planted from sod or plugs. Seek out the newer varieties with improved pest- and disease-resistance. Tolerates shade.

>> **Zoysia grass,** *Zoysia* species. Stiff blades, fine or coarse, depending on the variety. Slow-growing but very tough once established. Planted from sod or plugs. Goes dormant in winter.

Knowing when to shop

As you ponder your new–lawn installation, it's important for the success of the project that you proceed at the right time so that the plants have the best chance of prospering. The hottest months of summer are obviously not ideal because keeping a new planting damp isn't easy. Here are some guidelines:

REMEMBER

» **If you're buying seed:** You can purchase bags of grass seed or seed blends anytime you see them and then save them until planting time. Store them in a cool, dark, humidity-free place so they don't germinate or dry out.

Most bags of grass seed, if stored properly, keep fresh for two or three years.

» **If you're buying plugs or plants:** Begin by deciding what you want and then find and contact a local source. Perhaps the supplier grows to order and you need to arrange this (reserve) and pay a deposit. They'll also be able to advise you or answer your questions about timing and planting techniques.

» **If you're buying sod:** Same advice about conversing with a supplier about the details, with the added warning that sod dries out easily.

Grasses and grasslike plants always grow best — fastest and strongest — when planting time aligns with their growing season. That's the case whether you sow grass seed, plant plugs or individual plants, or purchase and roll out new sod.

TIP

Therefore, sow or plant cool-season grasses in the fall (or winter) when the soil and air is cooler, and sow or plant warm-season ones in spring. Here's what to do and when (good timing and good care is paramount!):

» **For seed:** Sow early in spring or in autumn, to avoid hot days and dry soil conditions that threaten the survival and growth of seedlings. The bag has directions about how and how much to sow as well as proper techniques and care.

» **For plugs and small plants:** They need to be guarded from drying out before they go in the ground; plan to plant them shortly after (within days of) bringing them home. If you must delay, hold them in a shaded spot and keep them hydrated.

» **For sod:** Your best bet is to discuss planting day with your supplier and arrange for a delivery the night before or the day you plant.

REMEMBER

No baby plant (of any kind!) ever likes to be planted in stressful conditions, so adjust your planting date depending on the weather. Stressful conditions include cold or frozen ground, periods of heavy rainfall, times of prolonged drought and, of course, the heat of midsummer.

Planting drought-resistant grasses

If you have a grass or grasses in mind and know when to plant, the following identifies what you need to know to actually get them in the ground:

>> **Prepare the site.** Don't get plants first and prepare second. Clear and clean up the spot, including adding organic-matter amendments if needed. Then plant as soon as possible after. Chapter 4 has details and instructions regarding site preparation and soil improvement.

>> **Work quickly.** Minimize the time the plants are exposed; get them in the ground.

>> **Provide aftercare.** This varies depending on what you planted; get specific advice from wherever you purchased. In general terms, mulch and irrigate new arrivals consistently until they're established, especially if there is no rain. Seeds need at least ten days or more of consistent dampness in order to germinate well.

SOWING DROUGHT-TOLERANT GRASS SEED

Sowing grass seed is the easiest and most affordable way to put in a new lawn area. You can undertake the endeavor in late fall, early spring, and maybe early summer, depending on where you live and your climate. To find out which is best, ask at the place where you bought the seed and/or follow the example of other gardeners in your area.

Remember: Just because you've chosen a drought-tolerant type or mix doesn't mean it doesn't need water to get going. Neglect will be fatal. Grass seed must be watered at the start, and to help it through dry spells in its first year until it becomes established and strong. Fortunately, the plants will become much more self-sufficient in the years to come.

Keep these tips in mind if you're sowing grass seed:

• **Determine how much seed you need.** Measure the dimensions of the area you wish to cover and then consult the bag, which has specifics. If the math is beyond you, take the dimensions to where you want to purchase seed and ask a staffer for help.

• **Prepare the planting area.** Clear away any covering (tarp, mulch), and loosen the soil. Use a garden fork. Optional: This is also the time to add amendments such as organic matter. Then level it with a rake.

- **Sow according to the rates recommended on the seed bag.** Work horizontally and then go back and sow in a vertical pattern. Yes, you can do this by hand if you're neat and careful and the area isn't large. Alternatively, borrow or rent a mechanical lawn spreader or lawn roller.

  Tip: Here's a nifty way to make sure you plant the seeds evenly: Divide the area into three or four somewhat equal areas by drawing lines with a stick. Then divide the seeds you purchased into three or four piles, and then make sure you plant no more and no less than one pile per each marked area.

- **Cover the seeds lightly.** Grass seed needs a little light to germinate. A thin layer of soil, mulch, or straw does the trick. Stay away from hay, which contains weed seeds.

- **Water lightly and evenly.** The object is just to dampen the area. A sprinkler works great; set the spray to light so water doesn't dislodge the seeds. (If planting in sandy or fast-draining soil, set the sprinklers to come on briefly — a few minutes — four or five times a day.) Keep the area moist until the seeds sprout and get growing — you'll probably need to water daily. This may take 10 to 14 days, at least.

Catching the Eye with Ornamental Grasses

Ornamental grasses were once a hot new trend in landscaping, but now they're commonplace and widely available, having earned many people's admiration. Thanks not only to that initial burst of popularity but because they've endeared themselves to gardeners in many places, you can now shop from a huge and varied selection. Blue-hued ones, rusty red ones, coppery-hued ones, tall ones, short ones, you name it.

Ornamental grasses are fundamentally different from regular lawn grass, and not just because you let them grow tall and even produce flowering stalks (you don't mow them down to a few inches, I mean). Ornamental grasses are *bunchgrasses*, which means they stay in place but will, of course, become bulkier over time. Most people are used to the clump-forming look of these plants, but if you're still feeling skeptical, just think of them as perennials rather than fixating on the word "grass."

Working with their look

To get coverage over a broad area, to line a walkway, or to landscape an embankment or slope, you can plant many of them in close proximity. Doing so won't replace a traditional lawn, but it's a nifty look nonetheless. Otherwise, ornamental grasses adapt well to life in mixed beds with all sorts of other plants, from shrubs to flowering perennials and succulents.

Emerging from or covering the clump, stalks bearing grass flowers may appear. Sometimes that doesn't happen if your growing season is too short to allow flowering or when the plant is young. However these grasses certainly grab attention with their colors and perhaps airy or dramatic feathery forms.

Another thing ornamental grasses may do is undergo foliage color changes. Early growth may be reddish or purplish and then segue to a shade of green. Cooler fall and winter weather can cause the blades to turn gold, red, or a combination of autumnal hues. The same grass grown in one locale may have blue-green leaves and bright-green ones in another; it's a matter of soil type, available moisture, and/or temperature.

WARNING

Because the grasses termed "ornamental grasses" are bunchgrasses and thus form nice individual clumps, you may assume that they don't spread and aren't invasive. That's mostly true. However, where the growing season is long enough to permit production of flower stalks or plumes, seeds can be a problem. The wind picks up this bounty and spreads it around the area.

TIP

When you feel a clump, row, or area of ornamental grasses is getting too tall or exceeding its allotted space, or you just want a neater look, cut back. Established plants tolerate pretty drastic trimming, down to stubble a few inches high if you so wish. The plants will regenerate. Early spring is ideal because growth is just ramping up and the plants are most resilient and full of energy then, but fall is fine, too.

Considering the pros and cons

Here are the pros to ornamental grasses:

>> They're reliably perennial, which means they last for years. In some places, growth slows, halts, or dies back in winter.

>> They don't sprawl. They're manageable. They stay where you plant them.

>> They offer a range of colors, including fall-foliage changes and colorful flower spikes or plumes.

>> They contribute interest and drama when they flower, which is in the fall when otherwise the garden may not have a lot of blooms or color.

>> If left tall (not trimmed back), they provide shelter for birds and other wildlife, including in the winter months.

Meanwhile, here are the cons:

>> Unlike lawns, they can't take foot traffic. They're too bulky (clump-forming mounds).

>> The flower plumes that typically appear in autumn can add a lot of height to the plants, which may block other plants or sights in your home landscape.

>> Plants flop over if the soil is too rich or if you fertilize. (Like any floppy plant, staking can remedy the situation.)

>> The plumes, if your growing season is long enough for the seeds to ripen, can send forth lots of seeds on the wind, which can lead to unwanted seedlings. (Simple enough to prevent, though; snip off the plumes. Use them for bouquets.)

Eyeing top drought-tolerant choices

Not all ornamental grasses are drought-tolerant. Here's a selection of ones that are (just remember when a plant is young and new to your landscape, it requires regular watering until its root system gets established):

>> **Blue grama grass,** *Bouteloua gracilis.* Narrow, gray-green foliage. Mature plant size is 1 to 2 feet (0.3 to 0.6 m); purple-tinged flowers on stalks whose height is 16 to 20 inches (40.6 to 50.8 cm).

>> **California fescue,** *Festuca californica.* Slender green to blue-green leaves. Mature plant size is 2 to 4 feet (0.6 to 1.2 m) high and somewhat narrower in width; purple-hued flowers on 4-foot (1.2-m) stalks.

>> **Deer grass,** *Muhlenbergia rigens.* Slim, bright-green to silver-green leaves. Mature plant size is about 3 feet (0.9 m) tall and wide; yellow to purple flower stalks about 5 feet (1.5 m) high.

>> **Melic grass,** *Melica spp.* Stiff, flat, narrow blades of blue to blue-green. In most garden species, mature plant size varies from 1 to 4 feet (0.6 to 1.2 m) high and wide. Flower plumes are in scale and ornamental, varying from tan to reddish; birds love this grass.

>> **Mendocino reed grass,** *Calamagrostis foliosa.* Stiff, tidy gray-green to blue-green foliage, tinged purple in cooler weather. Mature plant size is 1 foot (0.3 m) high and 2 feet (0.6 m) wide; flowering spikes are about 1 foot (0.3 m) high, start out russet or purple and age to tan.

>> **Muhly grass,** *Muhlenbergia spp.* Green foliage. Mature plant size is typically 2 to 4 feet (0.6 to 1.2 m) tall and wide; flowering plumes rise 1 foot (0.3 m) or so above the clump, creating a spectacular flurry of pink to purple hues.

>> **New Zealand wind grass,** *Anemanthele lessoniana.* What gorgeous foliage! Graceful, threadlike leaves in shades of green transform in autumn's cooler weather to copper, gold, and bronze. Mature plant size is 3 feet (0.9 m) tall and wide; rosy flowers are in scale.

» **Purple needlegrass,** *Stipa pulchra.* Hairy, long green to gray-green leaves. Mature plant size is 1 to 3 feet (0.3 to 0.9 m) tall and somewhat less wide; flowers are carried on 2- to 4-foot (0.6- to 1.2-m) stems and begin purple before fading to tan.

» **Sheep fescues,** *Festuca ovina* varieties. Densely tufted mounds, generally 1 feet (0.3 m) high and wide, relatively slow-growing. Depending on where you live, you may find for sale Idaho fescue, *F. idahoensis,* Arizona fescue, *F. arizonica,* and others.

Some of these grasses also appear in the section, "Identifying top drought-resistant grasses," earlier in this chapter. To make them appear more ornamental, let them grow to full size and flower, rather than cutting or mowing them to manage their size.

WARNING

The one to avoid, even though it's wonderfully drought-tolerant and easy to grow, is pampas grass, *Cortaderia selloana.* It was originally introduced as a garden plant but has proven to be extremely invasive. In fact, many places have banned its sale. It forms huge clumps (12 to 15 feet, 3.6 to 4.6 m, high and wide) of narrow, razor-sharp-edged leaves. The unfriendly foliage is joined in summer by towering white plumes full of seeds! There's a pink-flowered variety around, but don't be tempted. To be fair, the plant is *dioecious,* meaning the males and females are separate plants. If you had a female plant, you'd have a great show so long as there were no males in the vicinity to help her produce seed.

TIP

If you want colorful-leaved ornamental grasses, you have many choices, including cultivars developed by the horticultural industry. Shop around to notice the beautiful variety!

LAWN-REPLACEMENT PROJECTS THAT AREN'T PLANTS

No rule says that after you take out your lawn more plants must go in. Here's a quick rundown of some *hardscape* (man-made landscaping features) ideas to consider. They're not only low water, they're also no water!

Note that the fact that the newly cleared area is probably flat and open turns out to be conducive to these types of projects. Normally, in other situations, you'd be advised to clear and flatten out the spot beforehand anyway. (By the way, if you need DIY instructions, consult the second edition of *Landscaping For Dummies* [John Wiley & Sons, Inc.], which contains several detailed chapters on preparation and installation of common backyard hardscape projects.)

Be forewarned, though, that any of the following may hold heat, raising the temperature of your outdoor space somewhat, particularly in hot, sunny weather and during the heat of summer (concrete and gravel, in particular, absorb sunlight and reflect it back):

- **Patio or terrace:** Whether concrete, brick, or flagstone, these can be a wonderful and practical addition to a home landscape. Lay out and install one yourself or call an experienced and recommended contractor. After it's installed, you'll find that you and other family and friends are more drawn to spending time outdoors.

- **Deck:** Decks are wonderful outdoor-living spaces, not only because they allow for lounging or dining but also because they can be designed in ways that elevate you above the ground or attach to the house, giving a whole new perspective on your yard. To integrate them, perhaps build around a large established tree or planted bed or, at least, decorate it with potted plants.

- **Gravel:** Refer to the information and ideas in Chapter 14.

Another option is installing a pool — a swimming, wading, or lap pool, or even a water garden. These ideas aren't as crazy or wrong as they may sound because after the initial filling, a water feature is mostly set, only needing occasional topping off due to evaporation, plus some seasonal maintenance. Read all about it in Chapter 18.

Considering Other Low-Growing Plants

After the lawn is gone, because you want to cultivate low, spreading growth in that area, you may turn your attention to groundcovers and other turf alternatives as a low-water, low-maintenance solution. Popular, practical choices include many succulents (especially stonecrop or trailing sedums) and carpeting herbs like thyme, monardella, and rosemary. Additionally, certain penstemons, salvias, daisy-like plants, and arctostaphylos are low-growers.

Because most of these alternatives don't grow as quickly or thickly as turf grasses, adjust your expectations and plans to a different, looser look. That said, they'll eventually provide excellent, even weed-suppressing growth if planted closely.

TIP

Unlike turf grasses, unfortunately groundcovers don't appreciate becoming the site of a kiddie soccer game, a place to sit down, or even an area to walk across to get from one part of the yard to another. You can install a path or stepping stones or set a bench in a lawn-replacement planting.

At any rate, rather than offering a long list of plants here — you can find lists in Chapters 6 and 7 — I instead offer some important, helpful tips:

>> **Make sure you select for sun.** The former home of a lawn is a sunny spot. Nurseries offer groundcovering plants for sun as well as shade; bypass the shade section.

>> **Eyeball plant names and descriptions, focusing on lower-growing selections.** You're looking for words like *trailing, prostate, creeping, carpeting,* even *dwarf.*

>> **Don't overlook shrubs.** Plants that are technically shrubs, forming a woody base and sending forth branches over the years, come in low-lying, thick-growing options. The operative words here are *creeping* (as in "creeping juniper") and *carpeting* (as in Flower Carpet roses).

>> **Plant closely.** How closely depends on what you choose and the size of the plants you bring home. Ask the nursery staff about their expected mature spread and how closely to plant them for groundcover use — and you're off and running.

>> **Have a watering plan.** Putting in lots of small plants close together calls for regular watering, at least until they get established. If you're landscaping a smaller area, consider soaker hoses or other options (see Chapter 3). Larger areas may need in-ground irrigation installed first (refer to Chapter 5).

>> **Mulch!** Mulch is a newly landscaped area's friend and this is never truer than with larger or mass plantings. Conserve soil moisture and try to keep weeds out.

Going Wild with a Meadow Garden

A popular alternative to a traditional, resource-sucking lawn is a meadow or, more properly, a meadow bed. These plantings use native grasses and prairie-type plants or native flowers, both annual and perennial.

Certain wildflower (pre-made) mixes composed of low-growing plants can also be used for meadowlike lawns. Meadow lawns are less formal-looking than most grass lawns but can be walked on or played on and have a wild beauty all their own.

REMEMBER

Even though meadow plants are taller, occasional mowing or trimming-back of your meadow will be in your future.

TIP

If someone else a street over has a meadow area in their yard, stop by, ask for a tour, and learn from their experiences!

Make no mistake: A meadow garden is still gardening. You can't just sow or plant meadow flowers and grasses, and then walk away and expect the results to prosper or stay looking the same. That said, doing this in your yard is no more difficult than installing and caring for other planting projects. The following sections explain how to make your meadow dreams come true.

REMEMBER

A compelling reason to do this is to create habitat for and offer sanctuary to pollinators, birds, and other ecosystem inhabitants. Chapter 11 mentions that a regular lawn doesn't do any such thing.

WHAT WILL THE NEIGHBORS THINK?

Despite their benefits and potential beauty, meadow gardens and beds remain controversial in some communities. To the untrained eye or the eye accustomed to traditional lawn grass or even beds of gravel punctuated by succulents, these plantings aren't welcome.

This prejudice isn't totally unfair. A meadow area that isn't matured (maybe its second year will be a peak show) or one that isn't well-maintained can indeed look like a jumble of weeds.

Meadows may be prohibited or frowned upon in densely populated neighborhoods. In planned communities with a homeowners association (HOA), they may be outright banned or at least regulated. Find out whether your area allows meadow gardens. You've probably heard stories of defiant or distressed meadow gardeners being fined or forced to mow it all down.

Sometimes they're prohibited in the front yard, and you can shift your plans to another part of your property. Certainly you ought to be able to landscape however you please in the back or along the sides of your home.

Assuming you get the green light and go ahead with the project, take good care of the area. Let your neighbors see you out there — that will help them understand it's a tended garden space, not a weed patch!

Getting started on your meadow area

When you're ready to begin, attend to these practical measures:

>> **Pick a spot.** Full sun and out in the open tends to be ideal. Repurpose some or all of your former lawn area, dress up a curb strip, or create a border along a driveway or walkway or along the front of your house.

>> **Define the area.** If your meadow garden has boundaries — edgings of stones, wood, fencing of some kind, even a buffer like a gravel moat — the whole thing looks tidier and planned, and skeptics will better receive it. Defining the area also makes the project more manageable for you.

>> **Put up an attractive and informative sign.** Order a customized one on www.etsy.com, saying something like "Teri's Meadow, Butterflies Welcome!," "Mi Pequeño Prado," "Habitat Restoration Project," "Pollinator-Friendly Garden," or "Low-Water Wildflowers."

>> **Do your homework.** Read and ponder this section's basic information. Visit nurseries and do some research online about meadow plants and design approaches.

>> **Figure out approximately how many plants you'll need.** The first step is measuring the site and calculating the area (length × width). Maybe make a sketch. Because you want thicker growth in a meadow scheme, plan for plants to be installed close together. Knowing their projected size will guide you.

Alternatively, armed with the site dimensions, go to the nursery and enlist the help of a staffer. You can always add more plants if you didn't buy enough on the first trip!

Preparing the site and soil

A meadow area or bed is a gardening project, not a toss-in-the-plants-and-go affair. Get the spot ready beforehand to boost success by doing the following:

>> **Evict weeds.** Weeds are aggressors and can overwhelm and shade out little growing meadow plants. Remove them by the roots whenever possible. You might not get all of them but give this a good effort — you'll save annoyance and work down the line.

TIP

If the area is full of weeds now or in the recent past, hit the pause button and beat back the problem first. Don't till, which brings both weed seeds and plant and root fragments to the surface where they can germinate and grow. You have options:

- Tarp or solarize the area (see Chapter 11 for instructions).

- Let a crop of weeds germinate, then mow them down (many are annuals and won't get tall enough to reseed; you're basically outsmarting them with this method!).

>> **Consider some soil improvement.** Even when you intend to install lots of native plants, the native soil in your yard may not be welcoming to seeds or seedlings. Low-water plants do need some tough love (that is, you don't want to pamper them with rich soil that leads to lush — and thirsty — growth), but a little soil improvement won't hurt in this case, particularly if your soil is poor or gritty. Improve it before planting anything by digging in organic matter such as compost, bagged dehydrated cow manure, and/or good topsoil. See Chapter 4 for more information.

>> **Install a watering system or have a watering plan.** Among your options are in-ground irrigation, soaker hoses, and watering gadgets as I describe in Chapters 3 and 5. Your water needs will be dictated by what sorts of plants you choose — really drought-tolerant plants won't require much. But, as ever, seeds and baby plants always do. So have a plan.

>> **Protect the prepared spot.** A cleared area, with or without some soil improvement, is an open invitation to opportunistic weeds. They can come in from seemingly nowhere, on a breeze, or from under the ground if you missed root fragments.

Even if the gap between getting the spot ready and planting time is only a couple of days, cover it! Tarp it, cover it with black plastic, spread flattened cardboard or old carpets over the area, whatever it takes. Anchor the edges. Don't remove the cover until planting day.

Choosing appropriate plants

Picking plants for your meadow display is fun. Your best bet is to pay a visit to a nursery that specializes in pot-grown native and meadow plants so the staff can advise you and answer your questions. Otherwise, nose around a more-general nursery and look for ideas.

REMEMBER

Local and regional plants are well-adapted and also offer food and shelter to area pollinators. Planting these boosts two goals: adding garden beauty and nurturing the environment.

Here are my best shopping tips:

>> **Be selective.** Choose wildflowers and native grasses. Planting a variety assures that you'll always be something to admire.

TIP

Aim for balance to get a more natural-looking meadow. Pick some grasses and some perennial and annual blooming flowers. (Time and experience will help you hone the look as you discover if your plans worked or need to be tweaked from one year to the next.)

>> **Don't be a purist.** When you go shopping, you'll see *cultivars* or *nativars*, which are cultivated varieties of native plants. They're variations and improvements on the original species — either spotted by a savvy horticulturist or developed at a nursery. Their growth habit may be shorter and less rangy. Or their flower size may be larger and/or flower production is higher. Color variations are available. For example, purple coneflowers now come in a rainbow of bright colors, including orange, magenta, red, and yellow.

Some plants aren't native nor descended from natives (instead they're from other low-water parts of the world), and yet they deliver the color and exuberant look you wish for, so go for it! Add some cosmos, zinnias, and different kinds of poppies to your meadow display. The goal is to have lots of pretty flowers tossing in a light breeze.

Keeping your meadow looking nice

Water is a need in the early days, but over time, your meadow planting will become more self-sufficient. Still, here are things you can and should do to keep it attractive:

>> **Mulch it.** As with all new plantings, mulch is key. It helps hold in critical soil moisture to help sustain young plants and helps keep out encroaching weeds. Lay down an inch or more, and if possible, maintain/replenish the mulch layer, at least until the meadow plants get taller, growing thickly enough to manage these matters for themselves.

>> **Maintain it.** Pass through and groom your meadow, even if doing so feels like busywork (many meadow plants are low-care, but you want to let your neighbors see you working in the meadow area). You can trim off spent flowers, remove excessive or spent growth, and cut back stems or branches that are crowding out other plants or pushing the boundaries of the area. Mowing at season's end might be a good idea.

>> **Assess balance.** The prettiest meadows in nature have both grasses and flowers. Although the look you wish is up to you, an equal amount at any given time looks nice. Grasses carry on most of the year (and may even bloom, though their flower spikes arguably aren't as showy or colorful as their companions) but flowers come and go. The look can change dramatically from one season to the next, and definitely from one year to the next — simply because some plants are stronger growers.

MAKING A MEADOW FROM SEED

Another way to install a meadow is to use seeds, sowing a meadow mix according to the directions on the can or label. Using these mixes can provide instant gratification when colorful annual wildflowers pop up along with grasses. Perhaps the annuals will go to seed in autumn, and offspring will show up the following spring.

However, it doesn't always work out that way. As in the wild, some plants dominate and others recede. You can let nature take its course and see how you like the second-year look or you can plow it all under and start over each year.

Tip: Be choosy. Buy your meadow mix — a curated mix — from a regional specialist, not a cheap blend at the hardware or big box store (which can contain invasive or climate-inappropriate plants). You want something that's locally adapted and features a balance of grasses and flowers.

TIP

Intervene to edit — trim or take out plants — when you feel the balance is off or when you notice some of the plants becoming too dominant.

TIP

For the first year, observe which flowers do best for you. Plan to reseed more of them in subsequent years, especially near to each other so you create little islands of each variety. This action actually mimics the way natural meadows look and will be more stable as the years go by.

Chapter 13

Considering Artificial Turf

Toc oday's *synthetic turf* — as it's commonly referred to by companies who sell it — isn't your childhood favorite miniature-golf course's Astroturf. The products have come a long way from shiny green, phony-looking, cheap outdoor carpeting material. Now you can put in something that not only looks real, but also feels real.

This chapter addresses everything from what synthetic turf is made of, to the pros and cons of installing it, to use and care suggestions and concerns. After you're empowered with the important details, you can decide whether to go this route.

A LITTLE HISTORY ABOUT ARTIFICIAL TURF

Synthetic lawn grass was invented in the mid-60s for use at an athletic field at a private school in Massachusetts (where winters can be long and snowy, with wet weather in fall and early spring).

Not long after, it was deployed at a much bigger athletic indoor venue, the Houston Astrodome — no sunshine indoors to nurture a grassy surface — and gained national attention.

The company? Monsanto — of Roundup herbicide fame or infamy. After it carpeted the Astrodome, the fake grass was dubbed Astroturf.

No judgment ahead. I merely remark that where water is precious and expensive and an area of green lawn is still desired, replacing your lawn with artificial turf can be an option.

Getting Real about Artificial Turf

The inspiration for inventing and putting in this green lawnlike carpet is still relevant: You can have a lush greensward where climate and weather limit or prohibit it, and it looks great year-round. Here I examine why people select artificial turf, the pros and cons of doing so, its composition, and features.

Understanding why homeowners choose synthetic lawns

In low-water regions, the main motivation is self-evident. Artificial turf needs no water. But that's not all. Other reasons range from practical to aesthetic, which include the following:

>> "It's better than a patchy lawn."

>> "Our lawn sees heavy use — the kids playing out there, lots of foot traffic. It was being worn down to nothing. There was no point in putting in any type of garden, either."

>> "I wanted a permanent solution."

>> "We don't have time to keep up a lawn. It's too much work. But we wanted one."

>> "Honestly? I like lush green. The colors and textures of dry landscaping plants don't thrill me."

>> "We are tired — tired of water restrictions and high water bills, tired of struggling to keep it going."

Seeing the upsides

This section discusses the positives regarding putting in artificial lawn grass. I assume a realistic-looking, good-quality product is installed. The pros:

>> **Tough and durable:** It's capable of holding up to whatever the weather and seasons dish out; therefore, it looks good, even flawless, year-round.

REMEMBER

>> **Low-care:** It doesn't need water, fertilizer, or mowing. It never dries out or turns brown; it always looks fresh.

Artificial turf is said to last from 20 to 25 years (often well past the typical 10-year warranty period) when it's a quality product, it's been installed correctly and with care, and you've maintained it properly.

>> **Nonfading, won't discolor:** It's UV-stable and exposure to sunlight doesn't cause it to lose its luster.

>> **Thick *and* uniform:** All the water, fertilizer, and gardening skills you could hypothetically bring to a lawn won't equal the nice, dense, lush look from one edge to the other. In this respect, artificial turf can look better than real turf.

>> **A problem-solver:** Artificial turf is welcome when water shortages or conservative use of water mean you can't sustain a green lawn. It's welcome when an area where you want to have a lawn simply isn't possible, such as on the shaded side of the house or where a major tree not only creates shade but also consumes all the resources of soil moisture and nutrients.

>> **Immune to pest and disease issues:** Obviously, fake grass can't become afflicted with grubs, dollar-spot disease, or other vexing problems that real grass is prone to.

>> **Increased property value:** Its dependable attractiveness and easy care adds value, including curb appeal, to your landscape. In some places, real estate agents contend that a quality artificial turf installation increases your property's value.

Knowing the drawbacks

While modern-day artificial turf is an impressive facsimile of real grass, there are some issues you should be aware of, including the following:

>> **Not ultimately environmentally friendly:** It eventually shows wear and breaks down and needs to be removed and replaced — another expenditure for more plastic. (Turf made of recyclable plastic is available, and it's more expensive.)

Artificial turf offers nothing to the ecosystem — no food, no pollen or seeds; no worms; no shelter from weather, sun, or predators; no place for creatures to mate, reproduce, or raise the next generation. Of course, to be fair, neither do many living lawns.

>> **A heat sink:** On hot, sunny days, the surface heat can become intense. Artificial turf can hold so much heat that it can get hotter than pavement or concrete! Don't send the kids or pets out there. Don't walk barefoot on it.

To cool off hot artificial turf, the manufacturers recommend that you hose it down with cool water. (So much for saving water? Well, actually, the water used wouldn't begin to equal the water a living lawn in the same setting would consume.)

It can actually melt on super-hot days. Not the entire expanse, but certain parts — and there's no repairing that damage and restoring the old look. Even reflected sunlight off an adjacent large or double-paned window can cause spot-melting.

>> **Odors:** At first, you may detect its own odor — reminiscent of that new-car smell — which dissipates. The surface can also trap and hold organic things that get smelly, spoil, or rot, such as ripe fruit, dead creatures, and pet waste (see the nearby sidebar).

>> **Too lush to be real:** The lawn itself looks quite real, but its consistently lush green surface stands out in the neighborhood or in the context of your otherwise low-water, live-plants landscaped property.

A way around critics and judgmental neighbors: Put the artificial lawn in the back yard so only you and your household see it. As for a way around the jarring impression: Emphasize green rather than gray-green and blue-green foliage in adjacent landscaping. Create a transition zone.

ARTIFICIAL TURF AND YOUR FURRY FRIENDS

If you have a pet or pets that go outside, consider the following:

- **Lounging/resting:** Some pets love to lie down on grass, to snooze, to keep an eye on you while you garden or paint the fence, or to roll around on their backs. Not a problem here, especially with some of the softer-textured options.

- **Pet waste:** Even if you make a point of walking the dog in other places or around the neighborhood, it happens. Rinse away urine with the hose as soon as possible, not so much because it will stain the surface (it probably won't), but because odor can build up or linger. Scooping poop can be tricky. Choose lower blades/lower pile height to make cleaning easier. Follow up by rinsing off the area with the hose.

Some dogs like to dig and some cats like to scratch, for various reasons (it's fun, it's instinctive, they're trying to bury their waste or a toy or treat, and so on), but they'll be frustrated with artificial turf. Today's artificial turf is tough enough to withstand their nails and won't yield. Of course, if they've used their noses, they understand it's not living grass over dirt and may not even try.

Grasping its composition

Artificial turf is made of plastic, yes, but all plastic isn't created equal. Here are the three basic options:

>> **Nylon turf:** Very strong and tough. Texture and grass blades are stiff. It can withstand high temperatures and heavy objects without losing its shape. Best for putting greens, not for landscaping. Also, it's expensive compared to the other options.

>> **Polypropylene:** Considered the builder grade of artificial turf, it's the cheapest — both in cost and appearance (it really does look fake). It's not very durable, and will crush when walked on. It can't withstand high temperatures. You may use it decoratively, but not as a garden feature.

>> **Polyethylene turf:** This is the best-looking turf, commonly used for landscaping and sport fields and arenas and the preferred material for residential use. It's softer underfoot than nylon. It's available in various colors and textures.

Finding out about desirable features

When you begin to look at artificial turf, consider these factors that will drive your ultimate choice:

TIP

>> **Face weight:** This term refers to how many ounces of grass fiber per square yard (blades + thatch, not the backing). Higher = denser.

>> **Color:** You can find lots of variation; there's no such thing as plain green. View the samples.

Some manufacturers have responded to the public's wish to have synthetic turf look more realistic — the feeling is that it can look a little too perfect, a little too bright green. Therefore, they've introduced dark or brownish tints to some products. Just tints! It does help.

>> **Fibers:** It's made up of yarn of polymer plastics. See the previous section about composition.

>> **Pile height:** The length of the blades. It generally varies from 1 to 1.5 inches (25 to 40 mm). Shorter blades are best for heavy/recreational use; longer blades, however, look more realistic. Tall ones look lush.

>> **Feel:** How soft and flexible the blades are — a matter of personal preference.

>> **Backing:** The part that underneath, of course, is also plastic, complete with evenly spaced punch holes to allow air and water through. The most durable backings are made from latex or polyurethane or both.

Avoiding undesirable features

Well, as with so many purchases in life, you get what you pay for. Stay clear of these features:

» **Cheaper turf:** It has the unpleasant ability to show a particular kind of wear — footprints and imprints of items such as outdoor furniture.

» **Cheap, abrasive materials:** Some types can tear, cut pet paws, or hurt human bare feet. The way to judge quality is to get samples, bring them home, and let everyone take them for a test drive, that is, step on them, touch them, and so forth.

Taking the Plunge with Artificial Turf

If you're tempted to invest in artificial turf, here's the information you'll need to proceed.

Recognizing how it's sold and installed

Installing artificial turf isn't a DIY project, even if you have the time and are exceedingly handy. That's because manufacturers sell the full package — product and installation. The matter of choosing usually turns out to be a proprietary product. When you decide on a product, you must go to the firm that installs it; they make and/or represent it.

These companies begin their potential relationship with you by coming out and giving you a free estimate. Get it in writing, of course, and make sure you're comfortable with the terms, timetable, and warranty or guarantee. After you come to an agreement about the job, they work with you and the site to make it fit, and then they install it.

Vet the company you select so you work with one that's experienced, ethical, and insured. Your early encounters will also show you that they understand what you want and are responsive to your concerns and ideas.

TIP

Get samples. Just like carpet or paint samples, dozens of turf options are available. Bring them home and spend time viewing, touching, and analyzing them. Typically they're 1-foot (30.5 cm) squares (*tiles*).

For installation, these products generally come in rolls of 15-foot (4.6 m) widths, which the installation crew will carefully cut to fit.

Checking out the expenses

The cost reflects all the related elements of the project: drawing up the plan, selling you the product, and undertaking the installation. The final cost depends on the type of turf you choose and the amount. You could be looking at thousands of dollars for a modest-size installation (say, a 20-foot by 40-foot, 6 m by 12 m) site.

TIP

To keep the expense down, do what people with living lawns do when they want to save money: reduce the size. Increase the size of the adjacent or surrounding landscaping and garden areas.

Finding out how long the process takes

Allow time for finding and assessing companies and collecting bids, a process that may take several months.

After you choose a company, they'll visit your property to meet with you, discuss your needs, wishes, and expectations, and measure and analyze the site. Review and sign a contract, which should include a projected timetable. The installation day, or days, may not come until the product is available in the quantity you need and a work crew is available.

Preparing for installation

Refer to Chapter 11 if your old lawn needs to come out first. Then ask the supplier-contractor what else you can do to prepare. They're bound to want the site cleared, leveled, raked, and perhaps even compacted.

If they don't offer these services and you don't want to or can't meet their standards, find a contractor who can. They probably can refer you to someone they've worked with before.

Understanding proper installation

This section gives you an idea how the installation happens:

1. **The workers put down between 4 and 12 inches (10.1 to 30.5 cm) of finely crushed gravel material on the subgrade.**

   They consider your native soil that underlies the project, the *subgrade*. This gravel is akin to a patio base. They compact and flatten this gravel before proceeding, either by watering or with a plate-compactor machine, or both. The object is to get it flat and even.

2. **They may lay down a thin layer of permeable but tough plastic — perhaps a proprietary product — atop the crushed gravel.**

These underlying materials don't just set the stage for a smooth lawn surface. They also prevent weed growth from below and allow drainage, as from occasional rainfall or garden watering.

3. **They roll out, cut to fit, and lay down the turf.**

   They know how to line up seams and work around shapes. They secure everything in place, with a special adhesive, staples, and/or nails.

4. **They may sprinkle and broom in some fine sand.**

   This helps the fibers stand up like natural grass.

WARNING

A good contractor will not only alert you but also deal with any potential speed bumps. They can include the following:

>> **A septic field:** Don't install artificial turf over a septic field because you or a contractor might need access to dig it up, ruining your investment. Instead, discuss alternate locations for the turf with your contractor.

>> **Big rocks or a rock-filled site:** Someone (either you or the contractor) will have to clear them.

>> **Too many trees or shrubs in the way:** The artificial turf will deprive their root systems of water and air. Are you willing to cut them down, that is, to sacrifice them so the project can go forward?

>> **Existing irrigation systems or sprinklers:** They have to either be removed or rerouted.

Remembering Some Maintenance Do's and Don'ts

Caring for artificial turf has a learning curve because it's so different from living grass. Here are some do's and don'ts when you have artificial turf:

>> **Do:** Keep it clean and tidy by lightly raking its surface to remove leaves and debris, either with a plastic-tined rake or a push broom.

>> **Do:** Clean it by hosing it down from time to time.

>> **Don't:** Use leaf blowers, which can loosen securing nails or staples.

>> **Don't:** Use hedge trimmers, which can mar or burn the plastic where they come into contact with it.

>> **Don't:** Use automatic sprinklers or leaky hoses nearby. Calcium deposits (from municipal/treated water) will spoil the turf's surface.

Chapter **14**

Pondering Rock Gardening

I f you decide to remove your lawn, like many people in low-water and hot-summer climates, you'll never look back. You can focus on covering your landscape, or much of it, with another primarily horizontal material — expanses of rocks, gravel, and/or stones. This approach definitely takes care of the water-use problem and can also create a desertlike look.

This chapter identifies whether this option is right for you and explains what's involved in making this transition. It also presents ways you can avoid clichéd looks and make those materials look more inviting and beautiful.

REMEMBER

Rock gardening isn't simply about rocks. You still have plants, décor, pots, furnishings, and so on. This chapter just teases stones large and small out of the mix, so to speak, in order to examine them and their possible roles — they're supporting roles for your landscape as a whole.

Taking a Hard Look at Rock Gardening

Even if you've reached this crossroads — lawn out, probably a rock garden going in — stop and think before proceeding. Your goal is to get away from high water consumption and all the work a lawn requires but understand that the new look has its own maintenance issues and aesthetics.

Here I spend a few moments going over the practicalities and the issues they raise, from the unique benefits to the unique challenges. Then I proceed to an overview of how others have deployed rocks and stones in their home landscapes — it's an eye-opener, in every way, believe me!

Reviewing the benefits

When you add or allow stones and rocks in your low-water landscaping, your landscape gains quite a few advantages. The primary benefit, in the context of this book, is that your water consumption and water bill will plummet.

Here are some other landscaping pluses to using stones and rocks:

>> They provide a more natural and harmonious look.

>> They bring unadorned color and character to your landscape.

>> They require little or no maintenance.

>> After the initial investment they save money (on the water bill).

>> They anchor elements.

>> They don't attract pests or diseases.

>> They withstand foot traffic.

>> They act as a trouble-free mulch.

>> They protect plants.

>> They prevent weeds.

>> They create privacy.

>> They're long-lasting, durable, and don't decompose.

>> They're affordable and a good investment.

>> They help keep damaging moisture away from your home's foundation.

>> They act as a fire barrier because they're not flammable.

>> They improve water retention and drainage (check Chapter 15).

>> They provide lots of color options.

>> They improve your property's value. (They're a great selling point for buyers who want low water bills and little to no yard maintenance.)

MY CHILDHOOD NIGHTMARES OF BAD LANDSCAPING

When I was a child growing up in suburban Southern California, my dad was fed up with our high water bills and took out the front lawn, laid down black plastic, and ordered a couple truckloads of gravel. He and some neighborhood friends raked the rocks smooth — and done. Or so he thought.

I have two thoughts about this episode now as an adult, a horticulturist, and an author of books on gardening. One, his solution looked awful. And two, it's amazing that I ended up in this line of work with a role model like that (sorry, Dad, love you!).

The new "landscaping" didn't work out. Things he did wrong:

- **He didn't prepare the area.** He did nothing to eradicate our patchy, parched lawn. **The result?** Our sad lawn did eventually die underneath that covering. The many weeds, however, being able to tolerate abuse and still thrive, poked up around the edges and in places where the sheets of black plastic loosely overlapped. Also, he didn't try to make the site level or to direct drainage, leading to the last problem in this list.

- **He didn't dig down to create a bed or basin to receive the stones.** So they were piled *above-grade,* that is, on top of the site, raising the raked-over surface of the finished product a couple of inches above the adjacent driveway, sidewalk, and neighbor's yard. **The result?** The gravel didn't stay in place, and the finished look didn't last long. It may have solved the water-use problem, but it became a maintenance headache. Soon he was paying us kids a penny a stone to retrieve them out of the neighbor's yard, off the sidewalk and driveway, and out of the street, and to toss them back where they belonged.

- **He didn't confine the gravel.** Even some bricks embedded horizontally around the perimeter would have helped. Nothing stopped the stones from straying, which they did, just by people walking on or past it (or kids running over it on foot or with bicycles), plus the rare rainstorm carried bits into the sideway, driveway, and street.

- **The black plastic wasn't permeable.** When rain fell, water pooled on the surface here and there. The stones shifted around and slid off. What a mess.

Avoiding unimaginative landscaping

Some people are reluctant to embrace low-water landscaping because they (falsely) believe that it won't be attractive. Certainly there are many dispiriting examples. Here are some rock-landscaping schemes (seen from California's Orange County to

Phoenix and Albuquerque to Las Vegas), that aren't very imaginative or attractive. You'd do your own landscaping a service by steering clear of them:

>> **Suburban swirl:** Putting down contrasting colors of gravel (some, actually dyed), for example, akin to a lawn-size yin-yang layout or a more elaborate stained-glass-window composition or other design. The contrasting sections are separated by black plastic edging, bricks, or scalloped brick edgers.

>> **Fake desert:** Highlighting one or more large cacti, a few big agaves, or a tall yucca or two in a sea of stones.

>> **Rosebush hell:** Plunking down some sun-loving hybrid-tea roses (vase-shaped plant forms, big flowers, long bloom period) in rows or here and there, underlaying the whole thing with (often) white gravel. The plants end up looking awkward and forlorn, often baking in the reflected heat and never reaching their beautiful potential.

>> **Weed surrender:** Some plants — invasive weeds — don't mind little or no water and heat from stones; indeed, they thrive and spread out.

Well, at least something's growing, an impression of greenery or even, at times, flowers. But once their root systems are intertwined with and embedded in the gravel, it's unbelievably tedious and frustrating to try to evict them.

>> **State of denial:** A gravel base is populated with plants that aren't low-water. The light and heat reflected off the rocks adds insult to injury and the Oriental poppies, daylilies, lisianthus, and so on, sizzle and die.

>> **Moonscape:** That would be what my dad was aiming for, I think (see the nearby sidebar) — nothing but an expanse of plain gravel, unrelieved by plants or outdoor furnishings of any kind. Even when done properly (dig a few inches down so the resulting bed is at the same grade as its surroundings, lay down a weed barrier, perhaps even create a border or boundary to help keep in the rocks), the result looks lifeless, unfriendly, and lonely.

Also, unlike the surface of the real moon, sometimes a gravel lawn can absorb and reflect sunlight to the point where it gets too hot to walk on or touch!

Working with stones and rocks the right way

You can landscape and employ rocks and stones in more ways than you may think. Now that demand for water-wise landscapes is high, ordinary homeowners and landscape designers are being more creative and innovative.

Here are some basic principles you can follow when using stones and rocks in your landscape:

>> **Rethink your use of color.** Gravel naturally comes in many hues (avoid dyed rocks; the color leaches out and/or fades). Large stones do too, and sometimes they're layered or multicolored. Choose with care. Really focus on hues that to your eye look good with your home's color and architecture as well as your plantings.

>> **Explore and work with texture.** Some rocks and stones are smooth, whereas others are rough or pock-marked. If your yard isn't large or you're landscaping a discrete area, keep it simple and stick to a theme.

>> **Place rocks and stones to support a theme in your landscape.** You can make a formal look, using them for neatly defined beds and edgings, or fill an area with similar-hued, similar-size stones for a uniform look. Or mix it up and strew stones large and small for an informal, natural-looking scene. See Figure 14-1.

>> **Put stones and rocks to practical uses.** Let them become literally the architecture of your landscape. Position them to create or define contours. Have them separate and define different garden areas.

TIP

Instead of placing rocks atop the surface of your yard — whatever that surface may be — embed them. Practically speaking, doing so secures them in place and makes them look like they belong, like they're emerging from the earth.

REMEMBER

Think about fences and walls (house and outbuilding ones as well as boundary walls). Think about harmony of texture and color. Consider contrast, too. One thing to avoid is making a scene too diverse or too busy, such as a terra-cotta wall around a yard full of different-colored rocks; assuming it encloses your entire yard, the wall is always going to dominate and you're better off following its lead.

FIGURE 14-1:
Make a composition with rocks more eye-catching by creating a color theme with adjacent plants.

Source: Artiste2d3d@shutterstock.com

FINDING IDEAS FOR SOME ROCK-GARDEN INSPIRATION

Look around before you decide on a course of action for your own landscape; doing so is fun and motivating. Keep a file (literally or on your laptop or other devices) that you can refer to.

Even as you try to focus on rocks and stones while you research and gather, inevitably you'll get to thinking about plant selections. Because, of course, you're aiming for a full picture and I want to assume you aren't just forming a plan that's nothing but a bed of gravel. For loads of plant ideas, refer to Part 2.

Here are some ways you can find inspiration:

- Keep your eyes open in your neighborhood and wherever you travel and snap photos of ideas or entire yards that you admire.

- Visit botanic gardens in the region. Heck, go to their websites or Instagram accounts and nose around; inevitably, they've filled their social media with images intended to entice you to pay a visit.

- Trawl Instagram and Pinterest and drool over all the beautiful photos.

- Even if you don't plan to hire a professional designer, look at the websites of ones in your region and even visit some of their completed projects if you can. (In the end, you may decide to get their expertise and creativity by hiring them for a design, but try to save money by doing some or all of your own work.)

- Buy books and magazines. Sitting leisurely and thumbing through colorful pages looking for ideas and learning from authors and photographers is relaxing.

- Don't forget to browse this book's color insert. Notice the rocks and gravel as much as the plantings and check out how they work together.

Identifying Your Materials Options

Plenty of choices are available, and you're sure to find something interesting and inspiring. When considering materials, you also need to contemplate space and your budget. I discuss these factors in the following sections.

REMEMBER

Using local rocks is better. They just fit in and look more natural. Don't worry, you don't need to know anything about your regional geology. You'll recognize them when you see them. They're the ones that are easy to find when you shop locally.

Considering the realm of gravel and small stones

Even if you've already done some looking around and research, the sheer diversity of options may astound you, especially when you pay a visit to a landscaping supplier. Even a big box store will have an array of selections, in different sizes/diameters ("grades") and colors.

Different grades give you yet more options and can change the look. Here are some of the many options:

- » Pea gravel
- » Crushed gravel
- » Washed gravel
- » Shore gravel
- » White gravel
- » Colored gravel
- » Decomposed granite

- » Crushed granite
- » River rocks
- » Brick chips
- » Marble chips
- » Lava rock
- » Flagstone
- » Crushed shells

Reflecting on decorative rocks

You have a lot of potential with using decorative rocks in your landscape. Groupings, contrasts, partnerships with plants and pots, pairings with garden décor and furnishings, and stepping stones — the sky's the limit.

In practice, of course, any natural rock can be decorative, depending on its color, size, shape, and position.

A popular trend is colored rocks, ones that are naturally colored as well as ones that have been dyed. (I'm not in favor of dyed ones — the color doesn't last.) Colored rocks open up avenues for mosaic-like compositions in terraces, pathways and walkways, front beds, and smaller areas (what landscapers call *vignettes*, simpler but attractive compositions of compatible plants and decorative items).

Don't go too wild. Most home landscapes aren't that large, and if you get too ambitious, you'll run up higher supply bills while creating a hodge-podge. See the nearby sidebar for inspiration.

Contemplating larger rocks

The landscaping industry defines a *boulder* as any big rock more than 10 inches (25.4 cm) around. Finding a place for one or several in a revamped low-water landscape is often possible, indeed fun.

If you're fortunate, you have some on your property ready. Maybe the boulders were excavated during some sort of project (new septic field, new garage, new garden area) and set aside. Or you know a place where you can go get rocks for free. Just don't steal them from public lands. At minimum, you'll have some explaining to do to someone if you damage your car or truck's suspension hauling them or if you drop one on your foot.

You may actually have to buy big rocks for landscaping. The upside is, when you go shopping, you'll find some beauties. Stores don't sell boring, crumbling, and unattractive big stones! Another upside is that you can just point to the ones you want and somebody else, hopefully young, strong, and with a good back, will pick it up and deliver and place it.

Looking at fake/faux products

You may want to put fake rocks in your landscape. They look perfectly realistic. They're usually made out of fiberglass composite, often painted with a UV-resistant coating to preserve their color. You can purchase these where landscaping supplies are sold.

They weigh a lot less than real rocks, making them much more maneuverable. Frequently they're hollow, which means you can use one to hide something from view, such as a well head or tree stump.

Perhaps of interest: Some fake rocks have Bluetooth music speakers so you can entertain yourself or visitors when outdoors!

Fake gravel or pebbles also exist. I can't see any special advantage to such products over the real thing, and they're mainly sold for drainage projects and not really for landscaping.

Installing Rock Materials and Rocks

If you're ready to install rock materials and rocks in your landscape, these sections can help you decide how to place those items.

REMEMBER

Does a dry streambed interest you, either as an attractive landscaping feature or as a way to route water through and within your yard or, ideally, both? If yes, flip to Chapter 16.

Putting in groundcovering gravel, step by step

You can cover a former lawn area, bed, slope, curb strip, front-yard approach, backyard, courtyard, and on with gravel or one or more of the gravellike materials listed in the section, "Considering the realm of gravel and small stones," earlier in this chapter.

You can accomplish the best results on fairly flat ground, simply because there's no tendency for the stones to slide downhill and pool at the base. Stick to these steps for a basic installation:

1. **Clear the area well.**

   Dig out and evict all the plants that were growing there and dispose of them. Remove weeds and larger plants by the roots. Pry out rocks, roots, debris, any other obstructions.

2. **Excavate.**

   Dig down into the cleared ground to a depth of up to several inches/cm. Tamp and rake until the area is as smooth as possible.

TIP

The best time to put in edging material of any kind, to define the area and help contain the gravel material, is beforehand. Press it in firmly or whack it into place with a mallet. (Use bricks, larger stones, or heavy-duty, UV-resistant plastic edging. Boards will work for a while, but eventually rot.)

3. **Line the bottom with black plastic or hardware cloth.**

   This suppresses weeds.

4. **Pour in the gravel material, aiming to fill a touch higher than grade (ground level).**

   Assuming you've prepared the area to receive several inches/cm of material, this means you'll overfill slightly, by an inch (2.5 cm) or less.

TIP

Managing the filling and smoothing-over that follows is easier if you deposit small piles at intervals throughout the area, rather than dumping it all at one end.

5. **Rake over neatly.**

   Work slowly and carefully so as not to displace the material. Your objective is to evenly distribute the material and create a generally level surface, giving the project a finished look.

6. **Add in-ground plants.**

   Scoot the gravel material out of the way, then slice an X in the underlying plastic to create a planting hole. Either fold the cut pieces under or slice them off entirely. Then use a trowel or shovel to create a hole for the incoming plant. Refer to Chapter 10 for planting instructions and advice.

7. **If you choose, add big rocks and any garden ornaments.**

   Clear a spot for big rocks and bury part of their bulk for stability.

   As for any garden ornament, depending on what material you've used and how substantial your garden gnome, sundial, or decorative lantern is, it may wobble if you just set it there. If it doesn't have one, attach it to a base, then seat and move the gravel material back over it so it's out of sight.

8. **Add potted plants if they're part of your overall design.**

   They're just fine arrayed on gravel material. If you have any worries about stability, just move the gravel material out of the way and set pots on the plastic-covered ground below.

TIP

Putting gravel materials on a slope can be tricky because the tendency (even in perfectly dry conditions) is to slide downhill. The key to success will be out of sight when you're done: Install a bottom layer of textured pavers meant for this job (ask where you buy the gravel). Also, use angular, not rounded rocks.

Maneuvering bigger rocks into place

If you move big rocks into position yourself, have a plan and be safe and smart. Get the new spot ready by creating a depression you can plunk or roll the rock into, deep enough to keep the rock in place and stable.

Lift with your legs and not your back. Or maybe use a small earth mover, sturdy wheelbarrow, and/or a helper or two to move and position it.

REMEMBER

A big rock will lose a little size in your landscape when you install it correctly because you'll have buried some of the bottom of it.

Avoid indecision, regret, and extra work with this project by having a positioning plan and an understanding of how to get the effect you want. Consider the following.

Positioning rocks

Even though you may not be a rule-follower, landscaping with rocks isn't the best time to freestyle. Here are some techniques and ideas that'll save you trouble:

- » **Bigger goes lower.** Always place larger rocks at a lower elevation. It looks natural.

- » **Support the leading actor.** Array smaller stones around a big rock to give it a settled look in the landscape.

- » **Face in the original direction.** Sometimes the south side of a big rock is lighter in color than the rest of it; stick with that in its new home. Sometimes it's evident which face was in contact with the ground; keep it that way. The result looks more natural.

- » **Taller trumps wider.** Placing a large rock that's taller than wide with the focus on its height is an interesting look. Just make sure it won't topple over.

- » **Go with a keystone boulder.** A *keystone boulder* is just a solo large rock, out in the middle of your landscape or anchoring a corner or special area. Because it's the only or biggest one, it has a commanding presence.

Installing mother rocks

You can place a large rock to protect or shield vulnerable plants at its base or along one side. The big rock, often referred to as a *mother rock*, can offer a little shade or shelter from winds.

Avid gardeners who enjoy growing special little alpine plants pioneered this idea — or, maybe it would be more accurate to say, actual big rocks out in nature accomplished it first. Anyway, using mother rocks in your landscape can be quite practical and attractive.

Looking at offbeat ideas

Here are a few fun, attractive design and positioning ideas for larger rocks that you may want to try:

- » **Put large rocks to work.** Maybe they can become seating or resting spots. Maybe you can fashion a bench by laying a board across two supporting similar-size rocks.

- » **Create a cairn.** A *cairn* is a short stack of rocks, largest on the bottom and smallest at the top. It must be stable or it won't last; it's both an art and a science. You can watch some good instructional videos on YouTube.

- » **Make low walls or create elevation changes with rocks.** Look online for "rock walls" or "stone retaining walls" for all sorts of inspiration and information.

Being Aware of Practical Considerations

No surprise here, you have to think about a number of factors as you move to add rocks of any kind to your home landscape. I discuss the main ones here.

Shopping for rocks

Nothing can substitute going to see and touch the rocks you're considering using. Asking around — other gardeners, landscaping services, wherever you buy your plants — and searching online (including reading reviews) can also lead you to sources. The value of the rock(s) dictates whether it's sold by the pound or the ton.

You can purchase rocks at three typical outlets:

>> **A local rockyard or stoneyard:** Most likely they offer the most choices.

>> **A landscape supply yard:** If you're not looking for anything unusual or special, such places offer popular materials.

>> **A big-box store with a large gardening section:** Selection may be limited and prices tend to be higher than the other two sources.

Gravellike materials are usually sold by the cubic yard and the prices vary quite a lot. The machine that scoops up the gravel typically has a one-yard bucket, leveled off. Watching them scoop your order may not be a bad idea. (This reminds me of British ale enthusiasts who give the barkeep the eagle eye while they draw them a pint, making sure they get the full 16 ounces!)

You can sometimes get the materials delivered in heavy-duty plastic sacks.

Big rocks, of course, are sold individually. Rates range from $100 to $600 per ton. Sandstone weighs less than granite or limestone.

REMEMBER

Inquire about delivery: How soon, how much more will it cost, and will the person(s) who brings it to you unload it where you direct them to or will they dump it curbside?

TIP

Even if you get a variety of materials, save expense and trouble and arrange for only one delivery. Be sure to be there to receive it, so you can check that all is as expected.

Contending with rocky challenges

Rocks, of course, aren't living things. They aren't organic. That means in your lifetime, they aren't going to decompose and contribute any nutrients or other benefits to the site's soil.

More pressing is the problems they can create. Here's a rundown, with mitigation suggestions and possible solutions.

>> **Problem:** Rocks and stones (especially pea gravel and volcanic rock) absorb and retain heat by day and reflect it back or release/radiate it by night. That's not always a good thing. Their immediate area becomes hot, affecting adjacent plants and, if they're near your house, heat into your walls.

   Solutions: Either don't site vulnerable plants near *heat sinks* (any element that absorbs and/or holds heat, such as a stone wall or concrete walkway), or put in ones that relish the heat, such as many succulents (see Chapter 7). Don't place rocks too close to house or building walls.

>> **Problem:** The areas of rock start to get dirty, especially obvious if you've chosen lighter colors.

   Solutions: Always underlie a bed with rocks with plastic or hardware cloth, so the soil underneath can't enter the display. This also keeps out moisture from the ground below; however if sitting puddles from a rainfall appear to be staining or marring your stones, the solution is to route drainage away from the area.

>> **Problem:** The rocks sink into the ground over time. They're heavier than soil, and gravity is the law. If you change your landscaping plans later, removing the rocks is hard work or impossible.

   Solutions: Spread out the weight by clustering several smaller rocks or a variety of sizes rather than one large one. Underlay the area with plastic or landscape fabric, which won't completely stop the process but will slow it. Avoid watering nearby because ground moisture softens the ground and hastens sinking. Stay out of the area, so you and other household members and garden visitors don't step on or press on the stones.

>> **Problem:** Projectile injuries are a risk — not just kids picking up and playing with or throwing rocks, but also during garden maintenance. If your rock area is next to an area that is mowed or weed-whacked, the machine can fling around small rocks.

   Solutions: Scold the kids (well, divert them to other entertainments). Protect yourself when mowing or weed-whacking: wear sturdy boots, long pants, and goggles and work carefully. Put in barriers or buffers between gravel-filled areas.

Keeping rock displays looking fresh

Rock-filled displays aren't ever as much work as a green lawn, but neither are they maintenance-free. Here's the short list of things you need to do from time to time:

>> **Keep ahead of the weeds.** Despite precautions you may have taken, weeds always seem to appear and you must keep after them.

WARNING

A site that hasn't been weeded regularly soon becomes unmanageable. Weeding between rocks is hard, tedious work and only gets more difficult the bigger and more extensive the weed growth becomes.

» **Clean, with a hose.** Yes, your era of high water use is over, but an occasional sweeping spray of the hose rinses off dust and debris and refreshes the rocks.

» **Rake gently.** Push stones back where they were with a rake and level everything and fill gaps. Your yard will look better.

» **Replenish.** Sometimes more stones are needed here and there. If you didn't have any leftovers, return to your source.

NEW TREND: GRAVEL GARDENING

Gravel gardening (not the most glamorous name) gives a huge role to gravel. Indeed, what you create is akin to a yard-size raised bed filled with gravel!

To do this right isn't a small or inexpensive undertaking. You need to clear and excavate the yard or planting bed beforehand, and install some kind of strong, confining edging (bricks or stones). Then pour in a whopping 4 to 6 inches (10.1 to 15.2 cm) of gravel.

That's not a decorative-gravel delivery. Nor is it a mulch delivery, though it will certainly do the jobs of discouraging weeds and holding in soil moisture. Runoff is greatly reduced and water remains in your yard; it's directed down to the soil below.

The planting method you choose makes all the difference. You set young plants (pint- or quart-size pots) directly into the waiting gravel. But first, you gingerly loosen and dunk their root systems in a bucket of water and/or gently shake them, so that the roots go into their new gravely home with *no soil mix on them*. This induces them to reach downward for the soil.

Extra-diligent, even generous water is delivered to them for weeks. Plants that size don't take long to reach the soil level below. Once there, voilà! They're far more independent. And untroubled by weeds.

Practitioners find there's little maintenance — just some periodic tidying up. They contend a gravel garden is 80 percent less work than a conventional garden with similar plants!

4

Landscaping with Watering Needs in Mind

IN THIS PART . . .

Examine various ways to prevent runoff and water loss.

Consider the beauty and practicality of a dry streambed.

Recognize the many benefits of mulching.

Contemplate good ways to supply needed moisture to potted plants.

Ponder including a pool, container water garden, or recirculating fountain.

Look at xeriscaping principles and how they continue to apply to low-water landscaping.

Chapter **15**

Appreciating Mulch and Other Helpful Products

'm happy to reveal that the low-water landscape has some splendid allies, at the most down-to-earth level, literally.

Chief among these is mulch; honestly, no other material is as important and useful. This chapter takes a deep dive into all things mulch: the diverse kinds, their benefits and uses, and ways to shop for and apply mulch properly for maximum effectiveness.

I also include a practical overview of a couple other things you may find helpful: water-absorbing crystals (available as powder or included in soil mixes) and coconut coir (available in forms requiring rehydration, but then available to help you save garden water).

Much Ado about Mulch

Of all the allies a gardener needing to conserve water can have, mulch tops the list. Sometimes it's free, sometimes you have to buy it, sometimes it's a one-time investment, and sometimes you have to get a bit more and top off periodically. No matter where you get it, it's all good.

REMEMBER

Mulch is a material applied onto (atop) the soil surface. By contrast, soil-improvement materials are dug into, incorporated into, the native soil. I admit that distinction can be a bit confusing because you can use some of the same materials both ways.

Here I explain why mulch is so important in conserving water and contributing to the health of your plants. After that, I walk you through what and how to buy and apply.

Eyeing how mulch helps

Mulch brings a lot of important and desirable benefits to your landscape — so many, in fact, that I hope after you review the following list you'll be convinced that you must have some!

>> **Mulch reduces evaporation.** Mulch holds, indeed hoards, moisture close to the soil surface. Because many plants have roots close to the soil surface, mulching around them is a game-changer. According to the California Waste Management Board, just 2 inches (5 cm) of mulch cuts water loss by 20 percent.

>> **Mulch moderates soil temperatures.** According to the same report, 2 inches (5 cm) of mulch lowers the temperature in the top 4 inches (10.1 cm) of soil by as much as 10 degrees F (about 5 or 6 degrees C).

REMEMBER

Mulch acts as a buffer or barrier between the soil below and the world above. It absorbs, regulates, cools, dissipates, and generally softens the fluctuating blows of heat (and cold). Thus the plants don't suffer (as much) from extremes. By contrast, unmulched plants exposed to extreme conditions are harmed and can die.

>> **Mulch slows runoff.** Mulch soaks up moisture rather than letting it get away; essentially, it approves penetration. When the mulch is right over a plant's root system, the moisture it has absorbed obeys gravity and eventually most of it works its way down to the plant's roots where it's needed and absorbed.

>> **Mulch lowers the moisture needs of plants.** Mulched plants are never as desperate for water as ones that are exposed and unmulched. Mulched

plants are able to stay more evenly hydrated and to go without water for longer periods of time.

Mulch is especially beneficial for shallow-rooted plants, which inhabit the first few inches (cms) of soil and thus are more vulnerable to drying out.

>> **Mulch discourages weeds.** Weed seeds and root fragments that germinate or sprout in the soil and work their way to the surface will be inhibited. They'll be buried and stymied, perishing under the smothering blanket of mulch.

Weeds that enter your landscape from above (hitchhikers on new potted plants, birds or other creatures moving them around, or remnants of past gardening efforts) can find a layer of mulch too thick to penetrate.

If you've already mulched and weeds happen to appear, the good news is that if you act quickly, they're surprisingly easy to pull — because their root systems are no deeper than the mulch and are easy to yank out of mulch (as opposed to hard, dry ground).

Weeds that are able to get a foothold in your landscape aren't just a threat to its beauty and tidiness, they suck up valuable soil moisture (and nutrients) from the ground. Also, if they're allowed to grow, they can crowd and shade out desirable plants. Mulch can be an excellent deterrent. "An ounce of prevention is worth a pound of cure!"

>> **Mulch helps tie your landscape together**. From a design standpoint, putting down the same sort of mulch in various areas and beds in your yard does wonders for creating a sense of unity.

>> **Mulch makes your yard look tidy and cared-for.** Neatly applied and regularly replenished mulch appears neat. Your plantings immediately look better and weeds are suppressed, so the whole scene is pleasing to the eye and attractive.

>> **Organic mulch helps improve your soil.** Most soils in drier areas could use a little improvement! Mulch gradually breaks down and enters the soil below, contributing some organic content and helping to improve the texture. It facilitates air exchange with the soil and allows water to get through — all to the good.

Don't make the mistake of considering mulch a way to upgrade poor and lean soil or a substitute for soil–improvement work. It won't be sufficient and it acts too slowly. For information on soil improvement, flip to Chapter 4.

Figuring out how much mulch to buy

Rather than guessing and having to return to the source, do a little math beforehand when you're getting mulch.

I can't give you estimated prices because prices vary so much, not just by material but also in terms of quality, amount/quantity discounts, your location, whether there's a delivery charge, and so on. Avoid sticker shock; do online research and make calls!

Mulch is an investment in the health and water-retention of your landscape. Payback is significant: You *will* save time, money, and effort if your plantings are mulched well. Mulching isn't a place to economize, so don't be penny-size and pound-foolish.

To figure out how much mulch you need, follow these steps:

1. **Calculate the square footage (square m) of the area you plan to mulch and determine the depth (inches or cm).**

2. **Convert that number to feet (or meters) and then multiply all three figures to obtain the estimated volume needed in cubic feet (m).**

   Most mulch bags are 1.5 to 2 cubic feet (that's 0.042 to 0.056 cubic m).

   Here's a sample scenario: Suppose your garden area is 10 × 10 feet, and you'll mulch to a depth of 3 inches (.25 feet).

   10 × 10 × .25 = 25 cubic feet needed.

   (3.05 m × 3.05 m × 0.07 m = 0.7 cubic m needed)

3. **Divide to figure out how many bags of mulch to buy.**

   To continue this example, assume you'll buy bags of mulch that are 2 cubic feet each.

   Divide 25 ÷ 2 = you'll need to buy 12.5 (well, 13) bags.

   (Assuming 0.056 cubic m mulch bags: Divide 0.7 by 0.056 = you'll need to buy about 12.5, well, 13 bags.)

When you have a bigger area to cover, a truckload mulch delivery (from, say, a local landscaping service or garden center) makes more sense than buying, transporting, and opening a large quantity of individual bags. Note that truckload mulch deliveries are usually quoted by the cubic yard (so convert your cubic-feet-needed figure to cubic yards; simply divide by 27). Bear in mind that a typical pickup truck bed can haul around 3 cubic yards; if your mulch needs are bigger than that, more trips or a larger truck will be necessary.

Sometimes you can get free mulch! (You can't always specify how much — just accept it gratefully.) Local utilities cut down and shred a lot of brush and trees when clearing power-line corridors or bush-hogging roadsides. Give them a call to ask if you can have some or pick up some up at wherever they deposit it. They might say "certainly!" Just clarify that the free material is wood chips, not chopped-up weeds or vines.

No matter how your mulch arrives — bags or a truck delivery — don't deposit it on garden ground. Doing so smothers whatever is there, plus a pile could be in the way. Instead keep it in the driveway or on a patio, and/or place it on a large tarp. This also makes cleanup easier.

Reviewing the types of organic mulch

Good news: Options abound! You can buy mulch, you can make your own, or you can recycle materials on hand. You can use different mulches in different spots — you can mix it up. You can give a certain type a try and then switch to something else, until you judge that you and your plants are happy with the effectiveness as well as the look.

Of course, your budget and what's locally available will dictate what you use. Typically these materials are available in bags wherever gardening supplies are sold; you can order larger amounts by the truckload.

At any rate, here are the common *organic* kinds (derived from living materials), with commentary to help you better understand each one as you think about your choices (for inorganic mulch, consult the section, "Using stones as mulch," later in this chapter):

>> **Bark mulch:** Dry shredded bark. It may be a mix of various hardwood or softwood trees. It looks natural and smells wonderful.

>> **Cocoa-bean hulls:** Trendy, expensive, dark brown color, and wonderfully aromatic! Can be long-lasting. Can form mold on the surface. (Not safe for use around puppies or dogs who might nibble.)

>> **Compost:** Referred to as *black gold* (because the color is dark and the material is so valuable and wonderful). Take it from your own compost pile when you need it and it's free; alternatively, you can buy bags of commercial compost. Whatever your source, compost looks great and delivers all the benefits I describe in the section, "Eyeing how mulch helps," earlier in this chapter, plus its nutrients are continually leaching into the soil below.

Quality matters. Don't use compost from any source that might contain chemical contaminants or weeds. That may mean you can't use free local municipal compost.

>> **Composted leaves:** Also called *leaf mold*. Whole leaves mat down; you need to use chopped-up ones — you can do this yourself by running a lawn mower over a dry pile.

>> **Pine bark nuggets:** Attractive and long-lasting. One small potential drawback: the pieces float (and can drift away) in water, so don't use them where water pools or flows.

>> **Red cedar:** Pretty, natural reddish color. Nice, earthy aroma. It's fine-textured, naturally pest-resistant, and doesn't break down as fast as other organic mulches.

WARNING

When a bark mulch color is too vivid — bright red, or dark black, for example — the look may be too good to be true. Even though the mulch material itself may be organically based, usually shredded bark, it has been dyed. After rainfall or when you water, the dye leaches into the ground (and groundwater), not a strong poison to soil life but not good either. Just say no. (Also, why would you want your landscape to have a fake-looking color?)

>> **Spent hops:** Do you live near a brewery? They may give the waste material away or sell it for cheap. Your yard will smell beery until the aroma dissipates. Nice color and fire-resistant.

>> **Wood chips:** Natural look, doesn't blow away, doesn't compact readily. However, they can be a fire hazard.

TIP

If you're applying mulch to an area devoted to a short-lived or temporary display — annuals for quick color, for example — don't invest in or bother with a thick organic mulch. Instead use a thin layer (an inch or less, 2.5 cm; any deeper and the material can mat or get moldy) of dried grass clippings or chopped-up dry leaves.

WARNING

Nitrogen deficiency can happen if you mix organic mulch into the ground at season's end. Tiny soil organisms use soil nitrogen to break down the mulch in place. If plants in that area show signs of nitrogen deficiency (slow growth, yellow older leaves) — confirm with a soil test — you can either discontinue the practice or fertilize a bit to make up the difference.

The good news is that this little problem is confined to the thin interface where the mulch and soil meet and typically doesn't dramatically affect nutrition reaching your plants.

TIP

Lighter-colored mulches reflect rather than absorb sunlight, which helps to maintain cooler soil temperatures. Dry grass clippings and straw are two good examples. You might keep some on hand and sprinkle about on the mornings of especially hot days.

Using stones as mulch

Inorganic mulches — mulches that aren't derived from living materials, such as stones — have their places and uses. A real advantage is that they can increase water infiltration, important in low-water plantings.

Popular options include gravel, pebbles, and pea gravel. Check out different grades and hues. Typical sources include home-supply box stores, large garden centers and nurseries, stone yards, and landscaping services. (For the sake of simplicity, I refer to them all as stones in the following discussion.)

TIP

Stone mulches are a good "leave them be" choice for garden beds and landscaped sections where you won't be actively digging or moving plants in and out. That's not only because they're stable and inert, but also because you don't want to be disturbing or knocking them about as you tramp in and out of the area.

These materials can be quite long-lasting in their appointed spot (provided neither weather, the passage of time, and/or playing children deplete or move them around). They can also be attractive, adding color and texture to the look of your landscape.

Stone mulches do have two potential drawbacks:

>> They absorb and hold warmth, heating up their immediate vicinity and the soil surface, potentially to the depth of an inch or two (a few cm). Some plants don't appreciate this, especially shallow-rooted ones. Others do; succulents certainly do — see the lists in Chapter 7.

>> You have to buy stone mulch; few yards have enough material naturally on hand.

REMEMBER

Individual pieces should be a half-inch (1.3 cm) or less to get the benefits of weed suppression and moisture retention. (Larger pieces are fine if your main goal is spiffy appearance; refer to Chapter 14 for more information.)

Applying and replenishing mulch

For mulch to deliver the benefits you want, the benefits your landscape needs, you must apply enough and apply it correctly (several inches atop garden soil). An intervening layer of landscape fabric is optional and helps keep weeds at bay. Refer to Figure 15-1 to see how it should look once in place.

REMEMBER

Mulching with organic materials, in particular, is a constant landscape chore because it's temporary. Consider every delivery an opportunity for quality time with your plants, so you can see how they're doing and respond if they need anything else, from water to grooming to pest control.

Organic mulches generally need to be replaced or topped up once or twice a year.

CONSIDERING OTHER MULCH OPTIONS

These mulch options hold in soil moisture at the ground level, at least, and inhibit weeds:

- **Black plastic:** Inorganic. Keeps moisture in and thwarts weeds, but it's not attractive and eventually deteriorates. You can put some down first, and then cover with an organic or inorganic mulch.

- **Landscape or weed-inhibiting fabric:** Inorganic. It's not literally fabric, but rather woven plastic fibers or a perforated plastic sheet (usually polyester, nylon, or recycled plastic). Practical for letting air and water through and reducing erosion, but not attractive. Best to put some down first and then cover the area with an organic or inorganic mulch.

- **Loose dried leaves or pine needles:** Organic. Don't allow them to mat down or compact. Can be a fire hazard.

- **Paper:** Craft paper, newspaper. Organic. Don't use colored paper, inserts, catalogs, and the like, which contain dyes and may also be coated. A too-thick layer of paper on the soil surface (more than a half-inch/1.3 cm) limits oxygen and air exchange with the soil. Dampening it slightly helps hold it in place and encourages it to break down slowly over time.

- **Shredded rubber.** This material is mainly made from recycled and defective tires — better than sending that stuff to the landfill, right? It looks good over a long period of time, resists compaction, and doesn't blow away. However it may contain toxins, contributes nothing organic to the soil, and can become stubbornly embedded.

- **Straw:** Organic. If you like the look and it won't blow away, by all means use it. Just don't use hay because it contains weed seeds.

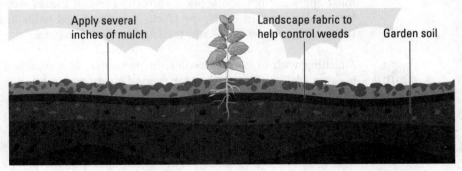

FIGURE 15-1: Mulch in action.

(c) John Wiley & Sons, Inc.

Knowing when to apply

You can put down mulch at any time. Just don't do it on a windy or rainy day, of course.

REMEMBER

Always keep an eye on areas mulched with organic materials because they break down or may be blown or washed away. Be ready to replenish and maintain.

Put down mulch at these times:

REMEMBER

>> Over a newly cleared bed or planting area because the covering helps protect the soil and keeps weeds at bay until you're ready to fill it.

>> Around a newly installed plant because it's a helpful welcome to their new home.

>> Around fall transplants because it keeps the soil warmer, allowing them a bit more time to put out root growth to anchor and sustain them. It also helps protect from the coming colder weather.

>> Where *frost-heaving* (this is when water in soil freezes and causes the ground to expand and swell upward) due to freeze-thaw cycles are an issue, mulch helps the plants cope better with the soil-temperature fluctuations.

>> When you want to delay spring growth, mulch protects your plants from sprouting before cold weather is over. In this case, mulch after the ground freezes.

Understanding how thickly to apply mulch

Although every garden is different and you may want to try to see how little you can get away with, more mulch is invariably better.

Mulching to a depth of 2 inches (5 cm) should be considered the minimum — it may not be enough to get all the desirable benefits I discuss earlier in the section, "Eyeing how mulch helps," in this chapter.

To get the best water-saving, weed-suppressing benefits of mulch, I urge you to go thicker. Make it a practice to lay down 3 to 4 inches (7.6 to 10.1 cm) if you can.

Deeper mulch than that and roots can get suffocated, plus water has a harder time getting through, so find the sweet spot.

Looking at ways to apply mulch

The object is to put down mulch everywhere it's needed in an even and thorough manner. How you accomplish this feat depends not only on the material, but how much area you intend to cover.

Basic methods include walking around shaking it out of the bag it came in, tossing handfuls, distributing shovelfuls, hurling bucketfuls, and trundling around with a wheelbarrow making deposits.

After it's more or less in place, spread it out more evenly by hand (wear gloves) or with a short-tined rake.

Here are a few pro tips:

>> Don't lay mulch over weeds. Get rid of them first, ideally by the roots.

>> Start by distributing piles throughout the area via bag, bucket, or shovel, then get down on your hands and knees and finish spreading the material around by hand.

>> If you rake mulch around, use a rake with short tines, which are better at breaking up clumps and spreading.

WARNING

Special alert for shrubs, hedges, and trees: Don't push mulch right up against their trunks. Keep about 4 to 6 inches (10.1 to 15.2 cm) back. Mulch in too-close contact traps moisture and can encourage decay and fungi. Also, rodents may take up residence in or below the layer of mulch and chew the bark, girdling and eventually killing the plants.

Coping with mulching problems

Occasionally mulching has a few issues, which I discuss here, but none are serious or challenging enough to deter you from using mulch.

Dealing with runoff

Time, weather, wind, fast-moving storms — nature conspires to deplete your mulch! If it keeps getting away on you, here are a few things to try:

>> Switch to a heavier-weight mulch.

>> Dampen it when it's dry to help it stay in place.

>> Confine it by installing edging (see Chapter 16 for options and installation advice).

>> Weight it down with strategically positioned rocks and stones and/or garden décor.

Addressing slime mold

Blobs or foamlike masses of yellowish or yellow-brown stuff — sometimes white, tan, orange or even red — form on the surface of your mulch. It appears suddenly and spreads quickly. (I was amused to see the problem cited in an article in the *Dallas Morning News* with the headline, "Did the dog throw up in your mulch or is that just slime mold?")

The good news is, this fungus is nontoxic and totally harmless to you, your plants, and your pets. It's caused by overly damp, humid conditions in organic mulch that it establishes and feeds upon. To the extent that you can prevent it, don't oversoak your mulch.

To get rid of slime mold, just scoop it up with a shovel. Take care not only to get all of it but to work gently so you don't inadvertently scatter its minute spores around. Don't toss it elsewhere in your yard, not even into the compost pile. Send it away with the household trash.

Alternatively, if you don't mind the look, you can certainly leave it be. It's just working away decomposing organic material. If your soil could use more organic material, you can consider slime mold a garden ally!

Preparing for fire danger

Using mulch in areas with high fire risk is a conundrum: Mulch holds moisture and inhibits weed growth, but mulch is often also flammable material.

Your best bet, therefore, is to use rocks and stones as mulch (consult Chapter 16 for all the details). If you prefer to use organic materials, though, only use heavier, chunky, composted bark chips or plain old compost — nothing lightweight and dry.

Water districts in fire-prone areas are always trying to educate the public on ways to mitigate or prevent fire damage, including offering landscaping tips. Figure 15-2 shows what you should and shouldn't do.

Here are a few more cautions:

>> **Locate beds of mulched plants away from structures.** Most fire districts recommend 5 feet (1.5 m) away — even more is better.

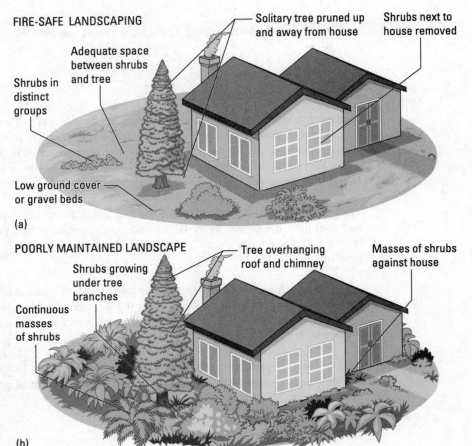

FIRE-SAFE LANDSCAPING

Solitary tree pruned up and away from house

Shrubs next to house removed

Adequate space between shrubs and tree

Shrubs in distinct groups

Low ground cover or gravel beds

(a)

POORLY MAINTAINED LANDSCAPE

Tree overhanging roof and chimney

Masses of shrubs against house

Shrubs growing under tree branches

Continuous masses of shrubs

(b)

(c) John Wiley & Sons, Inc.

FIGURE 15-2: Well-maintained landscape to mitigate or prevent fire damage (a). Common landscaping mistakes (b).

>> **Don't apply mulch too thickly.** Keep layers to 2 inches (5 cm) or less. Should a thicker layer catch fire, it tends to smolder, which is hard for firefighters to notice and hard to extinguish.

>> **Don't mulch widely or in a continuous way throughout your fire-vulnerable landscape.** Beds and patches can become combustible stepping stones.

WARNING

Should fire threaten, don't waste water or compromise water pressure by running out and soaking your mulched beds. (An advancing fire will cause them to dry out quickly regardless.)

Assessing Water-Storing Crystals

Here I discuss the non-organic, non-natural material that's widely marketed as a way to conserve landscape and container-grown plant water. There may be a time and a place for these products. Read further to decide if you want to try them.

Understanding what they are

These non-organic materials are synthetically produced water-storing crystals, sometimes called *hydrogels* or *moisture beads*.

Poured into your hand, they resemble granulated sugar or small chunks of sugar. That's not very surprising because both are crystals. Like those of sugar, the individual crystals are very tiny. Composed of highly absorbent polymers, they actually consist of a long, repeating chain of identical molecules bonded together (like plastics and resins).

The tiny crystals bind with water molecules, which causes them to swell dramatically like a sponge. They then look like goo or jell — they expand to a whopping 300 to 400 times their original size! (Sound familiar, parents? It's the same technology used in disposable diapers.)

In the soil of your garden or the soil mix of your potted plants, the crystals slowly release the absorbed water back into the root zone of plants and moisten the adjacent soil. Manufacturers of these products say they degrade in 3 to 5 years, depending on how much you use and your particular yard's conditions.

REMEMBER

The absorbent polymer crystals don't actually *conserve* water, though they're certainly a big help in areas where water must be conserved. Instead they hang on to the water, sequestering it so the plants can use it. The precious moisture would otherwise get away and be lost or wasted — it would otherwise leave via evaporation and runoff. Thus they increase your soil's water-holding capacity.

Considering the pros to using crystals

Here are reasons for using crystals:

>> They're efficient. They release water slowly and steadily, thus preventing both overwatering and underwatering.

>> They're affordable (refer to the section, "Adding crystals to your shopping list," later in this chapter).

>> They spare you the time and expense of watering as often.

Using these products doesn't absolve you of the chore of watering your plants. Your plants still need supplemental irrigation at times, especially during prolonged hot spells.

>> They're out of sight. Unless someone digs in your garden beds or pushes their fingers into your potted plants' soil mix, they aren't obvious or visible.

>> Because they expand when they absorb moisture and contract as they release moisture, they help to keep the soil aerated and prevent soil compaction, thereby assisting drainage.

>> If you use water-soluble fertilizer, they absorb the boosted water and release it back slowly to your plants' roots. Thus they act as an agent of slowly delivered nutrition.

>> Moisture-induced garden problems are fewer. Mealybugs, fungus gnats, fungal infections, mold, mildew and root rot are all much less likely to attack and harm your plants.

>> Studies have shown they *don't* adversely affect life in the soil, such as soil microbes.

>> Studies have shown they *don't* adversely affect aquatic life in reservoirs, lakes, streams, and aquifers.

One of the most valuable and popular uses of these products is in the soil mix of outdoor potted plants, particularly in hot, sunny settings or if you're heading out of town for a short vacation. The plants have a better chance of survival, to be sure. (Chapter 17 discusses container-grown plants.)

Eyeing the cons to using crystals

The arguments against using the crystals/possible risks are as follows:

>> Soil texture where they're used can become disconcertingly slippery or goopy.

>> People are understandably squeamish about or hesitant to put polymers in the ground, especially gardeners who want to keep their landscapes natural and to do no harm. (However, so far, no environmental-science research shows definitive long-term harm from these products.)

>> In addition to bonding to water molecules as they degrade, these crystals may bond with other molecules in the environment. Of particular concern is acrylamide, which has been implicated as a neurotoxin and carcinogen. However, so far, studies only show this to be a "negligible, insignificant" problem.

>> If they're dug up or discarded before they've completely broken down, they can't be disposed of as organic waste or added to a compost pile.

>> They aren't a substitute for watering.

>> Small children and pets may discover or unearth them and, worst-case scenario, ingest them or stick them in their ears or nose. Once in the presence of internal moisture, just imagine how dangerous the crystals could be as they expand their size dramatically. Emergency removal would be needed.

>> Overwintered plants continue to be hydrated rather than slowing down or going dormant. Cold weather can harm or kill plants with fresh new growth at the wrong time of year.

Adding crystals to your shopping list

You can purchase water–storing crystals in the following two ways, neither which is expensive (just read the label with care to make sure you aren't mistaking them for similar–looking products):

>> **Small packets or in bags:** Available wherever gardening supplies are sold, either locally or online. Just as an example, a 12-oz bag of crystals is around $20. The packaging has instructions regarding how much to use and how to either mix it into garden soil or add it to plain potting mixes for container-grown plants. Make sure you don't overdose.

>> **In potting-soil mixes:** Your cue is the wording "Moisture Control." Due to the weight, buy the bags locally wherever you shop for your garden. They aren't costly: A 1.5 cubic-foot bag of moisture control potting mix that contains the material typically is priced less than $10.

Understanding how to use

If you want to try using absorbent crystals, be sure to use them correctly in order for your plants to derive maximum benefits. Heed the following guidance:

>> **Container-grown plants:** Add the crystals to the potting soil before filling the pot (follow the directions on the bag regarding amount/proportion) and then add the plant. Water only when done.

If a plant is already in the pot and you'd rather not take it out or repot it, prep a small amount of crystals pre-mixed with soil mix. Create evenly spaced holes in the surface of the potting mix with a stick or pencil and then carefully decant in the new modified soil mix. Water only when done.

If using a moisture control potting mix, simply fill containers and add plants as usual. Water only when done.

>> **In-ground plants:** Pre-mix the crystals with garden soil according to the rates given on the bag, then add to the planting hole. If a plant is already in place, carefully dig down in the vicinity of its root system — taking care not to damage or snap off growing roots — and add, refill the dug-out area, and tamp down firmly. Water only when done.

WARNING

Although you may be tempted to just sprinkle some crystals around the base of certain potted plants or in-ground plants in your landscape, don't do it. When they absorb water and expand, they'll look odd and goopy hanging out on the surface and, just as importantly, they won't be doing an efficient job of delivering water down to the roots.

Examining Coconut Coir for the Garden

Those who maintain landscapes in places where coconut palms grow already know this secret — the highly absorbent coir has many practical uses. If you don't live near coconut palms, you'll have to go out and buy some. Here's the lowdown.

Knowing what coconut coir is

Part of the multilayered fruit of the coconut palm, *coconut coir* (pronounced "core") is the natural, brownish husk found between the inner shell and the outer coat of the coconut. Its texture is fibrous or wiry. Other names for this material include *coir fiber*, *coco coir*, and *coco peat*.

In times past or by those who were ignorant of it or simply not thrifty, this layer was considered a waste product. No longer. Nowadays it's harvested wherever coconuts are processed.

Understanding its dry-garden potential

Coconut coir can absorb and retain up to ten times its volume in water. No wonder gardeners and landscapers are so interested in it!

Among its other virtues are the following:

>> It improves soil aeration, letting in air. Plant roots suffer or even die when compacted and coconut coir helps to prevent that.

>> It doesn't attract insect pests.

>> It's earthworm-friendly.

>> It's pH neutral (neither very acidic nor very alkaline), making it an easy, adaptable addition.

>> It's an environmentally friendly, biodegradable, renewable resource.

It has a few drawbacks, however, which are as follows:

>> It doesn't contribute any nutrients.

>> It's not ready-to-use (see the next section for some shopping tips).

>> It might be salty, due to the environment from which it was harvested. And the last thing dry-garden plants need is extra salt. Avoid very cheap sources: Quality coir isn't discount-priced.

Here are some ways you can use coir:

>> **Raise seedlings or pot houseplants and outdoor-display potted plants.** Blend it into the soil mix (in lieu of the nonrenewable resource, peat moss). You can buy bags of mix that specifically list it as an ingredient.

>> **Increase water retention in hanging baskets.** Buy sheets of it and line a hanging basket or buy pre-formed pieces that fit neatly into hanging baskets and frames. The container must allow drainage, however, or the absorbent material will stay too damp and your hanging-basket plants may rot.

>> **Line raised beds.** Line a bed or stir in coir fibers, no more than 40 percent, because your plants also need ingredients that supply their nutritional needs.

>> **Include in the ground.** You can add fibers to planting holes of incoming shrubs, trees, and perennials, but don't be overzealous — no more than 40 percent. Alternatively, you can dampen some fibers and place them around the base of plants that appreciate the evaporating moisture as well as coir's ability (like any good mulch) to retain some soil moisture.

REMEMBER The main benefit of using coconut coir in your garden is its water-holding capacity; it's otherwise inert (no nutrients), so use it in concert with other, beneficial amendments.

Shopping for and rehydrating coconut coir

Coconut coir is sold in a variety of forms. The stringy, wiry fibers are loosely stuffed into bags; a popular brand is CocoLoco. Or they may be compressed into chips, little round disks, or bricks.

Because it has been utilized to make rope, stuff upholstery, and make doormats, among other creative uses, you can find coconut coir in craft-supply stores. It's also sold as dry, compressed bricks; you can find them anywhere you buy gardening and landscaping supplies.

To rehydrate in preparation for using:

1. **Choose a big container.**

   Expect it will expand dramatically — it can gain up to ten times its original volume. Select one that's too big, rather than too small.

TIP You can rehydrate a brick in a large bucket. A bale (about 2.5 cubic feet) is best rehydrated in a large trash can or even a kiddie pool!

2. **Place a brick, block, or bale in the container and pour in water.**

   Let sit for at least 15 minutes. Check back and top it off as needed until you're satisfied that it's reached its maximum size.

3. **Remove, drain, or squeeze out excess.**

4. **Tease it apart into usable pieces.**

Being aware when using coir

Heed the following cautions when using coir:

>> Don't try to cut, slice, or saw a dry brick. It's too hard.

>> Discard duds — occasionally a brick or bale simply won't rehydrate well.

>> Don't waste perfectly good unused portions. Coconut coir stores well for years.

Chapter **16**

Keeping Water in Your Yard

This chapter tours the practical ways to retain water right in your landscape. Fortunately others before you have confronted the common challenges and come up with a variety of effective and ingenious approaches and solutions. I describe the best ones I know of, noting benefits (and flaws and cautions, where applicable).

You can apply one or more of the good and worthwhile ideas in this chapter to your low-water landscape. If you can't stop water from getting away, at least you can slow it down.

REMEMBER

While you may mainly be focusing on keeping moisture in your landscape for the needs of your plantings, doing so is a good idea in other ways. Kept in place, water is better able to percolate into the soil, where it's naturally filtered (purified) before returning to the aquifer or a nearby stream or reservoir. Water that moves through soil rather than running off also contributes less pollution to the environment. All good!

Improving Absorption

When water is scarce and/or expensive, watching it run off, or realizing that it's evaporating, is vexing. Runoff is a common issue in compacted ground or soil that is high in clay. Also, many suburban and subdivision house lots are slightly elevated above street level; the intention was to protect the home and basement from water damage. But this design also slopes downhill, having the unfortunate result of sending water out of such yards and into street gutters, storm drains, and away.

Endeavor to increase how much water actually soaks in where you want it to. You can take slightly different measures for different areas as you work to increase your landscape's ability to hold on to moisture. When soil absorbs water, it acts like a sponge, essentially buying time for your plants to get some before the water gets away due to evaporation or runoff. Remember that mulch (Chapter 15 discusses mulch in greater detail) is your best partner; try the following ideas, but don't forget about using mulch.

An important benefit of working to retain what water you have in your own yard is you also end up reducing erosion — you retain soil and/or mulch, which no longer washes, blows, or drifts away. Improving absorption thus becomes a win–win for your dry landscape.

REMEMBER

Observing water running off, when you irrigate or during a rainfall, is a sign that the water is being delivered faster than it can be absorbed.

TIP

Rain in the forecast? Huzzah! But if it falls hard and briefly, most or all of that precious water gets away. Two things you can try:

>> **Moisten your planted areas beforehand.** Damp ground is more absorbent.

>> **Install rain barrels.** They collect and hold rainwater. You could leave them out in the open and hope for the best, but routing your roof's gutters directly into them is most efficient and successful. See Chapter 2.

In mixed beds

You have a few recourses to improve water absorption in mixed beds (planting areas with a variety of different plants) and implementing some or all may be worthwhile. The following identifies what you can do:

>> **Create basins around the perimeter of plants that need more water.** These surround the root zone area and make sure the water soaks in right there rather than running off. Refer to Chapter 2.

» **Improve the organic content of the soil.** Doing so slows fast drainage, increases absorption in heavy clay, and helps the ground retain moisture.

» **Deliver water slowly and deeply.** Doing so encourages roots to quest deeper into the earth. Water in soil does obey gravity and sink down, so you want the roots to be there to receive and use it.

On slopes

Let me say it again: Water obeys gravity and thus heads downward, which makes watering plants on a slope frustrating. Try these ideas:

» **Place plants that need more water at the base of a slope.** The problem is now a solution.

» **Create terraces on the hillside.** In the end, the plants within each terrace will be easier to tend, plus the area may look better. Soil improved with organic matter and physical barriers/borders for each level (stone, concrete, wood) help hold in precious moisture.

» **Add more plants.** Their roots will not only use the water that comes their way, but they'll also help prevent erosion by holding the slope or hill in place.

» **Dig routing trenches.** Aim on sending — or delivering (as with soaker hoses) — water where it's most needed. Yes, this tactic attempts to exert control over the flow. Careful observation of what's already going on can help you decide if this option is viable, and if so, what diversions you want to attempt.

» **Create berms, install runoff ditches, or put in a French drain.** These earthworks projects are worth investigating when excess water running through your property is a frequent problem — frankly, not often the case in low-water regions.

In lawn areas

If you still maintain a lawn and runoff is a problem, adjust your watering system and institute stop-start watering. For example, allow the area water for no more than 15 to 30 minutes, and then shut off your irrigation system and let the moisture soak in. Return in an hour or so and repeat.

TIP

Alternatively, if you have a programmable watering system that divides your landscape into zones, change the settings for two or three shorter deliveries, moving from one zone to the next before circling back.

If you're redoing your lawn, take the opportunity to level the grade before installing the new drought-tolerant grasses. (I describe and discuss these in Chapter 12.)

Adding Borders and Buffers

When you live in a place of sparse or episodic rainfall, worrying about too much water isn't your concern. In places where water is more plentiful, you may be bemused to hear that there are rules and laws about not routing water out of your yard — you aren't allowed to send it into the street or a neighbor's property.

That said, preventing runoff is clearly desirable here. Don't let valuable water get away. Here are some landscaping tricks that help confine what water you have to your own property.

Plant edging plants

Rather than letting the perimeter of your property peter out in mulch or stones, which eventually seem to end up straying, bit by bit, onto the adjacent sidewalk, driveway or walkway, landscape right up to the edge as Figure 16-1 shows. Planting at property boundaries means water that would have left your yard can now be put to good use, plus the plants help hold in mulch and prevent erosion.

FIGURE 16-1:
Help keep and use water on your property by installing plants at the boundaries.

(c) John Wiley & Sons, Inc.

Here are some of the advantages to edging plants:

>> **Edging plants soften boundaries while helping to prevent erosion.** The aboveground portions of edging plants, with their bulk or trailing growth, soften hard edges. The belowground portions — the root systems — hold soil and moisture in place, reducing attrition and erosion.

>> **Edging plants also help define bed and property lines.** If you want a literal living fence along a border, turn to the lists of shrubs in Chapter 8.

>> **Edging plants looks neat.** It announces to all who pass by or visit that a garden, a cared-for landscape, commences here.

>> **Living edges consume water.** A border or boundary of living plants isn't going to let excess water slip away onto the sidewalk or into the street, or to evaporate. They need it and they'll use it.

Install edging materials

Defining the edges of your planting beds looks nice but also has practical advantages — they protect the plants and show off the plants within (see Figure 16-2). Here I discuss what these materials can do and what your various options are.

Recognizing the benefits to using edging materials

You can help stop water from draining away or running off by putting in some physical barriers. Such edging barriers have various benefits, including:

>> They can be decorative or make your yard look neater.

>> They define areas.

>> They integrate well with similar materials also in your landscape.

>> They hold plants in place.

>> They keep different types of plants from encroaching on each other's territory.

Considering your options

Any well-stocked garden store or landscape supplier will have an array of choices, such as bricks, pavers, concrete sections, stones, and paving stones, including ones that fit or dovetail together for making continuous lines.

FIGURE 16-2:
Install edging
materials at the
perimeter of
planting beds.

To place these materials so they're effective at keeping water in your yard, seat them firmly into the ground, not merely set atop it. Make sure they present a united front, that is, fit them closely together. Remember to take dimensions into account when shopping; submerging edging material as deeply as 4 or so inches (10.1 cm) works great for stability, but you may still want to see some of it, so buy larger or longer pieces.

REMEMBER

These materials may have the ability to actually absorb some in-ground moisture. In that regard, they're helping, particularly when you have plants growing by them.

Alternatively, from the same sources, you can get nonporous edging materials made of plastic, metal, or rubber. Materials that are UV-stable are a wise choice. Aluminum or steel are also options — these materials don't become brittle, rust, or rot.

You can purchase them in longer sections or, if you prefer, as interlocking pieces. Deeper is better (4 inches, 10.1 cm, down is the general rule), so you can insert them firmly into the ground where needed and they'll be stable and still have a substantial attractive aboveground lip showing.

Although plant, metal, or rubber edging materials don't absorb any moisture, they can trap at least some in the adjacent ground, so nearby plants stand to benefit.

WARNING

Avoid using wood, even if you admire its natural look and strong lines. Over time, with exposure to dampness, lumber eventually rots in place. Pressure- and CCA-treated wood and/or dyed or painted wood may be a temptation, but the chemicals can leach into or flake off into your ground; probably not good for edible plants in the vicinity and anyway potentially harmful to soil life. Creosote-soaked railroad ties, in particular, are a no-no.

Consider trenches, swales, basins, and berms

Moving earth around, digging or using (or bringing in) extra soil to mold to your desires are options when you're trying to make your home landscape more water-retentive.

Projects of this nature route and control water on a much larger scale at big construction sites, public parks, and golf courses, and in road-building, so cast your mind to those and see what ideas you can borrow.

A few quick definitions are in order here (all these projects are similar or related):

>> **Trench:** A shallow, elongated excavation used to control where water flows

>> **Swale:** Basically a ditch, similar to a trench but often deeper, and without any exit

>> **Basin:** A bowl-shaped hole in the ground

And all the soil you removed to create a swale or basin? Use that to make a *berm*, a rounded mound of soil that can block or divert water but perhaps also provide an opportunity to grow some plants.

Landscaping earthworks projects can:

>> **Divert moving water.** A trench can direct landscape water to where you want it, including not just back into your yard but directly toward planting beds. It may be left empty (except when water is flowing) if encroaching weeds or erosion aren't problems. Otherwise, line it with plastic or water-permeable landscape fabric and/or fill it with gravel or rocks.

>> **Capture stormwater.** To be sure, an influx of stormwater isn't an everyday event, but when it comes, rainfall can damage existing plantings as the water courses through your landscape before heading for the street or downhill and away. The classic way to retain is to dig a large basin or hole and fill it with stones. Location is key; if the water won't end up there naturally, you need to create channels for it to follow so it does. In a bigger yard, creating a swale may make more sense.

>> **Block escaping water.** Length varies, obviously — but a berm acts like a dam to prevent water from getting past. Water should never go over it, so make it tall enough for the worst-case scenario (less than 2 feet, 0.6 m, high is typical). Water shouldn't wash it away, so make sure it's strong and compacted (some people use fill, gravel, rubble, and/or clay). If you're digging a basin or swale, use the excavated soil to form a berm — see Figure 16-3.

WARNING

If you think your landscape would benefit from this sort of molding and reshaping work but you lack the time, expertise, confidence, energy, or equipment to do it yourself, don't blunder along. Instead call in a qualified, well-reviewed, insured contractor for a site visit and discuss, with an eye to hiring them and leveraging their experience and expertise. It's better to have it done right with the proper machinery and techniques.

FIGURE 16-3: When you dig a swale or basin, you can use the excavated soil to create a berm.

(c) John Wiley & Sons, Inc.

Installing Dry Streambeds

Whoever first brought this naturally occurring feature into home landscaping was a genius. It's so practical and yet potentially so interesting and attractive. Here I examine the benefits, explain what to consider when planning a streambed, and tell how you can build your own.

Seeing the benefits

A dry streambed reduces runoff from your property. Basically, it acts as erosion control, channeling water when it flows through, as during an occasional seasonal cloudburst. No flash flood damage in your yard!

But a dry streambed is more than merely useful. Done well, it's potentially a beautiful solution, one that garden visitors will always be drawn to and admire. In fact, if and when it comes time to sell your home, a dry streambed adds appeal and therefore value; potential buyers will love the look and grow to appreciate the way it helps retain and direct precipitation in the yard. Take a look at the one in the color insert.

Planning the site/course

Unlike drainage trenches, a dry streambed has a natural look — as if it belongs, as if it's always been there, as if it happened on its own.

REMEMBER

To get that look, first and foremost go with the flow. The best channel is where water already naturally drains across your landscape.

As for the design, consider how naturally occurring streams flow. Their courses vary, and you can mimic that for an authentic look. Parts of the course can be slower-moving water — shallower and wider; faster-moving parts become deeper, steeper, and narrower.

REMEMBER

Space permitting, your streambed's course should have a chance to meander. This not only looks more natural that a straight-arrow channel, but it also helps to slow down the flow.

TIP

Look at what others have done. Check yards in your neighborhood and town for dry streambeds. Trawl social media, especially Pinterest. Focus on details as well as the overall design.

Installing a dry streambed yourself

With your design in mind, it's time to implement it. Assuming the size of the project isn't too daunting, yes, you can do this yourself. Just follow these steps:

1. **Mark its boundaries.**

   Define your layout on the ground. Use stakes and string, lengths of rope or cord, or flexible hoses. Stand back and assess and adjust until you're satisfied with the design.

2. **Gather a variety of different types and sizes of rocks and stones.**

   Boulders can go at the top or base and at the outer edges; smaller ones can occupy the streambed. If the stream will be wide enough to accommodate them, include a few big ones midstream to break up the flow (literally, when water is flowing, but also visually). Pea gravel can fill the entire course, end to end.

   TIP

   For a more natural look, choose stones that are rounded rather than angular or sharp-edged.

3. **Using a shovel and/or a small earth mover, dig out your stream's trench.**

   Stick to your design and lines, including creating areas that are wide and others that are narrower.

4. **Line the course.**

   If you want the water to proceed quickly to a stormwater basin (refer to the section, "Considering trenches, swales, basins, and berms," earlier in this chapter), line its course with heavy PVC or the rubber liners sold for underlaying ponds and pools. If your goal is to have the streambed actually hold and absorb water, line it with water-permeable landscape fabric.

   WARNING

   Skip lining the bed at your own risk because if weeds are able to grow from below or find ground to sprout in, eradicating them from among a varied bed of stones becomes a maintenance headache.

5. **Add the stones at last.**

   Pour in the base of pea gravel first, and then follow with the larger ones. Use *stepping down* to make their arrangements look more natural — that is, cluster smaller rocks around bigger ones.

6. **You may add plants along the banks, but if you do, choose wisely.**

   They shouldn't look out of place, and you'll have to consider their watering needs; native plants are often your best bet.

Putting in a Rain Garden

A rain garden (see Figure 16-4) is an increasingly popular way to capture rainwater to sustain a small garden bed. The scheme mitigates storm runoff, reduces erosion, and diminishes flood damage. Once established, the plants thrive with little extra attention.

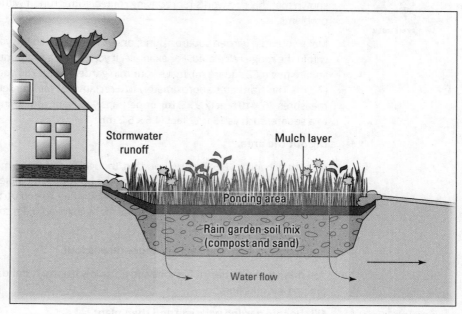

FIGURE 16-4:
This rain garden routes gutter water to a small garden area.

Stormwater runoff

Mulch layer

Ponding area

Rain garden soil mix (compost and sand)

Water flow

(c) John Wiley & Sons, Inc.

Basically a trench or garden bed, a rain garden receives rainfall runoff from your home's roof, driveway, or yard. The runoff goes directly to the area that's filled with plants. Water thus remains in your own yard, sustaining the plants and also, as it percolates through, naturally replenishing the groundwater. For example, water from your home's gutters is routed with a pipe into the rain garden area.

Follow these steps to create your own rain garden (if you're not up to the task, hire a contractor experienced in these projects):

1. **Walk around your property to identify an appropriate spot.**

   The best one is in a flat or slightly sloping area. Avoid getting too close to your house (you don't want moisture congregating near your foundation or basement) and avoid your septic field if you have one.

2. **Dig a test hole about a foot (0.3 m) deep, fill it with water, and observe how long it takes to drain.**

   It should drain off in a day or less. If it doesn't, pick a spot that does.

3. **Calculate the size/footprint of your rain garden, based on the footprint of your home.**

REMEMBER

   A rain garden should be about one-sixth the size of your house. Research has shown that this size works for receiving routed gutter runoff without any major problems.

   Make your rain garden square, round, or oval, whatever shape you like, just within the range calculated. For example, if your home's footprint is 1,600 square feet (488 square m), make your rain garden about 260 square feet (7.3 m). This translates approximately to a rectangular rain garden that measures 26 × 10 feet (7.9 × 3 m), or perhaps you want something closer to a square, such as 15 × 17 feet (4.6 × 5.2 m).

4. **Dig out the area.**

   A depth of 6 inches (15.2 cm) is standard, though if you plan to mulch the plantings, dig a little deeper. Work to keep the bottom of the hole fairly level; it doesn't have to be perfect, but you don't want water to end up pooling in a corner. If the area is on a slope, use some of the excavated dirt to create a berm on the downside to stop runoff.

5. **Run a pipe in from the nearest house downspout.**

   You may choose to bury it from view in a shallow trench. A standard PVC drainpipe works fine.

6. **Fill the rain garden with soil and then plant.**

   Adding some organic matter to the native soil increases water retention. In an arid climate, go with native shrubs and perennials, though ones that like a bit more moisture may find a home here. Get advice at your local nursery.

Leveraging Shade to Conserve Water

You may be pleasantly surprised that some shade can make a difference in conserving water in a landscaped yard. Shade mitigates evaporation and is always a bit cooler. It's hard to generalize here (too many factors), but shade is always welcome in the quest to use less water.

TECHNICAL STUFF

When a plant is shaded, basically two things happen:

>> **Transpiration slows down.** *Transpiration* is the process of water moving through a plant, from roots on up, and eventually entering the air. To help you visualize this, a shaded plant sips water more slowly.

>> **Shade helps whatever a plant is growing in to lose/evaporate less water.** In-ground or potted can make a difference.

A close look at your yard may turn up various opportunities to use shade to help your plants, some natural (other plants), some already present (buildings), others store-bought. Consider the following:

>> **Big plants shade:** Tall, leafy trees, from majestic oaks to palms to crape myrtles, have the ability to create shelter from the blazing sun under their canopies. In-ground and potted plants that struggle in full sun will appreciate such a location.

>> **Little plants shade:** Even in a mixed bed of, say, perennials and native wildflowers, positioning the more vulnerable plants or newer arrivals to the north or east side of taller neighboring plants can bring a little relief and protection.

>> **Shade cloth:** This product is available wherever gardening supplies are sold. Laid over garden plants, it can provide temporary or partial protection. Just be careful you're not also restricting air circulation. You don't need to completely swathe plants in this material; draping it gently over one side or rigging it above the plant(s) may be sufficient.

TIP

Not all shade cloth is created equal. It comes in different colors — black obviously absorbs sun, whereas lighter colors don't. Perhaps more importantly, shade cloth comes in *shade factors,* which refer to how much sunlight it's capable of blocking — usually between 25 and 90 percent. Your raised bed of salad greens and baby herbs may like a 50 percent shade cloth, whereas some flowers are fine with 30 percent. Ask a garden center staffer to help you choose.

>> **Row covers:** Even though these are sold for use in vegetable gardens, they can certainly be deployed anywhere you're worried about sun blasting your plants. Just make sure there's air circulation underneath. Note that they don't come in all sorts of grades like shade cloth does.

>> **Shade structures:** A shade structure can be a crate, lawn chair, or an open-bottom box you rig out of shade cloth (over a wire or PVC pipe frame), and its purpose is to provide temporary shade to whatever is beneath it. On a grander scale, a shade structure can be a simple slatted overhang or even a hefty pergola, which means it not only shields plants but also provides a comfortable place for people to gather or lounge outdoors on hot, sunny days.

>> **Shade from buildings:** This welcome protection is built into every home landscape. It's up to you to be observant about degrees of shade and position plants who really need part-day relief (and outdoor furniture), such as in a flowerbed next to a garage or shed.

Getting Help from Hardscape

The concrete and stone patios and terraces that were once so common are unforgivingly hot and dry places because they absorb and reflect sunlight. Adding insult to injury, when it happens to rain, water runs right off poured concrete and interlocking pavers. In fact, the compacted base material upon which they rest isn't meant to hold or drain water but rather to prevent water from draining through. In short: water is over and out!

Good news: Some innovative alternatives are available. You can find the products I discuss here wherever garden and landscaping supplies are sold (if you need help installing them, you're sure to find contractors who are experienced with these materials when you go looking):

>> **Permeable pavers and stepping stones:** These products allow water through, via joints between them — larger gaps than what you're used to seeing with traditional pavers. (A difference you may notice, but you won't see after they're in place: Their sides have raised bumps to enforce the gaps.) They come in a range of different colors, patterns, and styles.

These pavers are set into a permeable base. Thus water, rather than running off, is able to percolate into this layer. Ultimately the water is bound for the subgrade soil down below and back into your local aquifer. Most contractors create the base from a mix of stone sizes rather than one certain grade, and they may add additional layers of crushed stone if extra holding capacity is needed.

>> **Porous patios and terraces:** These are made from the pavers rather than a traditional poured concrete slab. And yes, you can allow grass or creeping thyme or petite succulent groundcovers to occupy the spaces between the pavers for a unique and naturalistic look.

TIP

Some municipalities offer incentives to encourage residents to install permeable options, including a break on your property-tax bill, expedited permitting, and changing the old codes to allow you to cover over more ground if you use these. Contact City Hall to find out.

Chapter **17**

Succeeding with Potted Plants

Maintaining containerized displays in the stressful conditions of long, hot, dry days where water is limited isn't always easy. Plants in pots dry out fast. The hot sun bakes their contents. What looked so fresh in the morning looks nearly dead later that same day. Heaven forbid you leave some of your plants alone for a few days or a weekend.

All this begs the question: Are pot-grown plants simply a bad idea in these conditions?

No, truly, they're not. Take heart. In this chapter, you discover ways to sustain your collection and help the plants look great. After explaining how to get potted plants off to a good start, I share some watering ideas and products to lighten your load of worry and work and a quick list of favorite container plants for low-water conditions — and some nifty design suggestions.

Giving Your Potted Plants a Good Start

In dry, hot, sunny growing conditions, container gardeners need to make a few adjustments in order to help their displays succeed. These requirements may or may not apply elsewhere, but all are essential here. The following sections begin at the beginning.

Identifying good pots and bad pots

When you go shopping for pots, or simply forage in the garage, at yard sales, or at craft sales, you need to keep some basics in mind:

>> **Choose pots that are better at holding precious moisture.** Plastic pots top the list. Glazed pots are also suitable.

>> **Avoid pots that wick moisture away from roots.** Clay pots and terra-cotta or earthenware ones, pretty though they may be, are terrible in this regard. Stone pots absorb dampness, too.

TIP

If you like the look of stone — say, stone urns — consider resin facsimiles. They're cheaper, lighter, and easier to maneuver!

>> **Confirm that the container has drainage holes.** You may not intend to overwater, but containers without drainage are a disaster for potted plants, especially drought-tolerant ones. Containers without drainage holes lead to *wet feet* (soggy root systems). Plant roots will rot in place. Drainage holes allow water to move through and exit.

TIP

Here are two ways to provide drainage in a container that lacks it:

● Drill holes in the bottom or sides, down-low.

● Alternatively, fill the bottom of the pot with a layer of coarse gravel or small rocks (an inch, 2.5 cm, thick or more, depending on the pot size). The idea is that water will pass through the soil mix above and end up there, below the root zone, to slowly evaporate.

>> **Make sure the container has a saucer or tray underneath it.** Why? A saucer allows you to see when excess water drains out the bottom, so you know when to stop watering. Rather than dump the excess, though, leave it to either slowly evaporate (raising humidity around the plant — some appreciate this) or so the roots can take it up later as needed.

TIP

Try nesting! Seat a suitable pot inside a slightly larger container that isn't suitable or is purely decorative. You can then grow something in a plastic pot and nest it in terracotta or stick a potted plant inside an whimsical container such as an old tea kettle or retired gardening boot.

SOME RANDOM THOUGHTS ON POT SIZE

Generally speaking bigger pots are more practical. They hold moisture in their soil mix longer than little ones; little ones dry out super-fast.

How about installing a big, deep planter box on your patio or deck, rather than an array of vulnerable, high-maintenance small pots?

However, if you really like small plants in small pots, cluster them together. Maybe they can share a drainage tray, which also helps conserve moisture. This strategy has a small but significant effect of reducing evaporation and holding in a bit of local humidity — there's strength in numbers.

Shopping for appropriate soil mixes

A well-drained potting mix is essential to success. Choose a lightweight one labeled specifically for containerized plants. Thanks to additives like perlite or pumice, these mixes strike the sweet spot between offering sufficient moisture and letting excess water pass through so roots don't stay too wet.

Note that if you're planting cacti or succulents in containers, you can buy sand-based, fast-draining mixes specially formulated for them.

TIP

Are you interested in utilizing water-retentive crystals or moisture-control potting mixes as additives? These mixes can be helpful to your plants and save you worrying about the roots of your potted plants becoming parched. Flip to Chapter 15 for all the details.

Potting your containers the right way

Placing your plants in containers is nothing mysterious. Simply handle with care. Follow these steps to avoid any hassles:

1. **Prepare the container by adding potting mix.**

    TIP

    Don't just pour in potting mix. Rather, dump it into a bucket or pot, add water, and then fill the container with hand-squeezed handfuls. This simple technique assures that the mix is properly moistened for the new arrivals yet not soggy.

2. **Water the plants before moving them to their new home and let the water drain away.**

3. **Coax the plants out of the pot they came in without tugging on their foliage or stems, which could snap off or break.**

4. **Repot them in their new home at the same level they were growing in the nursery pot and add soil mix firmly in around them.**

5. **Give them one more drink of water and place in a protected spot with some shade so they can adjust.**

   You can move them to their appointed location in a day or two.

REMEMBER

New arrivals, even low-water selections, do need a bit more water in the days and weeks after moving into their containers because they dry out so much faster than in-ground plants.

Managing Water Consumption in Pots

The amount of water you need depends on the type of plant you're growing. Succulents and cacti don't need much water wherever you grow them. Certain native plants, once established in a container, are pretty tough, requiring only the occasional drink.

REMEMBER

Overwatering kills more drought-tolerant plants, especially container-grown succulents, than other issues.

Certain herb plants and popular flowers (such as nasturtiums and mums) on the other hand, require a consistent source of moisture or they struggle and even throw in the towel (see Chapter 9 where I discuss herbs). And if you want to raise vegetables or small trees in containers, your success will depend on a good, steady water supply for them.

Here I take a closer look at the watering options for potted plants.

Hand-watering potted plants

Some people enjoy or prefer delivering water to their potted plants one by one. It *is* a good way to keep an eye on them and a satisfying activity, but you want to do it prudently and properly. Here's how:

>> **Water in the morning.** Doing so plumps up the plants before the heat of the day causes stress.

>> **Deliver water gently with a watering can or watering wand.** If water hits the potted plant too hard, soil mix and nutrients will wash or spill out, plus you may dislodge the plants.

>> **Group pots of plants with similar needs together.** Doing so cues you on how much and how often to water (you don't have to remember or keep track of each and every one's special requirements).

>> **Try bottom-watering.** Set pots in trays or pie tins and deliver the water there; they'll take up/slurp up what they need, as they need it.

>> **Water potted succulents and cacti sparingly.** They use less water. Let their soil mix completely dry out between waterings, and water sparingly, stopping as soon as you see water seeping out from the base.

Considering self-watering systems

Self-watering systems can be game-changers for many plants — flowers, vegetables, many herb plants, tropical plants, and so on. In fact, they may make it possible for you to grow plants you thought you couldn't sustain or didn't have time for. Here I discuss a few options.

WARNING

Self-watering planters that supply water evenly and constantly aren't appropriate for cacti and succulents; those plants need to dry out between waterings.

Self-watering pots with reservoirs

The basic design for this type (see Figure 17-1) has a water reservoir residing inside, which is a bonus because weight provides stability. You can fill it from above or from the side, depending on the size and design.

An evaporation grill, wicking fabric or a capillary strip is above the reservoir. Above the grill is the potting mix with the growing plant. Moisture is provided steadily and evenly to the growing root system!

REMEMBER

Make sure you refill the reservoir every few days or as needed. Some of these systems come with ways of alerting you that the reservoir is low, such as a gauge or a color change. (I wasn't able to confirm that "there's an app for that," but I suspect it won't be long in coming.) Another practical feature to look for is an overflow hole, in case you overfill the reservoir or there's rainfall. You can get big patio-size ones, railing planters, pots of various sizes, and even hanging baskets.

Drip irrigation systems

Pioneered by the greenhouse industry, these systems are available complete with water timers for home use. You can even get a kit that lets you water several containers on the same hose connection. A line from the water source has nipples you push down into the pot soil, and the water drips in slowly. Some assembly is required — so if you're handy, you'll have no trouble.

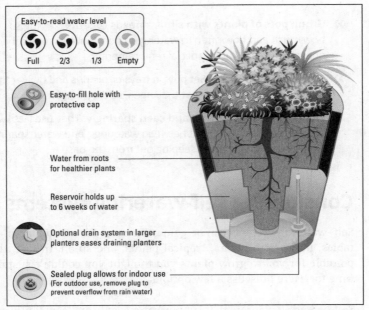

Easy-to-read water level

Full   2/3   1/3   Empty

Easy-to-fill hole with protective cap

Water from roots for healthier plants

Reservoir holds up to 6 weeks of water

Optional drain system in larger planters eases draining planters

Sealed plug allows for indoor use (For outdoor use, remove plug to prevent overflow from rain water)

FIGURE 17-1:
An example of a self-watering pot with a reservoir — note the clever features.

(c) John Wiley & Sons, Inc.

Taking Good Care of Potted Plants

Your potted low–water plants have special needs and concerns, which I discuss here.

Fertilizing your plants

Not every potted plant needs to be fed. Native plants, anything touted as drought–tolerant, and cacti and succulents are far less demanding than pots of flowering annuals, tomato plants, parsley, and other ornamental plants.

But if feed you must, here are guidelines:

>> **Use a balanced formulation.** Rarely do potted plants need any special fertilizer. A common 5-10-5 or 5-10-10 is fine.

>> **Feed only when plants are actively growing.** You don't need to feed them in the blazing heat of midsummer or when winter's shorter, cooler days arrive. In fact, adding a dose of fertilizer when they're stressed or it's time for them to slow down or become dormant is harmful and can even be fatal.

>> **Deliver fertilizer with water.** Mix it into the water according to the label directions (like aspirin, more isn't better). If you're using a self-watering planter, you can add it to the reservoir.

TIME FOR SLOW-RELEASE FERTILIZER

Larger, more substantial potted plants like perennials and small trees and shrubs do well with a dose of slow-release plant food at the beginning of their growing season in spring. As they grow and as you meet their watering needs, the nutrients release over a period of a couple of months.

Slow-release fertilizers look like little pellets or beads. You mix them into the soil mix when potting new arrivals and scatter some on the surface of established ones. The usual rate is a teaspoon for every gallon of potting mix, but consult the label to be sure and follow the directions.

Some potting mixes already have these pellets in them, so read the label to find out and don't double-dose.

TIP

Better, more even growth results when you feed potted plants at half-strength, twice as often. Just be sure to review the dosage instructions on the fertilizer label and do the math correctly.

WARNING

Salt buildup can happen in potted plants that have been fertilized. A bathtub ring on the pot is a sign. It means the plant isn't getting enough water to flush the fertilizer through the potting mix. Stop fertilizing when you notice this and flush the plant's potting mix or repot in fresh mix.

Placing plants to make them happier

It's possible to water more efficiently by the way you place, space, and group potted plants. Here are some principles and ideas to try:

>> **Thirstier plants:** Position them in morning sun and afternoon shade. Afternoon sun, even late-afternoon sun, is stressful.

>> **Sun-lovers, less-thirsty plants:** They can tolerate noonday and afternoon sun. Some don't mind a full day of sun, such as most cacti.

>> **Tall and short plants:** Clusters of potted plants can share humidity and offer each other a bit of shade. Place taller containers (which consume more water) next to shorter ones so the shorter ones can get their water.

>> **Plants that dry out easily:** To slow drying out from both wind and hot sun, set vulnerable plants close to anything bigger and taller — other pots, of course, but also walls, retaining walls, fences, garden furniture, an arbor. Corner spots are especially protected.

TIP

A base with casters/wheels, especially for a heavier potted plant, is so helpful. You can easily move it around in different seasons/months, or even over the course of a long, sunny day.

TIP

Turn, turn, turn. I'm sure you've noticed that windowsill plants lean toward their light source and can become lopsided unless you give them a quarter-turn periodically. Do the same with your outdoor potted plants — it really makes a difference and assures an attractive, balanced look.

Recognizing Some Plants for Pots

The following are all plants that do exceptionally well in containers in low-water situations. You can find many more plants and descriptions in Part 2.

POTS IN THE DRY GARDEN: A FEW DESIGN TIPS

Here are a few design tips to help your displays look great (not rules — just suggestions):

- **Get bold, colorful pots.** Strong colors for strong light! Consider cobalt blue, dusky purple, chartreuse, bright green, magenta, burnt orange, or bright yellow.

- **Get a multicolored pot.** Then choose one or two of its colors to echo in the plants choices within (not too many colors — too busy is hard on the eyes).

- **Match pot size and shape to plant.** Aim for equal volume or a vertical-habit plant in a tall/vertical pot.

- **Vary the compositions.** Arrange pots of mixed sizes, shifting them around so you still get a good view of each one.

- **Vary the heights.** A grouping of all-same-size-and-height pots blends together and it's hard for certain ones to stand out. Elevate a few on bricks, blocks, stones, or overturned empty pots so the display has some intriguing topography.

- **Throw in a wild card.** Tuck a whimsical garden ornament among the potted plants, tip a pot on its side (like an empty vessel), or tuck in some natural companions such as seashells, pinecones, or pretty rocks.

TIP

Think past flowers! Although most people love flowers, some of the best and most interesting potted plants have beautiful and colorful leaves and/or intriguing forms. Often these hold the stage in your landscape for much longer than a fleeting flower show, too.

Check out the following:

>> **Rosette-forming succulents:** Agaves, hens-chicks, echeveria

>> **Trailing sedums**

>> **Herbs:** Thyme, sage, rosemary, lavender (growing these in pots allows you not only to enjoy their beauty and harvest fresh snippings, but you can also put them where you can savor their scents)

>> **Annuals:** Million bells, portulaca, verbena

>> **Especially tough and beautiful flowers:** Chocolate flower, gaura, lantana, strawflower

IN THIS CHAPTER

» **Installing a basic pond, step-by-step**

» **Solving water-garden problems**

» **Placing and filling a small containerized water garden**

» **Considering fountains and birdbaths**

Chapter **18**

Including Water Features in Your Landscape

Believe it or not, adding some sort of element to your home landscape that features or relies upon water is *not* an outlandish idea. After they're filled, ponds and pools, big or small, with or without plants, fish and various extras aren't big consumers of water. Yes, you lose some to evaporation, but that's not a deal-breaker. The same goes for fountains; even a simple birdbath is a happy addition, not just for you, but for parched winged visitors.

Water features, by sight and/or sound, bring a soothing element to any garden area. And in areas where water is precious, they turn out to be especially welcome, a balm to the spirit and a joy to the eye. This chapter describes your options and explains what's involved. I also invite you to take a look at the beautiful example in the color insert. Your skepticism may evaporate.

TECHNICAL STUFF

A spot devoted to a water feature consumes at least 50 percent less water than the same area given over to a lawn or traditional flowerbed. A group of avid water gardeners in Denver, the innovative members of the Colorado Water Garden Society, confirmed and promoted this years ago. Interestingly, Denver is also the place where the term *xeriscaping* (landscaping and gardening responsibly in dry-climate conditions) was first touted — see Chapter 19 for more details.

Putting in a Pond or Pool

In nature, ponds and pools are in-ground and fed by groundwater, springs, rain, snowmelt, and/or streams. When gardeners recreate something like this for beauty and interest in their home landscape, it isn't part of or connected to other water systems or features. Instead a garden pond is a contained system.

REMEMBER

Water's only escape or exit from a garden water feature is evaporation. That's because the base is lined with something impermeable. A range of liner options — PVC plastic (UV-treated), flexible but heavy-duty synthetic rubber, or fiberglass — is available. Even concrete is possible in areas where the ground doesn't freeze in winter and there isn't a risk of the pool being pushed upward or damaged due to freeze-thaw cycles.

Using such rugged materials prevents leaks (but should leaks occur, act fast to repair them so the whole thing doesn't drain). Installation also involves putting garden pools in slightly above the grade of the surrounding ground so silt and runoff don't get in the water feature. Use bricks, rocks, pavers, flagstones, and/or landscaping to enforce, secure, and hide the edges.

The following sections explain the basic installation steps and discuss some options/variations and possible concerns.

Pondering a recirculating pump

These outdoor/garden-use pumps are a water feature's friend. They keep the water moving, which provides beneficial oxygen to plants and fish and other life in the water and also discourages algae. In other words, they help keep a display healthy. And of course they conserve and recycle water by keeping it always within the system.

They're a good idea if you have a larger water garden and necessary if you include a waterfall or cascade feature. Outdoor wiring and maintenance (including cleaning and changing filters) complicate the picture, but gardeners who have installed one praise the way it keeps the water clean and the display looking good. If you're interested in one, discuss it with your water-garden supplier or contractor.

Installing a basic pool

The following instructions assume a typical homeowner project, an installation of a preformed liner manufactured for this purpose, measuring 4 x 6 feet (1.2 x 1.8 m) and with a depth of 18 inches (46 cm). When full, this pool will hold an estimated 150 gallons (68 kg) of water.

WHAT ABOUT A STREAM OR WATERFALL?

A stream or waterfall can give your landscape not only the lovely sight of water but also the sound, whether trickling and gurgling along, cascading, or steadily pouring.

However, installing such features isn't a job for an amateur. A professional will help you identify the best spot in your yard, bring in equipment to grade and dig, install the liner and pump, and finish the job. They'll also explain maintenance or offer a service contract.

A stream or waterfall does have drawbacks in a low-water landscape setting. They can look oddly out of place — in your region's climate and even in the context of your yard's plants/other landscaping. And because they're occupying and passing through a broader area and are shallower than a pond or pool, evaporation happens much faster.

If you really like the look, you can consider installing a water-free one, that is, a dry streambed. Check out Chapter 16 for details, installation instructions, and advice.

Recruiting helpers — extra pairs of eyes and hands — makes the project go much more quickly and smoothly.

If the project isn't too large, you can do it yourself — if you want to. Otherwise, find and vet an experienced contractor. If you do it yourself, stick to these steps:

Step 1: Choose the site

The best spots are out in the open because direct sunlight is important for the health of a pool as well as its inhabitants (plant and animal). Also you don't want to run into tree roots or have trees or shrubs dropping leaves or fruit into the water. A fairly level spot makes the job easier. That said, you can tinker to make a site level in the digging process.

Avoid the lowest part of your yard. In a flash flood or heavy rainfall, all the water will go there and you'll have overflow and runoff issues.

Make sure the chosen spot is within reach of the hose, not just for the initial filling process, but for topping off water lost to evaporation.

Step 2: Create the outline

If you'll be sinking a preformed liner shape into the earth, drag it over to the site and mark the top edge of the outline on the ground. Chalk, white spray paint, or even a line of sprinkled flour works; alternatively just use a length of rope or a long outdoor extension cord. After you have an outline, go back over it, scoring the ground with a shovel or trowel.

Step 3: Dig the hole

Excavate using a shovel from the outer boundary, making the hole an inch or two (2.4 to 5 cm) bigger on all sides and in depth, as Figure 18-1 shows. Remove all sod, rocks, and debris as you work. Reserve the soil because you'll need some of it for filling back in around the liner later.

FIGURE 18-1:
Dig a hole in an open area, ideally free of tree roots and rocks.

Step 4: Level it

After you get close to the finished depth, slow down and work on leveling the hole. To do so, flatten and tamp down the base; use a piece of lumber to smooth it. Lay a board across the top of the hole, set a carpenter's level on it, and check from various points. If the top isn't level, it's often easier to adjust the soil at the yard's surface than to change the depth of the hole.

Step 5: Put in a base layer

A base layer helps you seat the liner properly (see Figure 18-2). Builder's sand is great because it helps you jigger the liner into place, plus it makes a nice smooth surface for the liner to rest upon. If the soil you've exposed by digging is rough (despite your best efforts to smooth it) with stones, you can lay down an old carpet or carpet remnants and then add the sand.

FIGURE 18-2: Pour a base layer of sand into the hole to help seat and protect the liner.

Step 6: Settle the liner into place

Wiggle and jiggle the liner until it fits and then check again with the board and carpenter's level across the width and length till all is level.

Step 7: Add water

To equalize the pressure from the water and the surrounding soil and to prevent bulges, simultaneously fill the pool with water and surround the liner with reserved soil. Set the hose in the bottom and start filling it slowly with water, while backfilling the gap between the ground and the pool from your pile of excavated soil. Tamp the dirt in place with a trowel or board, working your way around until the gap is filled evenly on all sides and the pool is filled.

Step 8: Add finishing touches

Hide the edges from view, not just to make the scene look more natural but also to protect the liner from UV rays, to help anchor your pool in place, and to block runoff from your yard. Use bricks, stones, or flagstones. You can then add plants in the pool and around the edges.

Recognizing pool variations

Liners are available from a variety of outlets, from big-box home stores to nurseries that specialize in water-gardening supplies. Here are some variations you may encounter:

REMEMBER

>> **Preformed liners:** These come in heavy-duty plastic as well as fiberglass. Shapes include round, oval, rectangle, and the ever-popular kidney and amoeba forms.

If you foresee adding plants to your pond (water-garden plants must be potted in heavy garden soil then lowered in; you can't just plunk them into the water), choose one with interior side shelves. You can include plants that don't like deep water — for example, irises, cattails, and sedges. (True, including side shelves makes digging the hole and backfilling after a bit trickier, but it can be done!)

REMEMBER

>> **A free-form pool:** This option allows you to design your own shape. For the lining, use a big sheet of heavy material intended for this purpose.

Get the dimensions, including depth (18 inches, 45.7 cm, is considered minimum) and then buy a piece that's too big by at least a foot (30.5 cm) on all sides. You'll trim it after filling the pool with water — never before.

TIP

If it's hard to maneuver on installation day, try leaving it out in the hot sun for a few hours, which softens it and improves its flexibility.

>> **A gazing or reflecting pool:** This type of pool can be sunken or aboveground:

- Sunken ones are supported by the surrounding earth (refer to the steps and drawings in the section, "Installing a basic pool" earlier in this chapter). Alternatively, you could set one into a paved area, patio, or courtyard where earth and/or masonry help support the considerable weight of the water.

- Aboveground ones require substantial side support in the form of a frame made of stone, brick, or even concrete.

Considering potential issues

Occasional problems surface. Here's a quick rundown along with comments about solutions (water loss doesn't make this list because it's understood that water features lose water to evaporation and occasional topping off is needed):

>> **Leaks:** Rips, punctures, and ordinary wear can cause a leak. If it's not a bad one, you can lower the water level until you find it and then patch it.

>> **Mosquitos:** These pests breed in water. Add the fish that dine on them or consult your water-garden supplier for chemical remedies that won't endanger pond life.

>> **Hungry birds:** If you have fish, birds come fishing and consume everything from cheap goldfish to expensive koi. Decoys and/or waterlily pads for the fish to hide under are remedies — as is a cat or dog in the yard.

>> **Vandal mammals:** Muskrats and raccoons can enter the pool and make a mess. Netting settled over the pool when you're not home or are indoors or asleep can discourage them.

>> **Clogged filters (if you have a pump):** Find out proper pump maintenance at installation time and don't be neglectful.

>> **Freezing winter weather:** Should water freeze in your pool (and it's not so deep that this couldn't happen in some locations), remember that ice expands. Lower the water level and take out pond décor before winter arrives. As for pond plants, consult your water-garden supplier for specific advice; sometimes you can trim them back and lower them into deeper water, and other times you must remove and keep them in a greenhouse, screened porch, or conservatory for the winter months.

Eyeing recommended water-garden plants

The best thing about adding plants to your display is that their most basic need — water — is all taken care of. Choose ones that look like they belong, like the conditions, and help keep the display attractive over long periods.

Here are some fine choices but, as ever, cross-check with your local nursery supplier to confirm that they're appropriate for your area. Many more, including some suitable native plants such as sedges and cattails, are suitable. This list is just to get you started with popular and colorful selections:

>> **Waterlilies:** You can find two kinds:

- Tropical: Often larger flowers; flowers rise above the water surface; not tolerant of cold weather.

- Hardy: Smaller blooms; flowers float on the water surface.

Both types are available in many colors and forms. Some are sweetly scented; some bloom in the cooler evening hours. In milder climates, tropical varieties are best.

You may include waterlilies for their blossoms, but their foliage (lily pads) is very important in a water display. They help cover your pond's surface, offering shade and shelter to fish and other pond life. Also, shielding the water's surface from hot, direct sun stifles algae growth and cools the water.

>> **Lotus:** Getting them to produce their unique and elegant umbrellalike leaves may not be difficult, but getting them to flower is trickier. Ask your supplier to recommend a variety known to do well in your area — and to sell you some appropriate fertilizer for extra encouragement.

>> **Irises:** Not all irises thrive in a water garden (for example, bearded and Japanese irises) but certain ones do (yellow and blue flag), and they bloom enthusiastically and also come in spectacular colors, including purple, yellow, and magenta. When they're not in bloom, their erect, bladelike leaves look great in your display.

>> **Cannas:** These love to have their feet in the water. Foliage can be plain green or dramatically colorful, and the flowers come in many bright hues.

Making a small, containerized display

If you don't want to take the full water–garden plunge, try a container. All you need is a sunny spot because most water plants love full sun — a corner of a patio or deck, maybe. Here's how to proceed:

>> **Choose the right container.** A large pot is best because most water plants aren't diminutive. Pick one that's strong enough to support heavy water and sturdy so it doesn't leak. Water-garden suppliers have such pots, but you may also find suitable ones elsewhere (if you find a good one but it has drainage holes, plug them).

The ever-popular half whiskey barrel can be used but must be lined so it won't leak, of course. Water-garden suppliers sell plastic liners that are a Cinderella fit, or you can line a big pot with heavy plastic, stapling or fastening it in place along the rim.

>> **Select suitable plants.** Depending on the size of the container, you can tuck in at least one water plant, maybe several. Avoid overcrowding because they do grow, and you don't want to end up with an unmanageable jumble.

Miniature waterlilies and miniature lotuses are available. You can also find small-size water irises, dwarf cannas, short cattails, and sedges. Just make sure, when you're browsing, that the plant is a suitable size for the pot you're using.

Adding Pretty and Practical Water Features

You can add a touch of water to a dry garden in other sensible yet pleasurable ways. Fountains and birdbaths consume minimal water. Without doubt they're more affordable and easier to maintain than the more substantial watery projects that I discuss in this chapter. Best of all, you still get to savor the big payoff of a lovely sight and lovely sounds in your landscape. These sections delve deeper into your options.

Enjoying a private fountain

If the gentle, soothing, bubbling, or splashy sound of a garden fountain strikes your fancy, do yourself a favor and indulge the wish. You can pick from among those different styles, and some offer adjustable settings.

Recognizing the different types

Fountains intended for outdoor display come with internal (hidden) small pumps to circulate the water. Two main options are as follows:

>> **A plug-in fountain:** You plug in the pump into a grounded outdoor electrical outlet.

>> **A solar-powered fountain:** When you get a solar-powered fountain, you greatly expand placement possibilities! Because it doesn't need to be plugged in, it can be set up far from your house, even tucked into a back corner.

Start by looking at all the many options and designs. Local nurseries, landscaping-supply yards, and big-box stores should offer some. Also look online, and check Instagram and Pinterest for ideas.

Prepare to be inspired. You can find everything from traditional pedestal fountains to small frog bathtubs and gnome grottos to cascading-stone designs. There are wall fountains, that is, ones that you can mount at eye level on a wall or fence. Other options include tiered bowls, spurting urns, and stone balls over which water makes a whisper-quiet, graceful sheen.

Purchasing and converting a large piece of original pottery into a fountain using a kit may be possible. If you're not a DIYer, take it to somebody who does this work. Although this option is probably the most expensive, if you go this route, you'll have something special and spectacular.

Using fountains

Here are some useful tips regarding fountains:

- » **Be flexible about materials.** You don't have to spend a fortune on a heavy authentic stone fountain when you can get a reasonable resin facsimile that would fool almost anyone.

- » **You may need a foundation.** A flat, seated tile or paver helps keep a wobbly fountain stable, disperses the weight of a heavy one, and also elevates the fountain a bit for more attention.

- » **Protect it for winter.** Even if the temperatures never fall below freezing and there's no chance of snow, colder and occasionally stormy weather can be hard on the fountain and the pump apparatus. Drain and cover the fountain (cinch plastic or a small tarp around it) and store the pump indoors until spring.

- » **Check the warranty.** Typically pump-driven fountains are only guaranteed for two or three years. If you're diligent about the care and maintenance of the pump, you can prolong its life.

- » **Consider night lighting.** If a fountain doesn't come with a lighting option, you may be able to install some illumination adjacent or nearby, so you can enjoy it even in the evening hours.

Splishing and splashing — birdbaths

I've met few gardeners who don't love having birds visit, but the usual ways to entice them don't include water. Some gardeners put up bird feeders. They plant shrubs, trees, and flowers that can feed or shelter the feathered friends.

Offering water via a garden birdbath is a wonderful thing to do, especially when the weather is hot and dry, and natural sources of water may be few and far between. The sound may attract them, and they'll tell their friends and family. You're offering both a drink and a bath.

Here are some guidelines when you include a birdbath to your yard:

- » **Make the approach safe.** Small birds worry about predators such as eagles, hawks, and vultures, but they long to visit your birdbath. Set it in the open but not far from shrubs or trees that they can perch in first and flee to if necessary. They'll look to see if the coast is clear and ladder on down the vegetation till they swoop to the birdbath's rim. (If you have no takers, after a while, try a different location.)

- » **Provide secure footing.** Some birdbaths are sold with a footer; otherwise you can provide one. The birdbath shouldn't wobble or threaten to tip over.

- » **Keep the water topped off and clean.** Otherwise the birds won't come or stay.

IN THIS CHAPTER

» Looking at the term's origins

» Reviewing the basic principles

» Choosing and placing practical plants

» Considering modern-day best practices and improvements

» Making the results attractive

Chapter 19

Updating Xeriscaping for Today's Low-Water Landscapes

The term *xeriscape* isn't a new concept anymore. Credit for coining it goes to the Denver, Colorado, water department in the late 1970s. *Xeros* is the Greek word for *dry*, and pairing it with *landscape* handily signified landscaping and gardening responsibly in dry-climate conditions.

In retrospect, promoting xeriscaping about 50 years ago was certainly ahead of the times. The demand has increased for low-water landscaping because a changing climate has intensified prolonged droughts and extreme weather events.

This chapter addresses the foundational xeriscaping concepts you need to know and heed. I tuck in some updates and fresh information and insights. And yes, your choices and efforts can lead to beautiful results.

REMEMBER

The prize here is a mature or maturing low-water landscape that looks great and isn't demanding of your time and resources. Don't forget that newly installed plants require more intervention and water so they can get established, which ideally is a temporary situation.

Comprehending Just the Basics

When Denver set out to encourage water-wise gardening to its residents, above all the city touted being practical. Practical in your plant selections. Practical in your use of precious water.

The following seven basic principles were identified — and they continue to make good sense. I define and describe each one, and then make a few helpful comments about putting these things into practice in your own yard.

Improving your soil

Good soil nurtures plants, allowing them to grow, thrive, and bring beauty to your home landscape.

"Bad" soil is a judgment call, because — with few exceptions — most soils can support some kind of plant life. However, the relationship between some native soils and water leads gardeners to want to intervene, so that you can put in an attractive landscape. The following helps clarify what you can do with less-than-ideal soil:

>> **Hard, dry soil:** It may be or have become dry, or it may have been compacted (by constant foot traffic or by heavy equipment, for example), or both. It doesn't absorb water well. A long-awaited, much-needed deluge may come and you'll watch with dismay as the water just runs right off and washes away.

>> **Clay soil:** The tiny bits and particles that make up clay soil compact together, sometimes quite tightly. The ground may be impenetrable and/or water-logged. A rainfall may run right off.

In both cases, the remedy is to add organic matter to your soil. Doing so improves its texture, breaking it up and aerating it (allowing in beneficial oxygen) — and allowing it to absorb water.

Don't worry, improving your soil so it welcomes plants is actually straightforward. The needed organic matter comes in a variety of forms, and you can use it in various easy ways to build up your garden ground. Flip to Chapter 4 for the details.

Selecting suitable plants

Not all nice landscape plants are water hogs and difficult to keep alive in dry conditions. Xeriscaping introduces those plants that can get what they need with less water and less work on your part. They're tougher and more resilient, and yet, they can still look great. Consider these suggestions:

>> **Focus on natives or nativars.** Most of these plants are native, or derived from native plants (*nativars,* cultivated plants chosen or propagated for bigger, better, and/or more flowers, longer blooming periods, and tidier growth habits). Recent years have seen an explosion of choices. Be proactive:

- View them in local garden centers and nurseries and/or check online for mail-order sources.

- Look for them growing in neighbors' yards and area botanic gardens; when you see ones you love, find out their names and go get some.

>> **Seek other appropriate plants from similar regions and climates.** The Mediterranean region has had a big influence (examples include lavender, rosemary, and many salvias). So, too, have parts of Australia (examples include banksia and kangaroo paws). Finding such plants isn't difficult; just ask for them where you shop for your garden or seek out nurseries that specialize in them. These plants serve to greatly expand your plant palette.

>> **Consider herb plants.** They add beauty in your yard and are great for harvesting for use in your kitchen. After established, many — such as sage, thyme, rosemary, and summer savory — thrive on neglect.

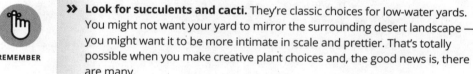

REMEMBER

>> **Look for succulents and cacti.** They're classic choices for low-water yards. You might not want your yard to mirror the surrounding desert landscape — you might want it to be more intimate in scale and prettier. That's totally possible when you make creative plant choices and, the good news is, there are many.

Common to all these plants is a preference for dry soil most of the time. Some need to dry out completely before you give them more water. Others can go all summer without water — they're used to doing so. California lilac, the beautiful ceanothus bush, is a classic example. For long annotated lists of recommended water-efficient plants, consult Part 2. You can also find a short list in Chapter 21 about ten great low-water plants.

TIP

Sometimes people fall in love with impractical plants — plants that need more water than you're willing or able to supply, or plants that are fussy about soil or light. One solution is to try growing such plants in pots and keeping them where you're sure to notice how they're doing and respond to their needs. Consult Chapter 17 for more details about gardening in containers.

Grouping plants appropriately

You can save yourself a lot of work and waste, while keeping your landscape's plants healthy and happy, by grouping them according to similar needs. Keep the following in mind:

>> **Water needs:** Place plants with similar irrigation needs in the same general area. That way, ones that don't need much don't get overwatered when you soak nearby ones that do. It's called creating watering zones. When creating zones, do the following:

- Ask about their water needs when you buy them and keep like ones together when you install them in your yard. Just take the time to find out.

- Place higher-water plants near the house where they can get runoff water from your roof, and you'll notice when they're in distress. Farther from the house, make a transition area for plants that need occasional water. The ones in your landscape's most-distant corners can be native plants that survive on natural rainfall alone. Chapter 16 discusses watering zones in greater detail.

>> **Light needs:** Plants can also be grouped according to light needs. Shade plants go in shady spots, sun plants can go in the sun, and some can go either way. Sometimes it's a learning curve — a plant struggles or fails or you have to move it, which is all normal. Your landscaping will improve and stabilize over time — you'll get there!

>> **Type of soil:** Soil requirements are another way to group plants, assuming your yard offers choices. Determine what type of soil you have: Is it a super-dry area? Put in super-drought-tolerant plants. Damp corner? Choose accordingly. Refer to the section, "Improving your soil," earlier in this chapter for more specifics.

TIP

Match up those plants who have things in common. Separate those that don't. Chapter 3 has more details and examples.

Mulching for maximum benefits

Using mulch is the best and quite possibly the most effective way to conserve water in your landscape. It's easy to acquire and apply — and affordable to boot! Here are the many important benefits:

>> Mulch holds in soil moisture and prevents or slows water loss due to evaporation.

>> It discourages weeds, interlopers that suck up water and soil nutrients that your desired plants need.

>> It stabilizes soil temperature. Without it, your soil will dry out, maybe even to the point of baking until it's rock-hard — clearly not what you want!

>> It looks nice and gives your yard and landscaping a tidier look.

To be effective, generously apply mulch; between 3 and 5 inches (7.6 to 12.7 cm) isn't excessive, just do what you can. Many natural mulches, from shredded bark or leaves to compost to straw or pine straw, are available. You could also use rock materials (crushed rock, gravel, decomposed granite, and so on). I provide a full list, complete with pros and cons, in Chapter 15.

REMEMBER

Organic mulches also break down over time and have to be replenished. The good news is that it's beneficial to your soil.

Pivoting to practical grassy areas

When Denver started promoting xeriscaping, suburban lawns were in their cross-hairs. Nowadays, decades later, the public has come to understand that sprawling areas of nice groomed green grass consume a lot of water, fertilizer, and effort — far more than any other landscape feature.

Getting rid of or greatly reducing your lawn is the best plan. That may have been hard to hear back then — and it's still hard to hear for some people. But these days, not just the arid West and Southwest have to reconsider or eliminate lawns. Other areas are now suffering daunting water shortages. These days, lush turf is definitely on the outs, and removal is no longer so shocking. Indeed, removing it may be necessary or required.

Lawn alternatives to consider include low-growing groundcovers of many sorts, meadow and pollinator gardens, creative new landscaping schemes, and even hardscape items like a terrace, patio, or deck. Part 3 confronts the entire matter — removing and replacing — in detail.

Ask yourself, is your current lawn area just a showpiece? Other showpiece landscaping ideas abound. Is it functional (a recreational area, for instance)? If yes, aim to keep it, but in a wiser, more efficient form:

>> **Go smaller.** Work to reduce your lawn area bit by bit over several years by gradually taking back some of that real estate and devoting it to one or more alternatives.

>> **Remove water- and fertilizer-hungry grass and replace it with a more resilient choice.** Bluegrass is a big culprit. Go with something like zoysia, bermuda, or bahiagrass. Maybe even a native grass or a blend. Research and choose a variety appropriate to your site.

- >> **Plant a groundcover that has a grassy look but is less demanding.** An example is liriope.

- >> **Put in artificial turf.** Yes, really. The materials and the look have changed dramatically for the better. Refer to Chapter 13 for the scoop.

TIP

Foot traffic may be your issue; if your current lawn gets walked over or played on and because of its location, the area will continue to be. Unfortunately grasses that tolerate foot traffic well also tend to be water hogs; drought-resistant grasses don't always hold up if tread upon often. Look at all alternatives: the grasses and grass blends, native and otherwise, that are now recommended for your particular region and climate as well as non-grass landscaping.

Irrigating efficiently

You don't need to waste precious water, potable or otherwise. Technology and techniques have come a long way since xeriscaping was first introduced. In fact, with a good inground irrigation system or even some low-tech ideas, you can enjoy a lusher, prettier landscape than the residents of Denver ever imagined. Today's innovations are terrific. Here are some highlights:

- >> **In-ground systems are super-efficient, with sophisticated monitoring controls.** They're very targeted and, properly installed and programmed, deliver the right amount of water to root zones.

- >> **Sprinklers and soaker hoses are better.** They're more durable, more efficient, and less wasteful.

- >> **Low-tech options have been mainstreamed.** Pipes, clay pots, and other ideas deliver water where needed. "What's old is new" and has been tweaked for modern-day North American gardens and landscapes.

- >> **Water-storing crystals are widely available.** Straight up or mixed into planting soil, these allow for efficient storage and plant water uptake (see Chapter 16).

- >> **Using nonpotable water has advanced.** You don't have to and shouldn't use valuable, expensive household drinking water. Among your options are rainwater, gray water, and reclaimed water.

REMEMBER

Part of efficient watering is making seasonal adjustments. Now standard with many irrigation systems are sensors that shut down or reduce water if rain happens to come — and of course they don't operate when you have a rainy fall, winter, or spring. Turn to Part 1 for more specific information.

Maintaining what you plant

Your attentiveness and active involvement can make all the difference in a successful low-water landscape. Chapter 10 has lots of good, useful information. Meanwhile, here are a few basic do's and don'ts:

>> **Do tidy up.** Cruise through the yard on a regular basis (how often depends on what you plant and the time of year — you'll get into a rhythm) and remove spent flowers and bedraggled foliage. If you don't want seedlings popping up here and there, including in spots where there is no room for them or conditions aren't right for them, clip off flowers and seedheads.

Keep up with pruning. Remove dead and diseased foliage and branches, and rein in excessive growth so plants look neater and require less resources.

>> **Don't fertilize or reduce fertilizing.** Don't install and spoil plants dependent on fertilizer when plenty of plants do fine without it. If you keep a lawn and mow it, leave the clippings on the grass to break down and help feed it. To offer nutrition to your plants, use compost.

>> **Do monitor plant health.** If you're watching, you'll detect pest or disease problems as they occur and can respond with more ecofriendly remedies.

>> **Don't allow weeds.** Although you may not ever achieve 100-percent control, neither should you allow encroaching weeds to get the upper hand. Weeds and unwanted plants not only mar the look of your landscape, but they also usurp water and soil nutrients.

Designing for Beauty

A key element of xeriscaping is design. Where should certain plants go, to thrive as well as to look good? How can you work with the natural contours of your site to route and hold water? How can you do all this and still have something that's attractive — a pleasure to behold and hang out in?

The short answer is, educate yourself to be sensitive. Sensitive to what's going on in your landscape — where water flows, where plants grow well, where butterflies linger. If you work *with* the land and your climate, you truly can create and nurture beauty. Chapter 16 addresses ways you can capitalize on your landscape's contours.

Other steps you can take to make your dry landscape pretty as possible:

>> **Go for colorful plants.** Not just bright, vibrant flowers, but find plants with good-looking, splashy, or variegated leaves. Consult the long lists in Part 2. Visit a large, well-stocked garden center. After you locate your discoveries, you can make attractive combinations and compositions.

>> **Aim for a lush look.** Mass plants (with *a little* elbow room between them, or you'll be clipping them back) rather than dotting them here and there. Mix shades of green.

>> **Add interesting elements.** Don't require plants alone to carry the load of your desire for an attractive yard. Incorporate rocks — big ones as accents, gravel as a base (Chapter 14 has tons of good ideas). Tuck in stylish and colorful garden décor (see Chapter 1). Relate your landscaping scheme(s) to your home's architectural style and color. Add sound: bird feeders, wind-chimes, or a small circulating fountain.

TIP

Seek inspiration and grab ideas — feed your imagination! Start by thumbing through this book's color insert. Move on to look in other gardening books on the topic of dry landscaping and to other gardens (public and private). Look online for photos from landscape designers or just other folks like you posting their successes on Instagram and Pinterest. It's fun and will help immensely.

A NO-WATER GARDEN — IS IT POSSIBLE?

Having a no-water garden isn't a joke. With planning (including following the principles in this book) and patience, your dry garden can live without supplemental water — in time. Reaching that goal depends on the plants you select as well as your local precipitation patterns.

Those who've succeeded with this say to give such a nearly independent landscape up to four years to establish. Water in new plants, at the start of the project and of course, if you introduce more later. Water everything less in year two, much less in year three, and see how it goes in year four.

You may need to spot-water certain plants from time to time, and resume irrigating when there's a severe and prolonged drought. But a self-sufficient landscape is possible. *Bonus:* You'll spend far less time maintaining it and much more time enjoying it!

5

The Parts of Tens

Discover and implement various large and small ways you can reduce your outdoor water consumption.

Explore and invest in tried-and-true plants that will thrive and deliver beauty in a low-water setting.

Chapter 20

Ten Ways to Avoid Wasting Landscape Water

Maybe when you made a mistake, your grandma would say tartly, "No use crying over spilt milk!" That old, not-very-comforting cliché really doesn't apply well to water in your landscape, though. Watching a rare torrential rain run right off, into the gutter, down the road and away, is definitely worth crying over. So, too, is a build-up of clouds that deliver nothing but a little sprinkling. Getting a huge water bill is also worth crying over. And heaven help you the fateful day when you turn on a tap and nothing comes out.

Here I help you stay positive . . . and proactive. Nobody wants to waste precious water. Your yard and garden can use every drop. This chapter identifies ways you can avoid wasting landscape water. I skip the most obvious mishaps, like leaving the hose running and going out for a few hours or even just having a very slightly leaky outdoor spigot that ends up over time dribbling away a significant amount of water. Even the nicest grandmother would call you out on those blunders.

Making Your Soil Better

A main cause of runoff is soil that simply can't absorb incoming water. Maybe it's dried out to the point of hardpan or dust, maybe it's just lean and gritty, or maybe it's got high clay content and water soaks in slowly if at all.

TIP

The remedy is the same: Add organic matter, which helps hold water and nutrients in the ground. Organic matter also promotes the biological activity that sustains healthy soil going forward — everything from beneficial soil microbes (including fungi) to big fat earthworms.

Organic matter added to lousy soil is a game-changer. It improves the texture of sandy ground so any water that arrives doesn't drain quickly away. It improves the texture of high-clay soils by helping the clay particles form aggregates, which in turn allow pores in the soil to open and water to be absorbed.

Adding organic matter is worth doing even when your yard's soil is somewhere between the two extremes. Dedicate yourself to ongoing soil improvement and never look back — there's no downside! Refer to Chapter 5 for full details.

WARNING

Although it's tempting to use inorganic fertilizers (such as Miracle-Gro) to get nutrients into poor soil, skip this shortcut. The benefits to your plants are temporary and the water-absorption problem isn't solved. That's because these products are water-soluble and plant roots can't access the benefits unless sufficient water is present. Furthermore, even though roots may grab some nutrition from this sort of fertilizer, much just leaches away. Yet another problem: Leaching-away fertilizer leads behind potentially harmful salts in your already not-so-great soil. Making your soil better with organic matter is always better!

Choosing Your Plants Wisely

Not all landscape plants need a lot of water. If you relocated to a dry climate after years in a lusher place or if your region is becoming consistently drier, let go of old assumptions about the idea of good garden plants and garden beauty. Stop wasting effort and money on landscaping that struggles, looks terrible, and fails — basically because it's not appropriate to the situation.

TIP

Save water and woe by installing plants that use less water and are adapted to the realities of your climate. And no, those plants aren't all cacti, or brown, or dull-looking. You'll be amazed at the range of vibrant colors, handsome textures, and interesting forms.

You're reading this book hoping you could find a better way. Thumb through the color insert for a quick sense of the possibilities, and then spend some time with the lists and descriptions found in the Part 2 chapters. I also include my top 10 in Chapter 21.

Planting in the Fall

Installing new and baby plants at a stressful time . . . is stressful. If your summers are baking hot, with little or no rain, why plant in spring and, within a couple short months, subject them to that stress? Nor would you plant when summer is in full swing.

REMEMBER

Planting in fall instead works out great because the soil and air are cooler. The newcomers won't experience heat stress, won't consume as much water, and the water they do get will be slower to evaporate. In fact, if you're fortunate to be in an area that gets autumn rainfall, you can basically piggyback your landscaping on that free water.

When plants are installed in the fall months, they naturally tend to put their energy into developing their root systems. Most plants simply aren't programmed to put out lots of new leaves and branches or to form flowers and fruit in the fall months. The result is the plants head into winter and the following spring with a rapidly establishing root system — they get a head start on their spring-planted counterparts. When spring rolls around, your fall-planted ones will grow robustly. Being a little older and more mature than their spring-planted counterparts also means they can head into the stress of a long, hot, droughty summer stronger.

Grouping Like Plants

When landscaping your yard or even just putting in a new flowerbed or patio-side planting, put similar plants together for several reasons. They may be of similar colors (foliage and/or flowers) or size, which looks nice. But the best reason is purely practical — they can be watered together, and all of them will be fine with that. The idea is not to mix up your landscaping so much that some plants get underwatered and some get overwatered.

TIP

Get to know the plants you like and choose; they're individuals and information about their characteristics and water needs are readily available — here in this book, in plant catalogs, at nurseries and garden centers, online, or anywhere else you research and check them out. Ignore water-need information at their peril; accommodate and plan around it and you'll definitely use water efficiently.

Mulching — and Mulching Some More

Mulch is The Stuff, low-water landscapers! By that I mean, it's valuable and essential. Water delivered to plants tends to be in the top few inches of the ground — and the surface, if bare (no mulch), is exposed to the hot sun and dries out alarmingly quickly. This remains true, by the way, whether you water from above or have an in-ground (buried) irrigation system.

Give the soil surface around all your plants a blanket of mulch and immediately evaporation is slowed and moisture is held in the ground. Mulch also helps discourage water-greedy weeds from sneaking in and usurping moisture.

If you do nothing else to conserve water and take care of your plants, at least mulch! Simple, affordable, and powerfully effective. All details — what to use, how thickly to apply, when to reapply, and so on, can be found in Chapter 15.

Investing in a Watering System

No other kind of watering is as efficient as an in-ground system. Granted, these networks of pipes, valves, and emitters have been more primitive or more complex and thus best-suited to people who considered themselves handy, so leaks, modifications, and so forth could be dealt with.

The present technology — and by that I mean not only the materials and the design options, but also the way these systems work and are monitored — have come a long way. Nowadays watering this way is intuitive (if you choose manual controls) or automated (smart and programmable controls). And efficiency is superb. Individual plant needs are accommodated, weather conditions and seasonal shifts are monitored, and not a drop of water is wasted.

Consider the particulars of your yard's topography as well as what sorts of landscaping you hope to sustain. And, of course, think about what you're willing and able to invest. You *will* save water — in many cases, dramatically.

Turn to Chapter 5 for an overview, nitty-gritty details, and more.

Using Watering Tricks

You don't need to reinvent the wheel. Water-scarce places throughout the world and throughout history have generated all sorts of techniques, work-arounds, and clever innovations for getting needed water to plants, from flowers to food crops to trees. Get on board with some of these techniques and cut your water use way back.

From creating a simple basin around the base of a plant (so water goes right down to the root system and nowhere else), to delivering water to root systems by inserting pipes or clay pots into garden ground, to clustering water-needy plants at the base of a slope, you can get the maximum benefit out of minimum water.

TIP

Gather or collect water, too. Hold rainwater in collection barrels. Put a bucket in the shower and a smaller one in the sink, and fill up as you can (avoiding soapy water). Dump dehumidifier and vase water on your plants. Route gutter water into a flowerbed.

Every time you turn on a faucet, indoors as well as out, use only what you need. You can save a lot, here and there, bit by bit, by just being attentive.

Chapters 2 and 3 contain the information you need.

Getting Rid of Your Lawn

A lush green lawn just isn't practical because it consumes a lot of water (and fertilizer) and needs mowing and grooming. Modern culture has embraced and enjoyed this paradigm for decades, but it's high time to let it go.

Taking out a lawn isn't as hard as you might think. Grass roots aren't that deep, and you can peel back and lift out sections. You'll be left with a blank canvas, an opportunity. Almost anything you install next won't even begin to guzzle the water and other resources that a greensward sucked up.

Consider this trend, or mandate, a gift. Be thoughtful and creative. Get to know, enjoy, and use your outdoor living space in brand-new ways. Discover how to live in harmony with nature in ways that your old lawn never allowed.

I predict that it won't be long before you concede that you don't miss the lawn. It might even be as soon as the arrival of your next water bill, which you'll see has plummeted, thank goodness. Get started! Refer to Chapter 11.

Throwing Some Shade

Water evaporates fastest of all in direct sun. Shade slows water loss. How can you leverage these basic facts in your landscape?

Where your landscape has no shade, find ways to create it or provide it, especially at high noon or on long, bright summer days. This can be as simple as buying some shade cloth at a garden center and tossing it over your vegetable garden or rigging a support for the cloth that creates shelter from the blazing sun. Awnings, laths, pergolas, shade houses — all bring some welcome relief to plants that suffer or struggle in full, blazing-hot sun.

TIP

You can also use living plants to provide cooling, water-conserving shade. If you want to cluster flowering plants under a tree or vine-covered pergola, have them in containers rather than in the ground so the root systems aren't competing for the same moisture. Chapters 16 and 17 present options and ideas.

Making a Shift

In a time of scarcer and scarcer water, it's only natural to prioritize. Showers, washing dishes, even just drinking water — indoor daily-life needs — become more important than maintaining the yard. If you feel you're approaching this crossroads, don't let your plants dry up and die. Don't pave over your yard, either (which, actually, will make your surroundings hotter and less comfortable). Your landscape is your domain, and you're its steward. It's an extension of your home — it is your home.

Make a shift now, while you can weigh options and be creative. Move to a low-water landscape that suits you and your household. It's possible and rewarding to live in beautiful surroundings using little water. A sense of harmony and shared responsibility between indoors and outdoors blooms — you'll feel it and feel less anxious, less stretched and stressed, and less busy.

Don't just avoid wasting water on your landscaping. Choose not to.

Chapter **21**

Ten Great-Looking, Low-Water Plants

You're on board with putting in plants that don't require a lot of water, but you also want color, beauty, and impact. There's a lot more diversity than you may realize. And the selection just keeps getting better, as gardeners, plant nurseries, botanists and botanic gardens, plant explorers, and professional landscapers continue to discover and introduce more choices.

Whether native or from a similar climate, you can find garden-suitable versions. If the plants don't already have bountiful, colorful flowers and/or don't naturally have a manageable growth habit, the horticulture industry has selected or developed appealing selections or *cultivars* (cultivated varieties). Those plants may appeal to you!

This chapter includes ten terrific, tough, widely available choices to give you an idea of what's available to get you started. Please note that I lead with the most widely used common name and, for clarity, supply the scientific name second. I recommend some cultivars, too. Narrowing down this list to just ten was difficult; it's like picking your favorite child or pet or student. You can find longer lists in Part 2 and, of course, much more when you go shopping.

REMEMBER

All of these plants are adapted to living with less water. Once established, they'll prosper and flower despite only occasional rainfall and infrequent irrigation, but — there's a but — you must give them supplemental water to start them.

Beardtongue, Penstemon

Once just a familiar Western wildflower, various species and cultivars have become all the rage in English and European gardens, and some years ago, one called *Penstemon digitalis* 'Husker Red' won the prestigious American Perennial Plant of the Year award (the name refers to the reddish foliage; its flowers are actually white). Now many, many choices are available, wherever perennials are sold.

It's a resilient, bushy plant that produces airy spires of nectar-rich tubular flowers in summer, in all sorts of vibrant colors. Bees, butterflies, and especially hummingbirds, adore it. Plant size varies. If penstemons do well for you, they'll increase their numbers by reseeding each year.

Consider these choices:

>> **'Elfin Pink':** Vibrant pink flowers in profusion in early summer, on a plant that gets about 2 feet (0.6 m) high and half as wide.

>> **'Margarita BOP':** Dark blue flowers, all summer long, against gray-green foliage — stunning. Plants get 2 feet (0.6 m) tall and wide.

>> **Pineleaf beardtongue, *Penstemon pinifolius*:** Green pine-needle-like foliage is joined by scads of bright orange flowers in late spring to summer. Around 12 to 18 inches (30.5 to 45.7 cm) high and wide.

>> **Rocky Mountain beardtongue, *Penstemon strictus*:** Long-lasting, tall, showy spikes of bright purple-blue on a bushy plant, 2 feet (0.6 m) tall and 3 feet (0.9 m) wide.

Blue Fescue, Festuca glauca

This ornamental grass forms a handsome green-blue to blue-hued mound. Straw-colored stalks emerge and wave yellowish flower clusters above the foliage — you may clip these off if you don't care for them. The clumps mature to about 12 inches (30.5 cm) high and wide.

Consider these choices:

- » **'Elijah Blue':** The most widely grown one; light blue blades.

- » **'Golden Toupee':** Funny name! Yellow to chartreuse blades.

- » **'Harz':** Olive-green blades; cooler weather nudges them toward purple.

Butterfly Weed, Asclepias

This native, orange-flowered American wildflower has enjoyed a burst of popularity now that any gardener interested in helping the dwindling monarch butterfly populations knows the butterflies need it — for eating, laying eggs, forming a cocoon, and hopefully producing the next generation. Native plant sales always seem to have a few, and native plant and general nurseries carry various butterfly weeds. Sizes/heights vary, depending on which one you choose and whether it is well-adapted to your area.

Consider these choices:

- » **'Gay Butterflies':** Bright red and reddish flowers. Plants get 2 to 3 feet (0.6 to 0.9 m) tall and 2 feet (0.6 m) wide.

- » **'Hello Yellow':** Sunny yellow blooms. Plants get 1.5 to 3 feet (0.46 m to 0.9 m) tall and 1 to 2 feet (0.3 to 0.6 m) wide.

- » **'Western Gold Mix':** Flowers ranging from gold to yellow. Bred especially for alkaline soils, such as are often found in the American West and Southwest. Plants get 1 to 2 feet (0.3 to 0.6 m) tall and wide.

Catmint, Nepeta

Do you love purple flowers and want pollinators and butterflies in your yard? Then this plant is for you. It's bushy, great for filling in flowerbeds in need of plentiful color, and shades out any weeds that may have designs on the spot. Wiry stems are topped with lilac to dark-purple flowers; these cover the plant for much of the growing season. Foliage is sage-green, which makes such a pretty backdrop. Plants do sprawl over time.

Consider these choices:

» *Nepeta × faassenii*: This plant has silvery-gray foliage and violet spires and stays shorter than 2 feet (0.6 m) high. 'Porcelain' has soft blue-hued flowers against blue-gray leaves. 'Snowflake' has white flowers.

» *N. mussinii*: Sometimes called Persian catmint, it's shorter than 1.5 feet (0.46 m) and features lavender-blue flowers. Those of 'Blue Wonder' are rich, dark blue.

» **'Six Hills Giant'**: Has dark purple flowers and gets 3 to 5 feet (0.9 to 1.5 m) high — not giant, but big.

» **'Walker's Low'**: It has lavender-blue flowers. Plants get 1.5 to 2 feet (0.46 to 0.6 m) tall and 1.5 feet (0.46 m) wide.

Coneflower, Echinacea

Coneflowers are handsome, trouble-free plants with big and beautiful daisylike flowers and strong stems. What's not to love? The original species, *Echinacea purpurea*, has light purple petals (well, technically ray flowers) that droop away from a prominent central cone (central disk or disk flowers) — think of the form of a badminton shuttlecock. Butterflies, bees, and other flying insects and pollinators adore this easy-going, generous-blooming plant.

Recent years have seen an explosion of cultivars — bright new colors and some funky flower forms. Plants grow knee-high or taller (2 to 4 feet; 0.6 to 1.2 m); many cultivars are shorter and more compact, so check.

Consider these choices:

» **'Butterfly Kisses'**: So pretty! Especially plush and prominent pink centers (disk flowers) surrounded by lighter pink petals (ray flowers).

» **'Hot Papaya'**: Fiery orange.

» **'Magnus'**: Orange centers, bright pink petals.

» **'Marmalade'**: Bright orange centers, lighter-hued orange petals.

» **'Solar Flare'**: Magenta-to-red with darker red centers, black stems — fabulous.

Can't decide? Buy a mix, like 'Warm Summer'.

TIP

Hens and Chicks, Echeveria

Tidy, plump little rosettes in various shades of green, gray-green, blue, and blue-green, they sometimes send up slender stems topped with jaunty little bell-shaped blooms in shades of pink, red, yellow, or white. That means your planting can sometimes gain a fun and appealing two-tone look for a while.

These plants look wonderful grown in patches, as a groundcover, tucked into or adjacent to terraces, steps, and pathways, or weaving their way in among other low-water plants. They spread out slowly over time via offsets, forming dense colonies. I consider them social succulents! Size varies, which makes a case for combining different kinds.

Consider these choices:

>> **Classic hens and chicks, _E. × imbricata_:** Blue-gray leaves edged in pink. Yellow and red flowers. Many variations; my favorite is the perfectly named 'Blue Rose'. They aren't big plants, individually, staying shorter than 4 inches (10.1 cm) and spreading the same or a bit wider, but they quickly form colonies.

>> **Lipstick echeveria, _E. agavoides_:** Green leaves, tipped and often rimmed in red with red and yellow flowers. Tends to stay under 6 inches (15.2 cm) tall and can spread out to twice its height.

>> **Mexican snowball, _E. elegans_:** Blue-green leaves. Flowers are pink tinged with orange. About 8 inches (20.3 cm) tall and somewhat wider.

Lavender, Lavandula

Although you probably recognize and like lavender and would welcome the beauty of its purple spires and its wonderful, sleepy fragrance into your yard, make sure you choose wisely. The plants need neutral or alkaline soil, good to great drainage, and plentiful sunshine.

Plant habit is usually bushy and size is generally between 2 and 4 feet (0.6 and 1.2 m) high and wide, so be sure to allow enough space and a little extra for the good air circulation they appreciate.

You can find many species and cultivars, ranging from dark purple, light purple, rosy purple, pink, and even white-flowered selections. Fragrance varies from rich to spicy to lightly perfumed. Even the size and form varies. Rather than list any by name, I recommend you peek into neighborhood gardens and check out the ones your local garden center or nursery sells.

Russian Sage, Perovskia atriplicifolia

This justly popular plant's combination of silvery-gray foliage and fuzzy, soft lavender flowers is enchanting. It grows broad and bushy. The flower spires are long and last for many weeks. The foliage has a pleasant, sage fragrance that only adds to the plant's appeal. The species grows 3 to 4 feet (0.9 to 1.2 m) tall and 2 to 3 feet (0.6 to 0.9 m) wide; selections vary in size.

Consider these choices:

>> **'Blue Spires':** Has deep blue spires and a neat, tidier growth habit.

>> **'Little Spires':** Gets only 2 feet (0.6 m) tall and wide, is a fine choice for tighter spaces.

Sage, Salvia

Culinary sages and ornamental sages are all grouped together into a huge, variable genus. Any and all are great for dry gardens, so long as the plants are grown in well-drained soil. The culinary ones, of course, are valued for the leaves, but even they can do double duty in your plantings, for example, 'Tricolor', which has gray-green leaves splashed with pink and cream.

The ones prized for their blooms tend to be bigger and bushier. Some are native to the American West, whereas others hail from far-off places like South Africa. Bees, butterflies, and hummingbirds flock to these flowers.

Consider these choices:

>> **'Hot Lips':** White-and-hot pink to red bicolor flowers, airy green foliage. Can get 3 to 4 feet (0.9 to 1.2 m) tall and wide.

>> **Mexican bush sage, *Salvia leucantha*:** Plume of purple or purple-and white on a bushy, rangy plant (4 to 6 feet, 1.2 to 1.8 m) tall and wide).

>> ***Salvia greggii:*** Blooms all summer — bright red, medium green leaves. Reaches 2 to 3 feet (0.6 to 0.9 m) tall and wide.

>> ***Salvia guaranitica:*** Green leaves and memorable brilliant, dark-blue flowers. Gets 2 to 5 feet (0.6 to 1.5 m) tall and wide.

Stonecrop, Sedum

These are mainly low-growing succulents, cute in containers and planter boxes, popular in rock gardens and for lounging over rocks and walls, and of course splendid as dry-garden groundcovers (and, trendily, useful for decorative green-roofs and living walls).

Stonecrops tend to stay shorter than 4 to 6 inches (10.1 to 15.2 cm) as they creep, spread, and sprawl. The succulent leaves come in a range of colors, including orange, dusky purple, and apple green. Flowers appear in spring and summer, usually little star blooms borne in clusters.

Consider these choices:

>> **Sea star, *Sedum pulchellum*:** Beautiful and easy. A nurseryman once said, "Once you have it, you'll always have it, because it reseeds." Leaf shapes vary, color is fresh green, and flowers form pink sprays.

>> **Spanish stonecrop, *Sedum hispanicum* var. *hispanicum*:** Dense mounds of simply beautiful purple-pink foliage.

Index

Bulbinella (*Bulbinella nutans* or *B. robusta*), 108

Bur marigold (*Bidens*), 112

buried clay pots
  installing, 52–53
  overview, 51–52
  spacing, 53

Bush penstemon (*Penstemon fruticosus*), 115

Butterfly Kisses, 336

Butterfly Weed (*Asclepias*), 335

C

cacti
  areole, 133
  Beavertail cactus, 135
  Black spine prickly pear, 135
  Blue columnar cactus, 134
  Blue flame cactus, 134
  Candelabra cactus, 134
  Candelabra spurge, 134
  Claret cup cactus, 136
  Fishhook barrel cactus, 136
  glaucous, 133
  glochid, 133
  Golden ball cactus, 136
  Golden barrel cactus, 136
  Hedgehog cactus, 136
  Mammillaria, 136
  Mexican lime cactus, 134
  Mexican post cactus, 134
  Old man cactus, 134
  Organ pipe cactus, 134
  Peanut cactus, 136
  Prickly pear, 134, 136–137
  rib, 133
  shopping for, 135
  short, 135–136
  Silver torch cactus, 134
  spine, 133
  Star cactus, 135
  Strawberry hedgehog cactus, 136
  tall, 134–135

Totem pole cactus, 135

Turk's cap cactus, 136

xeriscaping, 319

Calendula (*Calendula officinalis*), 118

caliche, 67

California aster (*Symphyotrichum chilense*), 114

California buckeye (*Aesculus californica*), 154

California buttercup (*Ranunculus californicus*), 108

California fescue (*Festuca californica*), 231

California fuchsia (*Epilobium canum: Zauschneria californica*), 114

California gray rush (*Juncus patens*), 226

California poppy (*Eschscholzia californica*), 118

CalTrans, 28

Camas (*Camassia*), 108

Campfire plant (*Crassula capitella*), 126

Candelabra cactus (*Myrtillocactus cochal*), 134

Candelabra spurge (*Euphorbia ammak* var. *variegata*), 134

Candellia (*Euphorbia antisyphilitica*), 130–131

cannas, 314

Cape rush (*Chondropetalum; Elegia* species), 113

capillary mats, 54

car washing, 42, 57

Catmint (*Nepeta*), 113, 335–336

centum cubic feet (CCF) billing units, 28

Cercis (Redbud), 155

Chaparral yucca (*Hesperoyucca whipplei*), 129

Chinese jasmine (*Jasminum polyanthum*), 151

Chocolate flower (*Berlandiera lyrata*), 113

cisterns and tanks, 37

Claret cup cactus (*Echinocereus triglochidiatus*), 136

clay soil, 60, 67, 70, 318

Climbing roses (*Rosa cultivars*), 151

Cluster lily (*Brodiaea*), 108

clustering, 191–192

cocoa-bean hulls, 269

coconut coir, 280–282

Coleus (*Coleus*), 120

collard greens, 164

collecting water
  cisterns and tanks, 37
  overview, 33–34
  rain barrels
    installing, 36
    lid, 35
    maintaining, 36–37
    outlet spigot, 35
    overflow pipe, 35
    overview, 34–35
    supplemental water for, 37
    using water from, 36
  rain walls, 38

color
  artificial turf, 245
  beauty and color, 17–18
  drought-tolerant plants, 15

Colorado River, 23

Colorado Water Garden Society, 307

compacted soil, 64, 67–68, 318

companion planting, 162

composting, 72–74, 269

Coneflower (*Echinacea*), 335–336

conserving water. *See also* rainwater harvesting; retaining water
  evaporation, 23–24
  fall planting, 329
  gray water, 38–39
  grouping plants, 329
  improving soil, 328
  irrigation systems, 330
  low-water plants, 328–329
  mulching, 330
  rainwater harvesting, 33–38
  removing lawn, 331

filters
  irrigation systems, 86
  ponds and pools, 313
finger test, soil moisture, 28
fire danger, mulch, 275–276
Firecracker penstemon
    (*Penstemon eatonii*), 108
Fishhook barrel cactus (*Ferocactus
    wislizeni*), 136
Flapjack plant (*Kalanchoe
    luciae*), 126
flex (poly) tubing, 88–89
Flower dust plant (*Kalanchoe
    pumila*), 131
Flowering tobacco (*Nicotiana*), 120
flowers. *See also* perennials
  for alkaline soil, 66
  annuals, 116–120
  overview, 103
foliage, watering, 56
foliar misting, 56
Foothill penstemon (*Penstemon
    heterophyllus*), 108
Foothill sedge (*Carex
    tumulicola*), 226
Forget-me-nots (*Myosotis
    scorpioides*), 120
fountains, 315–316
fraises des bois (alpine
    strawberries), 174
free-form pools, 312
French marigold (*Tagetes
    patula*), 119
Frowine, Steven A., 69, 159
fruit plants
  dwarf versions, 171–172
  overview, 170
  self-fertile trees, 171
  shrubs, 173
  strawberries, 173–174
  vines, 173

G

garden clubs, 184
garden fork, 212, 213
garden spade, 212

Gardening Basics For Dummies
    (Frowine), 69, 159
Gay Butterflies, 335
gazing pool, 312
Germander (*Teucrium
    species*), 108
Ghost plant (*Graptopetalum
    paraguayense*), 126
Giant coreopsis (*Leptosyne
    gigantea*), 114
glaucous cacti, 133
Globe amaranth (*Gomphrena
    globosa*), 119
glochid cacti, 133
Gold coin (*Pallenis maritima*), 108
Golden ball cactus (*Parodia
    leninghausii*), 136
Golden barrel cactus (*Echinocactus
    grusonii*), 136
Golden Toupee, 335
grains, 167–168
grasses
  advantages, 223–224
  cool-season grasses, 224–225
  ornamental, 12, 229–232
  planting, 228
  shopping for, 226–227
  sowing grass seed, 228–229
  warm-season grasses, 225–226
gravel gardening, 255, 262
gray water, 9, 38–39
Green aloe (*Furcraea foetida*), 129
grooming plants, 197
ground rock sulfur, 65
groundcover
  depth of watering, 49
  as lawn alternative, 12, 233–234
  rock gardening, 257–258
  on slopes, 58
groundwater, 25
group planting
  benefits of, 18
  conserving water and, 329
  water-need zones, 10,
    45–46, 192
  xeriscaping, 320

H

half-moon edger, 212, 213
hand-watering
  hoses, 57
  overview, 56–57
  potted plants, 300–301
  watering cans, 57–58
hardscaping, 232–233, 296
Hardy cyclamen (*Cyclamen
    purpurascens*), 115–116
harvesting water. *See* collecting
    water
Harz, 335
HCF (hundred cubic feet) billing
    units, 28
heat sinks, 243–244, 261
Hedgehog cactus (*Echinocereus
    viridiflorus*), 136
hedges, 148–149
Hello Yellow, 335
Hens and Chicks (*Echeveria*), 126,
    129, 337
herb plants
  for alkaline soil, 66
  depth of watering, 49
  overview, 169–170
  potted plants, 305
  xeriscaping, 319
Heuchera (*Heuchera* species),
    108, 116
Hill Country penstemon
    (*Penstemon triflorus*), 109
holding capacity, 64
Horehound (*Marrubium*), 113
Horned poppy (*Glaucium
    flavum*), 109
hose adaptor, irrigation
    systems, 87
hose bib, irrigation systems, 84
hoses, 57
hose-splitter (manifold), 84
Hot Lips sage (*Salvia microphylla*),
    109, 338
Hot Papaya, 336
hottentot fig (Ice plant), 127
Houseleeks (*Sempervivum*), 126

M

Macdougal's century plant (*Furcraea macdougalii*), 130

Macho mocha plant (*Mangave*), 130

Madrone (*Arbutus*), 154

Magnus, 336

mail-order shopping, 181–184

Malabar spinach, 167

Mammillaria (*Mammillaria polyedra*), 136

manifold (hose-splitter), 84

Margarita BOP, 334

Mariposa lily (*Calochortus* species), 109

Marmalade, 336

Matilija poppy (*Romneya coulteri*), 113

meadow gardens, 12, 234–239

Mediterranean cypress (*Cupressus sempervirens*), 154

Meerlo lavender (*Lavandula × allardii*), 113

Melic grass (*Melica spp*), 231

Mendocino reed grass (*Calamagrostis foliosa*), 231

mesh driplines, 92

metki (Armenian cucumber), 167

metric converter, 31

Mexican bush sage (*Salvia leucantha*), 109, 338

Mexican lime cactus (*Ferocactus pilosus*), 134

Mexican post cactus (*Pachycereus marginatus*), 134

Mexican snowball, E. elegans, 336

Mexican tulip poppy (*Hunnemannia fumariifolia*), 109

microclimates, 18

micronutrients, 69

Milkweed (*Asclepias* species), 109–110

millet, 167

Mimulus (monkeyflower), 110

mixed beds, improving absorption in, 284–285

moisture beads, 277–280

Mojave yucca (*Yucca schidigera*), 130

Monardella (*Monardella* species), 110

monkeyflower (*Mimulus*; *Diplacus*), 110

monoculture, 207

moonscape rock gardening, 252

Morning glory (*Ipomoea*), 119

morning watering, 50, 300

Moroccan daisy (*Rhodanthemum* cultivars), 110

mosquitos, 313

Moss rose (*Portulaca*), 119

mother rocks, 259

Muhly grass (*Muhlenbergia spp*), 231

mulching

applying and replenishing, 271–274

bark mulch, 269

calculating how much mulch is needed, 267–269

cocoa-bean hulls, 269

coconut coir, 280–282

compost, 269

conserving water and, 44, 330

evaporation and, 24

fire danger, 275–276

leaf mold, 269

meadow garden, 238

nitrogen deficiency and, 270

overview, 10, 265–267

pine bark nuggets, 269

red cedar mulch, 270

runoff, 274–275

slime mold, 275

soil and, 76

spent hops, 270

stones, 270–271

strawberries, 174

water-storing crystals and, 277–280

wood chips, 270

xeriscaping, 320–321

Mule's ears daisy (*Wyethia amplexicaulis*), 110

municipal water, 27–28

Myrtle (*Melaleuca* species), 154

N

N. mussinii, 336

Naked lady (*Amaryllis belladonna*), 114

Nardozzi, Charlie, 159

Nasturtium (*Nasturtium*), 119

National Gardening Association, 159

nativars, 16, 141, 238, 319

native plant clubs, 184

needle-nose pliers, 89–90

New Zealand flax (*Phormium tenax*), 110

New Zealand spinach, 167

New Zealand wind grass (*Anemanthele lessoniana*), 231

nitrogen deficiency, 270

no-water (dry) garden, 324

nozzles, sprinklers, 100

nurseries, 176–180

nylon turf, 245

O

odors, artificial turf, 244

okra, 166

Old man cactus (*Cephalocereus senilis*), 134

Olive (*Olea* europaea), 154

olla. *See* buried clay pots

Oregano (*Origanum vulgare*), 113

Organ pipe cactus (*Stenocereus thurberi*), 134

organic matter

adding, 71–72

for clay soil, 70

for intermediate soil, 70

for loam soil, 70

purchasing, 71

for sandy soil, 69

types of, 70

watering cans, 57–58

watering practices, 10–11, 195. *See also* irrigation systems

block planting, 48

bottle-drip irrigation, 53–54

broad areas, 48

buried clay pots, 51–53

clay soil, 60

deciding how deeply to water, 49

evenly saturated ground, 43

foliage, 56

hand-watering, 56–58

interval watering, 48–49

overview, 41

pipes, 54–55

plants distant from water source, 59–60

porous pipes, 55

purpose of, 42

before rain, 49

rescuing plants, 201

self-watering, 301–302

slopes and embankments, 58–59

solo watering, 46–47

standing water, 60

timing of, 50–51, 300

transitioning to low-water use, 43–45

water-need zones, 45–46

wicking systems, 54

waterlilies, 313–314

water-need zones, 10, 45–46

water-storing crystals, 277–280

water-use rights, 26

water-wise gardening, 9–10. *See also* low-water landscaping

weed-and-feed products, 210

weedkillers, 219

weeds

conserving water and, 44

disposing of, 76–77

meadow gardens, 236–237

rock gardens, 252, 261–262

vegetable plants, 164

well water, 29

Western Gold Mix, 335

Western wheatgrass (*Pascopyrum smithii*), 225

wicking systems, 54–55

wild-plant ethics, 185

winterizing

fountains, 316

irrigation systems, 98

ponds and pools, 313

wood chips, 270

Woolly sunflower (*Eriophyllum lanatum*), 112

Wright's buckwheat (*Eriogonum wrightii*), 114

X

xeriscaping

defined, 307

design tips, 323–324

dry garden, 324

grouping plants, 320

improving soil, 318

irrigation, 322

lawn alternatives, 321–322

maintenance, 323

mulching, 320–321

overview, 317

selecting plants for, 318–319

Y

Yarrows (*Achillea* species), 111

Yucca plants, 129

Z

Zinnia (*Zinnia*), 120

Zoysia grass, 226

About the Author

Teri Dunn Chace is an author, editor, and speaker on horticulture, gardening, and natural history. Among her nearly 40 titles are the second edition of *Landscaping For Dummies*, *Seeing Flowers: Discover the Hidden Life of Flowers*, and *Seeing Seeds: A Journey into the World of Seedheads, Pods, and Fruit* (the latter won a prestigious American Horticultural Society Book of the Year award), *How to Eradicate Invasive Plants*, *The Anxious Gardener's Book of Answers*, *Beautiful Roses Made Easy*, *Water Gardening*, and *Potting Places*. She's also written and edited for major consumer gardening/outdoor-living publications (*Horticulture*, *North American Gardener*, *Backyard Living*, and *Birds and Blooms*) and is presently the garden-and-nature columnist for the award-winning "Bottom Line Personal" newsletter.

Raised in Santa Barbara, California, and educated at Bard College in New York, she gardened for several years in arid southern Oregon. She currently resides in a small village in the heart of central New York's farm country; she and her husband also have a second home on a small island off the southwest coast of Nova Scotia.

The most intriguing job she's ever held? Monitoring rare turtles for The Nature Conservancy. Or . . . raising teenage boys. You can find more information at terichacewriter.com.

Dedication

I dedicate this book to the Santa Barbara Botanic Garden, where I got to know my first dry-climate plants by name.

Author Acknowledgements

Thank you to Chad Sievers, a patient and insightful editor. Thank you to all those who reviewed and contributed valuable ideas and information to this book, including Joseph Blau, Bill McDorman, Greg Horne, and Kathleen Pyle.

Thank you to Al Chace, who took me to The Hawk.

Inspiration and encouragement was an indirect but important factor in the work on this book, so a bow of gratitude goes out to the following folks: Craig Childs, Nancy F. Castaldo, the late John and Mary Mirgon, Nan Sterman, Saxon Holt, Barbara Lamb Hall, Renee Clark, Kathleen Kearns and Ned Lightner, Everett H. King, Colleen Collins, Ross Gay, Todd Snider, and Tinariwen. Katherine Chisholm, let's find time! Last but not least, apologies to Kagan, our red golden; while Mom typed, typed, and typed, he waited patiently to go out for walks.

Publisher's Acknowledgments

Senior Acquisitions Editor: Tracy Boggier

Project and Development Editor: Chad R. Sievers

Technical Editor: Bill McDorman

Production Editor: Mohammed Zafar Ali

Cover Image: © Dmytro Perov/Shutterstock